# Dream Not of Other Worlds

# sightline books

*The Iowa Series in Literary Nonfiction*

Patricia Hampl and Carl H. Klaus, series editors

*An Obermann Center for Advanced Studies Selection*

# Huston Diehl
# Dream Not of
# Other Worlds

*Teaching in a Segregated
Elementary School, 1970*

University of Iowa Press    Iowa City

*Huston Diehl*

University of Iowa Press, Iowa City 52242
Copyright © 2007 by Huston Diehl
www.uiowapress.org

"To You" and "Theme for English B," copyright © 1994 by the Estate of Langston
Hughes; "Migration," "Stars," "Long View: Negro," "Merry-Go-Round," "The
Dream Keepers," "As I Grew Older," and "Dream Variations" from *The Collected
Poems of Langston Hughes* copyright © 1994 by the Estate of Langston Hughes, used
by permission of Alfred A. Knopf, a division of Random House, Inc. and reprinted
by permission of Harold Ober Associates Inc. A section of "Where Is the Jim Crow
Section on This Merry-Go-Round?" and a short excerpt from "A Part of Me" were
previously published as "We're All Colored" in the *Massachusetts Review* 47:2 (Summer
2006) and were reprinted in 2007 in *The Messy Self*, edited by Jennifer Rosner.

Printed on acid-free paper

Library of Congress Cataloging-in-Publication Data
Diehl, Huston, 1948–.
Dream not of other worlds: teaching in a segregated elementary school, 1970 /
   Huston Diehl.
     p.    cm. —(Sightline books: the Iowa series in literary nonfiction)
   Includes bibliographical references.
   ISBN-13: 978-0-87745-996-5 (cloth)
   ISBN-10: 0-87745-996-7 (cloth)
   1. African Americans—Education—Virginia—Louisa County—Case studies.
2. Segregation in education—Virginia—Louisa County—Case studies.
3. First year teachers—Case studies.   I. Title.
LC2802.V8D54   2007
371.829'960755465—dc22       2006031401

07   08   09   10   11   X   5   4   3   2   1

FOR THE CHILDREN —

SUSANNAH,

JENNY, DAN, AND JAMIAN,

AND

ALL MY FORMER STUDENTS AT

MORTON ELEMENTARY SCHOOL

To You
To sit and dream, to sit and read,
To sit and learn about the world
Outside our world of here and now—
       our problem world—
To dream of vast horizons of the soul
Through dreams made whole,
Unfettered free—help me!
All you who are dreamers, too,
Help me make our world anew.
I reach out my hands to you.

—LANGSTON HUGHES

# Contents

# Foreword

*Dream Not of Other Worlds* is a memoir about my experience teaching in a segregated "Negro" elementary school in rural Louisa County, Virginia. The year was 1970, and I was a twenty-one-year-old white woman who had never lived in the South and who knew nothing about African American culture. I was my students' first white teacher. Their school, along with all the other elementary schools in the county, was to be integrated the following year under a federal court order, and they were understandably anxious about the impending change. To find out how they fared in the newly integrated schools, and to learn how three decades of integrated schooling have affected the education of black children in the county, I returned to Louisa at the beginning of the twenty-first century. My book ends with a description of my return in 2004 to the school where I once taught.

The way I tell my story is not the way I would have told it in 1970, for I no longer view my experience through the eyes of a rebellious "sixties" kid, intent on challenging authority, or a young idealist, confident of her ability to change the world. And I have learned many things—about the African American intellectual tradition, the history of the Negro schools, the Jim Crow South, black culture, and my own racial and class identity—since I was a naive twenty-one-year-old, foolishly imagining myself bringing enlightenment to the unfortunate. Unlike many teaching memoirs written in that turbulent time, mine does not end in triumph, but in failure. For many years I was ashamed of my failure, and even sought to conceal it, but I now believe that one of the ways I can contribute to the national conversation about race, minority education, and the multicultural classroom is to acknowledge and try to understand the many ways I failed the African American children in my classroom.

My book also tells about America's historic failure to provide adequate schools and equal educational opportunities to generations of black children. Woven into my narrative are stories from Louisa's past—about its white planters and their slaves, its freed blacks and the Freedmen's Bureau agent sent to educate them, its white leaders and the African Americans who lived under their Jim Crow laws, its segregated schools and the struggle to integrate them—stories that I use to shed light on my experience in 1970. But my focus throughout is on the ordinary lives of the African American children in my classroom—children isolated from the world's stage—and on their education in the county's largest Negro elementary school. Using the stories my students told me, the pictures they drew, the notes they wrote me, the assignments they completed, the journal and lesson plans I kept, and my memories of the many startling things they said and did in my classroom, I ask my readers to hear their voices and to attend to what they were telling me about their lives, their fears, their dreams, and their place in American society.

According to some educators, a teacher never forgets the students in her first classroom. Perhaps that is why, even though I cannot possibly remember every one of the thousands of university students I have taught in my long professional career, I can still recall with extraordinary clarity the fourth-grade children—my very first students—whose stories I tell here. Memory, of course, is a slippery faculty, grounded in subjective experience, shaped by emotion, vulnerable to suggestion, subject to revision, notoriously selective. A memoir like this one, which recounts an experience from a distant past, inevitably raises questions about the accuracy of its details, the truthfulness of its recollections, the validity of its retrospective interpretations.

All the incidents described in this book happened. Whenever possible, I have tried to verify the particulars through research and interviews. On the few occasions when my memory of a specific episode differs from someone else's, I make a point of acknowledging this discrepancy. I quote verbatim from the notes my students and their parents wrote me; none of these notes is fabricated. Some of the dialogue in my narrative has been reconstructed, but many of the more remarkable comments I relate here are exact quotations. To protect their privacy, I have changed the names of the children in my classroom, except when a former student has specifically given me permission to use his or her real name. I have also given fictitious names to some of the adults in my story. In my first chapter I tell how hard it was for me to understand my students' rural, black, Virginia dialect when I began teaching in Louisa County. Except when their way of speaking is relevant to my story, I do not, however, try to reproduce the distinctive rhythm, grammar, or idiomatic expressions of their speech when I reconstruct their conversations with me. In addition to my lack of fluency in this dialect, I have decided to render my students' speech in standard English because I want to eliminate any linguistic barrier that might interfere with my readers' ability to hear what my students were telling me about their lives.

"What happens to a dream deferred?" Langston Hughes asks provocatively in one of his best-known poems, and his poetry, suffused with the longing of the dreamer, is haunted by this question. Martin Luther King brilliantly turns Hughes's question around, bringing forth a rhetorically powerful vision of a transformed and hopeful future in his famous "I Have a Dream" speech. My title invokes both Hughes (the grandson of a Louisa County planter and an emancipated slave) and King, the tragedy of a dream deferred and the possibilities of a dreamed-of future. It does not, however, come from the African American literary tradition, but from a seventeenth-century English one, and my appropriation of it is ironic. "Dream not of other worlds," the angel Raphael warns an inquisitive Adam in John Milton's *Paradise Lost* when he asks about the mysteries of the heavens. "Be lowly wise." Whenever I teach this epic poem, my students are taken aback by Raphael's theologically informed instruction, which essentially advises Adam to accept his lowly position in a hierarchical universe and abandon his pursuit of knowledge that has been intentionally withheld from him. It seems to my students to contradict their most fundamental beliefs as American citizens: in the power of dreams; the opportunity to rise above one's station; the inherent value of knowledge and education; the pioneer spirit of discovery; the right to challenge authority.

In my thirty years of university teaching, however, I have never had a student respond so viscerally and so intensely to Raphael's words as an African American woman named Barbara, who was a student in one of the very first Milton classes I taught as a young professor at the State University of New York at Geneseo. Near tears, she could barely articulate her rage at this advice. No one, she declared with a vehemence that was almost frightening, could ever persuade her that Raphael's advice was legitimate or appropriate; no one could ever satisfactorily explain to her why Milton appeared to be advocating it. Her anger was especially surprising because, until that moment, she had been one of Milton's staunchest defenders, engaging in lively debates with other students less enamored with the poem or more critical of its cultural and religious assumptions. The other students fell silent, their discomfort palpable. They had, I was sure, no idea what had set Barbara off, no comprehension of why she could possibly be so disturbed by a few words of poetry from another era. But Barbara's reaction did not seem irrational, crazy, or excessive to me. I knew immediately that, like my African American students in Virginia, she must have been told all her life to "dream not of other worlds." Nearly ten years older than the typical undergraduate, she had grown up without any expectations that she would go to college. Taking a low-paying job as a clerical worker at one of the region's main industries immediately after high school, she entered the university only after she had been identified by her boss as exceptionally promising and had won a minority scholarship funded by her employer. I saw her very presence in my classroom as a triumphant act of defiance against all the people in her life who had tried to stifle her dreams. I use Milton's words in my title, then, to register her indignation and to affirm her refusal to obey them.

# Dream Not of Other Worlds

# A Part of Me

*You are white—*
*yet a part of me, as I am a part of you.*
*That's American.*
*Sometimes perhaps you don't want to be a part of me.*
*Nor do I often want to be a part of you.*
*But we are, that's true!*
*As I learn from you,*
*I guess you learn from me—*
*although you're older—and white—*
*and somewhat more free.*
*—from "Theme for English B" by Langston Hughes*

## Those Children

"Of course," Dr. Martin assured me as he shook my hand, "I don't expect you to teach those children anything." Speaking in the soft, courtly drawl of a Virginia gentleman, he emphasized, ever so slightly, the words "those children" so that I would understand and appreciate the unspoken difference between them and the two of us. "All I ask," he added, "is that you maintain order." And with no further instructions, I was hired to teach a fourth-grade class in a segregated, "Negro" school in rural Virginia. It was January 1970. I was twenty-one.

My interview with the superintendent of schools had not gone well. The office staff had misplaced my transcript, and Dr. Martin had no official verification that I had in fact received a B.A. degree a month earlier from a college two thousand miles away. Unperturbed that he knew nothing at all about my credentials, he showed surprisingly little interest in my qualifications for any of the numerous teaching positions he needed to fill before the beginning of the spring semester the following week. Indeed, he barely acknowledged my presence, directing nearly all his comments to my new husband, whom he had, to my surprise and dismay, invited into the interview. Bill had been teaching math in a junior high in Louisa County since September, his willingness to work in an impoverished, understaffed, rural school district having secured him a draft deferment at the height of the Vietnam War. As Dr. Martin chatted amiably with Bill about the eighth-grade arithmetic textbooks that at midyear had not yet arrived, it slowly dawned on me that he was not the least bit interested in interviewing me. Rather than treating me as a promising applicant for a teaching position, he saw me as a convenient solution to a bothersome problem: how to find enough bodies to staff the classrooms left teacherless by midyear resignations and leaves. If just about anybody would do, I served his purposes especially well, since by hiring me, he would be doing my husband a favor, thereby obligating Bill to check his anger at the absent textbooks.

I tried to direct the discussion toward the job openings that had been advertised. I had no teaching credentials and no classroom experience, but there was one position I thought I was reasonably well qualified for, a position teaching English in the newly integrated high school. I'd just graduated, a semester ahead of my class, with a B.A. degree in English; I'd done some tutoring in remedial English at an urban high school; and I'd taken an education course on teaching English in the secondary schools. Not a very high level of expertise, I knew, but enough to make me think I could do that particular job.

When I explained that I was interested in the high school position, Dr. Martin was visibly annoyed. "No, no; I can't let you teach in the high school," he declared curtly, his mannered gentility escaping him for a fleeting instant. Then, perhaps detecting my disappointment, he quickly sought to soften the effect of his blunt rejection. "That's not a suitable job for you," he explained patiently, speaking to me in the kind of tone a protective father uses when his young daughter asks to do something he considers dangerous. Then, after a short pause: "There are some real big colored boys in the high school."

I couldn't immediately grasp what he was telling me. The spring semester started in a few days, the district's opening for a high school English teacher was still unfilled, there were no other candidates in sight, and I met the minimal qualifications for the position. If that was the job I was best qualified for, why couldn't I have it? I tried once more to make my case, but Dr. Martin wasn't listening. My education and experience were irrelevant to him, trumped by the specter of black male sexuality and a southern ideal of white womanhood that I, born and raised in Pennsylvania, the great-granddaughter of a Yankee soldier, could only dimly comprehend. He swung his chair away from me to face Bill. "Trust me. You don't want your wife teaching in the high school," he advised, with some urgency, addressing him as if I weren't in the room. "An attractive young woman like her? It wouldn't be proper. Wouldn't be safe. Some of those boys, well, you know how they are." He paused, as if to let his point sink in. "I won't allow it. I think she should take the fourth-grade class over at Z. C. Morton. That's the Negro elementary school right next to the junior high where you're teaching, which would be very convenient for both of you." Then, turning to me, "Wouldn't you like to be able to drive to work with your husband? And have him near by in case you needed him?"

I was becoming increasingly alarmed at the prospect of teaching grade school. Fourth graders? I couldn't even remember how old they were. I had not set foot in an elementary school since I had left Hempfield Elementary for Penn Junior High ten years earlier. Reading, writing, elementary mathematics and science, social studies, spelling, handwriting—I hadn't a clue how to go about teaching any of those subjects to young children. But I needed a job and, newly arrived in this isolated, rural county in central Virginia, I had no viable options. I reluctantly agreed to teach a class of fourth graders whose teacher was taking a maternity leave. I was to begin my job at the Z. C. Morton Elementary School the very next week, observing the outgoing teacher for five days before assuming responsibility for the class.

It was snowing hard the following Monday as we drove into the school parking lot. I said goodbye to Bill and watched as he walked confidently towards the junior high, a graceless, two-story red brick building without a trace of ornamentation that, until it had been integrated a few months earlier, had served as the county's Negro high school. Then, far less confidently, I headed for the front door of the elementary school. It was separated from the junior high by a narrow driveway. The county's largest Negro elementary school, Morton had been built ten years earlier, replacing a number of one- and two-room schoolhouses scattered around the county. Originally conceived as a firewall to fend off school desegregation by providing African American children with an elementary school that was "separate but equal" to the county's white elementary schools, it was scheduled, along with the county's other elementary schools, to be integrated the next fall in compliance with a federal court order. To ease the transition, four white teachers had been transferred to Morton. I would be the fifth, and the first white teacher my students had ever had. I glanced nervously around before entering, taking in the drab brick exterior, the horizontal row of institutional windows, the empty fields that surrounded the isolated building and its companion school. And then I walked inside.

I remember their faces — curious, uncertain, anxious — when Morton's principal, Mr. Thompson, introduced me to my students. Heavy snow, highly unusual for that part of Virginia, had fallen in the early morning hours, was still falling in dramatic swirls outside the classroom windows, and the whole school was in an uproar. One of the local radio stations had announced that school had been canceled; another, that school was open. Buses had arrived late, or not at all. Some teachers had shown up; others had not. As the principal escorted me to Mrs. Stockton's classroom — my classroom — I could hear the din of children, exhilarated by the snow, the confusion, the unexpected disruption of routine. But when Mr. Thompson appeared with me in the doorway, his six-feet four-inch frame a commanding presence, the students fell instantly and utterly silent.

"What's going on in here?" he demanded sternly.

When he learned that Mrs. Stockton was absent, he turned immediately to me, shrugged apologetically, and said, "I'm afraid you'll have to be in charge today." He then announced to the students that I was Mrs. Hallahan, their new teacher, and abruptly left. I was on my own.

"Where are you from?" a boy in the back row asked.

I explained that I had grown up in Pennsylvania, but that I had just graduated from a college in Colorado.

The boy looked at me skeptically. "Where's that?"

Here, I figured, was a perfect opportunity for a geography lesson, and since I had nothing prepared and no clue what the kids were supposed to be doing that day, I quickly seized it. But as soon as I began trying to explain where the Great Plains met the Rocky Mountains, I could feel myself floundering. I needed some way to mark the distance between Virginia and Colorado, some way to help them visualize an unfamiliar part of the country.

"Do you have a map of the United States in the room?" I asked. A girl in the front row eagerly jumped up from her seat, marched over to the blackboard, and pulled down a large map hung on a frame above the board. Grateful for a visual aid, I turned to locate Colorado. But I found myself staring at a large map of Virginia. Taken aback, I pointed out that the map wasn't, in fact, a map of the United States, but of Virginia. The Rocky Mountains, I explained, were two thousand miles beyond Virginia. I fully expected the helpful little girl to realize that she'd pulled down the wrong map and to produce the correct one.

"It is so a United States map," protested a tall boy sitting in the far left corner of the room. "And the Rocky Mountains *are* on it." Rushing to the front of the room, he pointed triumphantly to the Blue Ridge Mountains. "See, right here."

"Yeah, the Rocky Mountains are right there, on the map," others began to shout as my impromptu geography lesson quickly disintegrated.

Bewildered, I tried to quiet the class.

"Your hair is beautiful," ventured one of the little girls, staring at my long brown hair. "Can I touch it?"

"Will you beat us?" another girl interjected, perhaps sensing the tentative way I was going about maintaining order.

Instinctively, perhaps foolishly, I assured the children that I had no intention of ever hitting them. The classroom erupted in hurrahs.

"Old lady Stockton beats us," one of the boys confided.

"She's beaten every kid in this class at least once," another declared. "Man, can she hit." Then everyone chimed in at once, the noise level of the classroom rising as they recalled ever-more-elaborate stories of palm-slappings, spankings, punishments, and perceived injustices.

"Can we look at the snow?" someone suddenly asked.

I glanced out the window. Great quantities of snow poured out of the sky onto the playground and drifted into fantastical shapes, eerie and magical. "Sure," I answered, thinking how rarely children in this part of country ever get to see snow. I naively assumed that they would turn quietly at their desks to stare out at the blizzard. But instead, they jumped out of their seats and made a wild dash to the windows, pushing and jockeying for position, shouting with glee.

"What on earth are you children doing?" boomed an incredulous voice in the hall. Mr. Thompson stood in the doorway, staring at my chaotic classroom in disbelief. I could tell that he was already worried about my competence. If the white superintendent had been oblivious to my lack of credentials and experience, my black principal clearly understood their ramifications. He must have known immediately that I was out of my depth. And he surely must have resented the way I had been hired by the white superintendent, without so much as a courtesy interview with him, let alone any consultation. Deeply invested in maintaining a disciplined and orderly school, he may even have foreseen the way my ineptitude would undermine his authority.

My struggle that Monday to keep the students quiet and in their seats must have been unsettling and disorienting to the students, too. Upon their teacher's return the next day, they sat quietly and obediently in the long neat rows of desks. Mrs. Stockton ran a tight ship. She expected her students to sit still, raise their hands, address her as ma'am, and do as they were told, and she didn't tolerate any challenge to her authority. At one point during my observation a small boy in the back of the room passed a note to the boy in front of him. Mrs. Stockton fixed her eyes on him, but the boy did not see her admonishing gaze.

"Ervin!" Her voice was sharp, her tone commanding and deadly serious. An extraordinary hush swept over the room. All the children became alert, tense, and unnaturally still. "Ervin," she said again, even more sternly. "Come here."

Ervin slid out of his seat and stood reluctantly beside his desk, hanging his head.

"Come here," she reiterated.

He walked slowly, solemnly towards her.

"Put out your hand," she directed.

He scowled, then held out his small hand, the palm faced upward, exposed. It shook ever so slightly. She picked up her ruler and hit it hard three times. Whap! The sound of the wood hitting the bare skin reverberated in the unnaturally quiet room. Whap! Whap!

"Go back to your seat," she ordered, without sympathy, glaring at him.

Fighting back tears, Ervin lowered his head and silently returned to his desk. The attentive eyes of his classmates followed him as he made his way to the back of the room. I watched, knowing I could never hit a child's bare hand, but remembering the chaotic scene of the previous day. How was I ever going to control a classroom of thirty-eight ten-year-old children?

I didn't fully understand the magnitude of this challenge until later in the week. One afternoon, as I monitored my students on the play-ground, I watched the children in Morton's other fourth-grade class walk in single file out of the school building and march with their teacher in utter silence around the boundary of the schoolyard. My students were shouting, jumping rope, playing tag, and making the most of their brief respite from the classroom, so I was immediately struck by the remarkably different demeanor of their counterparts. I watched, curious at first and then with increasing concern, as their teacher, a burly, middle-aged white man with ramrod straight posture and an authoritarian bearing, surveyed the column of silent students as if he were a drill sergeant inspecting his troops. There was some-thing bizarre, even menacing, about him. And his students were un-naturally subdued, as if they were afraid that a lapse in concentration might undo them. I had never seen a group of children so tightly controlled, so cowed. After completing their grim march around the perimeter of the schoolyard, they returned to the steps of the school, halted for a brief moment, and then, upon command, disappeared back into the building, their "recess" completed. What was I to make of this disturbing scene, the eeriness of the children's regimented and unhappy procession, the intimidating presence of such an unlikely elementary school teacher?

When I asked Mrs. Stockton to explain, I got only a terse answer. The teacher, she told me, was Mr. Snead. The year before he had been hired to teach at one of the white elementary schools in the county. However, after a series of complaints from parents about his style of discipline, he had been transferred to Morton. He was transferred, she went on, eyeing me closely, after he broke the arm of one of his white students. So skilled was Mrs. Stockton at dealing with me, the inquisitive white woman in her classroom, that I detected not a trace of emotion in her voice as she related this appalling story. She left unsaid everything that mattered about Mr. Snead's reassignment to Morton: the powerlessness of the black principal to prevent it; the fear of the children whom Mr. Snead taught; the anxiety of their parents; the outrage of the African American community at the white superintendent's blatant disregard for the safety of the children under Mr. Snead's supervision; the terrible message that his presence at Morton sent about the relative value of white and black children.

I eventually figured out that I was directly affected by Mr. Snead's reassignment to Morton. In response to the protests of black parents, Mr. Thompson had strategically placed only the most consistently obedient and pliant children in Mr. Snead's class. That meant that every child who had ever caused trouble, every child with special needs, every child prone to rebellion or hyperactivity or anxiety or restlessness, and every child with a reputation for sassing or questioning authority was, quite deliberately, placed in Mrs. Stockton's class. In effect, Mr. Thompson had attempted to keep out of Mr. Snead's sphere of power every single fourth-grade child who might in any way incur his wrath and thus be vulnerable to his abuse. Predictably, Mr. Snead's class was disproportionately female, Mrs. Stockton's—mine—was disproportionately male: twenty-six of the thirty-eight students in my class were boys. Mr. Thompson's solution was a brilliant one. Unfortunately, its success depended on a crucial factor: Mrs. Stockton. When he chose her for this difficult assignment, Mr. Thompson did not anticipate her maternity leave. And he most certainly did not anticipate that the superintendent of schools would replace his most effective disciplinarian, his most reliable teacher, with an inexperienced white woman like me.

## Seeing the Moon in the Daytime

Throughout the rest of that first week, I sat beside Mrs. Stockton's desk in the front of the room and looked out over the large classroom, trying to memorize the students' names, trying to get a sense of each individual child, trying to figure out the dynamics of the class. I easily learned the names of the class leaders and the class clowns and the troublemakers. But there were so many others, some quiet, obedient, and eager to please, others restless and having trouble concentrating. They sat at desks arranged in long, regimented rows, and from my vantage point at the front of the room, I could barely make out the faces of those in the back, let alone see what they were doing. I tried to get to know some of them before classes started in the morning, when they bounded off their buses, often after long, early morning rides through the remote countryside. The buses were still segregated that year, the bus routes byzantine and irrational in order to keep black and white children apart, and as a result, some students arrived at school a whole hour before classes started while others straggled in just as class began.

I quickly learned that, except for a short break at lunchtime, I would be in charge of the class from the moment the first students arrived on one of the early buses until the moment they all filed out of the school for the bus ride home at 3:00 in the afternoon. There were no art teachers, music teachers, or P.E. teachers to help out, no time set aside to collaborate with other teachers, and no curriculum specialists to consult.

Even worse, the county did not provide any textbooks for its students. Instead, it expected parents to purchase their children's schoolbooks. But most Morton parents were poor, and they couldn't afford to buy every child in the family all the required books. Some could not afford to buy any books for any of their children. And because the school board, freed from the financial obligation of purchasing textbooks from its own budget, routinely adopted new textbooks, parents couldn't even rely on the practice of buying books for the oldest child and handing them down. Because very few of the students in the class owned all of the required textbooks, every transition to a new academic subject was chaotic. Metal chairs scraped against the linoleum floor, pencils rolled off desks, girls beckoned their best friends to join them, and boys jostled with one another as students without books navigated a warren of desks in search of someone with a book to share. The students without books had no way of completing their homework assignments or reviewing for tests, so they were always at a serious disadvantage in class. Earlier in the year Mrs. Stockton had tried to pressure some of the parents to buy the required textbooks. In a note to Derrick's parents, she had written beside the failing grades on Derrick's report card: "Derrick simply must have his books if he is to do passing work this year." But Derrick, who was one of ten children, didn't have any books, and he was not making any progress.

Books of any kind were scarce. A dictionary and a few random reference works occupied the nearly empty bookshelves below the window in my classroom. Some battered and out-of-date textbooks — none currently in use — were stored on a shelf in the back closet. There was no school library, though a room in the building had been designated for one, and the only publicly owned books available to my students were housed in a county bookmobile that visited the school once a week. But it was small and cramped, its holdings were meager, and access to it was limited. Once a week, each classroom teacher was allowed to select three books from its small collection to use for the next seven days. None of these books could leave the school building.

There was a certain weariness in the way Mrs. Stockton conducted her lessons. The class was a handful, she was pregnant with her third child, and I could tell she was more than ready to begin her leave. Her instructional methods were decidedly old-fashioned. She asked students to read aloud, but she never asked them to discuss what they had read. Her tests required rote memorization and stressed the correct answer, not problem solving. She assigned a lot of busy work. And she marched her students, rather mechanically, through the exercises provided at the end of each chapter in the textbooks.

I watched in frustration as the students struggled with a set of exercises from the *Ginn Reader*. After reviewing the basic principles governing syllables and accents, Mrs. Stockton asked one child at a time to go to the blackboard. As each one picked up a piece of chalk, she spelled out a word which the student transcribed on the board. Then she asked the child to pronounce it, divide it into syllables, and put an accent mark on the accented syllable. Jeanine went first. Her word was "D-e-l-i-g-h-t." "DE-light," Jeanine said aloud, stressing the first syllable. She confidently divided the word into two syllables — "de-light" — and put an accent over the "de," just as she had pronounced it. Mrs. Stockton glanced at her teacher's manual. I watched her finger move down the page to where the correct answer was printed. "Wrong," she announced decisively, ignoring — appearing oblivious to — the difference between Jeanine's pronunciation and the manual's rendering of standard English. Jeanine looked baffled, but Mrs. Stockton offered no explanation, simply announcing to the class that the accent was on the second syllable. This scenario was repeated over and over. Whenever a student pronounced a word in a way that did not correspond to standard English pronunciation and then identified the accented syllable correctly as he or she had pronounced it, Mrs. Stockton declared the answer incorrect. She never addressed the differences between the standard pronunciation and the students'; she never explained dialects. The students became more and more frustrated and confused, and Mrs. Stockton more and more annoyed. "This isn't hard," she insisted. But even the smartest students were stymied. Told repeatedly that she was wrong when, in fact, her ability to accent words according to her own pronunciation was flawless, a very smart little girl named Sharon finally burst into tears. "I just don't understand accents, Mrs. Stockton," she sobbed.

Math lessons were even more discouraging. Required to use a brand new textbook that featured the "new math"—an experimental pedagogy based on set theory and mathematical reasoning rather than simple computation—Mrs. Stockton had clearly been given no training in the new method and, like many other elementary teachers across the nation, she didn't understand its basic premises. Adept at computational math, she seemed particularly destabilized by the textbook's emphasis on the reasoning process. Rather than ditch the book and teach the fundamentals of math as she had been taught them (a violation of district policy for which she probably would have been disciplined), she dutifully and gamely attempted to use the new math textbook, with disastrous results.

During one session she called on individual students to read a word problem in the textbook and then asked them to go to the board and work out the problem according to the model in the book, a model that required them to show how to use set theory to think through the problem. While each child struggled hopelessly to arrive at the answer using the new methods, I watched as she secretly worked out the problem in the traditional way on a tablet she kept hidden on her lap. She worked quickly and accurately, but hiding her own methodology from her confused students, she was, of course, never able to explain to them why they could not arrive at the correct answer following the book's method. Virtually every child dreaded math class. Math, they ardently believed, was a mystery beyond their capacity to comprehend, a kind of magic permanently denied them.

The class was studying American history in social studies, but Mrs. Stockton showed no interest in connecting the lessons in the book to the world in which the children were living. Early one morning Ramonia rushed excitedly into the classroom to show Mrs. Stockton and me a map her mother had given her. The map she unfolded depicted Southeast Asia. With her friends gathered eagerly around Mrs. Stockton's large wooden desk, Ramonia proudly located Vietnam, where, she explained, her father was in the air force, fighting in the Vietnam War. But then a wave of anxiety swept over her.

"I forget, Mrs. Stockton," she admitted sheepishly, "which side are we fighting for?"

Mrs. Stockton paused for a moment and then answered hesitantly, "The North." Another pause, and then, more confidently, she repeated, "Yes, we're fighting for the North."

Taken aback, I was unsure how to respond. I didn't want to do anything that would embarrass or undermine Mrs. Stockton, but I didn't want Ramonia going around telling everyone her father was fighting for North Vietnam. "Actually," I offered, as casually as I could, "we're fighting for the South." She did not seem to mind being corrected. "I never did pay much attention to those things," she admitted.

Once, during a silent reading period, Matilda encountered an unfamiliar name in her textbook. "Does this," the little girl asked, pointing to an illustration of a travel poster featuring palm trees and an ocean, "say 'Puerto Rico' ?" She sounded out the words printed on the poster slowly, tentatively, but correctly. Mrs. Stockton inspected the page Matilda held out to her. "No," she said. "Well," Matilda persisted, "what does it say?" Mrs. Stockton looked uncomfortable. "Oh," she replied flatly, with a shrug, "some other foreign country."

Mrs. Stockton taught science strictly from a textbook, a book that was poorly written and deadly dull. She was furious when she discovered that James and Reginald had sneaked into the back closet before school started to play with some neglected lab equipment. The instruments and equipment abandoned in the closet, it turned out, had been bought with Title I funds provided by the federal government. This program was designed to improve science education for children in impoverished school districts, but it earmarked funds to buy equipment without providing any support to train teachers. The broken and fragmented remains of the high-priced lab equipment carelessly shelved in the back closet primarily served as a reminder to children like James and Reginald that the exciting worlds of aeronautics and medicine and research chemistry lay tantalizingly beyond their reach.

Towards the end of one long day, Mrs. Stockton asked the students to take out their science books and turn to a chapter about the solar system. One by one, the students took turns reading aloud, most of them in slow, halting voices as they grappled with unfamiliar words and new concepts. Reginald squirmed in his seat. He was restless and bored. Then, suddenly, his hand shot into the air.

"Yes, Reginald."

"How come you can sometimes see the moon in the daytime?" he asked.

His question aroused his classmates from their late afternoon doldrums. "Yeah," they murmured, their curiosity piqued. "How come?"

Mrs. Stockton looked annoyed. She gave an exasperated sigh. "Why, Reginald," she exclaimed derisively, "do you mean to tell me that you've seen the moon in the daytime?"

Reginald held his ground. "Yes."

She directed a withering gaze at the boy. "Don't be ridiculous," she exclaimed sarcastically. "You can NOT see the moon in the daytime. Whatever gave you such a strange idea? Now, stop getting us off the track with your silly notions."

"But, Mrs. Stockton," Reginald began, the expression on his face a mixture of anger, confusion, and defiance. "I . . ."

"You most certainly cannot see the moon in the daytime," she repeated with absolute conviction. "Now cut out this chatter and let's get back to our science lesson." For the rest of the science lesson, Reginald stared sullenly out the window.

I watched this episode in stunned silence, thinking of my father, a doctor, and the countless times he sought to explain my questions about the solar system with elaborate demonstrations, the dinner table instantly converted into a laboratory. Grapes became moons circling apple-planets which in turn rotated around a gigantic grapefruit-sun as my father tried to convey the marvelous complexity of the solar system. Or a flashlight materialized to shine the sun's light while I analyzed the shadows cast by orbiting balls. How, I wondered, can a curious child like Reginald make sense of his world if his questions are mocked, his empirical observations denied? And who had mocked the child who grew up to be Mrs. Stockton?

Observing a class and teaching it are not the same thing, of course. Even when I could see the inadequacy of some of Mrs. Stockton's pedagogical techniques, I couldn't necessarily think of an alternative solution. Marcus was unable to recognize even the most basic words, and I could see that Mrs. Stockton's efforts to teach him to read were futile. Isolating him from the rest of the class during the reading period, she gave him separate assignments. Actually, she gave him the same assignment every day: a list of the first ten words from an alphabetical list of common words. The list began with the word "a" and continued something like this: "about, all, an, and, around, at." Every day, Mrs. Stockton handed Marcus his list of words and instructed him to learn them. At some point in the reading period, she would call Marcus to her desk and ask him to read his words out loud. Although the other students were supposed to be reading by themselves, they always eavesdropped as Marcus stumbled and stuttered, unable to master these simple words. And every day Mrs. Stockton subjected him to public humiliation, berating him for his stupidity. At the end of each exchange, she would dismiss him with the same words: "Go on, Marcus. No use your taking up my time any longer. If you're not going to study, I'm not going to help you. And if you don't care about getting any farther than those first ten words, then we'll study them right through to June." The first day I observed this ritual encounter, she turned to me and proclaimed loudly and contemptuously, in Marcus's presence: "Marcus's been trying to learn these same ten words since September." As the other students laughed and jeered, Marcus returned to his seat, frustrated, embarrassed, and seething with resentment.

I knew by his fluency with the spoken word that Marcus was a bright child, though without any training in the field, I had no way of diagnosing his problem learning to read. I volunteered to work with him. I invited him to read a simple story about a fox that I had selected in part for its vivid illustrations. As soon as he saw the first picture,

Marcus began to weave his own imaginative fox tale. He wasn't reading a word, but he was telling a great story. I located the word "fox" in the text for him, told him what it meant, played a little with its sounds, then encouraged him to sound out the word in front of it. The letters meant nothing to Marcus, but he had no trouble coming up with a list of appropriate possibilities: furry fox? red fox? sly fox? clever fox? mean fox? bad fox? I watched him—alert, engaged—"read" the illustration for clues, his imagination compensating for his inability to recognize the letters or sound out the words. I suspected that with close, carefully planned, one-on-one instruction, Marcus could learn to read. But I was at a loss to know how a teacher in charge of thirty-eight students could carve out the necessary time to achieve this. I realized sadly that I had none of the specialized materials or technical training necessary to help a ten-year-old boy who was functionally illiterate.

Still, I was full of ambitious plans about what I would do when I took over the class. I zeroed in on what I saw as the weaknesses of Mrs. Stockton's pedagogy, but I was blind to the limitations of my own. I never once considered how our different teaching philosophies were rooted in our separate and distinctive cultures or imagined that mine, the product of my middle-class white upbringing, might not be appropriate for the poor black children in the class I was about to take over. Quick to judge Mrs. Stockton, I didn't yet know that the story I would later tell about Morton Elementary would not be about her failings, but my own, and those of a county that systematically denied African Americans like her a quality education.

If I was critical of Mrs. Stockton, I also marveled at how masterfully she managed this very large class, handling the daily barrage of administrative forms, attending to her students' countless requests, following a carefully structured schedule of classes, grading scores of tests and homework assignments, dealing with a series of small crises, and keeping thirty-eight energetic ten-year-olds quiet and focused on their work.

Once that week even the unflappable Mrs. Stockton encountered a disciplinary problem she couldn't handle on her own and had to summon Mr. Thompson for help. During recess Reginald, Kevin, and Louis had ventured off the small asphalt rectangle on the playground where the children were confined on days when the open field behind the school was too wet or muddy. Monday's snow had melted, the ground was sopping wet, and by the time Mrs. Stockton noticed them, the three boys were roaming far out into the muddy field. Putting me in charge of supervising the other students, she angrily ordered the three boys inside to be punished. The other students watched warily as she marched the offenders into the school building.

"They're in for it," Clinton observed. His friends nodded somberly.

Not too long afterwards, Kevin and Louis returned, chastened but also excited. They had a story to tell. The other boys quickly gathered round them.

"Man, is Reginald in trouble," Kevin announced. "BIG trouble."

"I can't believe he had the nerve," nodded Louis. "Wait till his parents find out. He'll get another licking, for sure."

Everyone wanted to know what had happened, and having piqued the crowd's curiosity, Kevin and Louis happily obliged.

"Me and Louis each got five whacks with the paddle," Kevin explained to the children crowded around him. "Boy, did they ever hurt. But when it was Reggie's turn, he ran away from Mrs. Stockton. She was holding him by the shoulder, hard, but he squirmed away from her, and quick as a rabbit, he just started running."

"Did she chase him?"

"All over the room. She was so surprised. He was shoving chairs out of his way and racing around the desks and doing whatever he had to do to keep that paddle from getting anywhere close to his behind. Old Mrs. Stockton, I think she was scared of Reggie, scared of what he might do next."

"And she was mad too," Louis added. "REALLY mad. I wanted to laugh out loud when I saw her chasing him. She looked so silly. But I kept eyeing that old paddle of hers and I figured I'd better keep my eyes down and my mouth shut and stay out of the way."

"He actually ran away from Mrs. Stockton?"

"And kept on running and running . . ."

"He'll be sorry. Mr. Thompson came storming into the room and hauled poor Reggie off to his office. I *never* saw him so mad. Reggie's in for a terrible beating."

The others listened in awe. As the story got repeated around the playground, Reginald's rebellion began to take on a mythic dimension. The boy's bold defiance, the teacher's uncharacteristic loss of control, the principal's angry response, and the imagined scene in Mr. Thompson's office—the scene in which the imposing man with the dreaded paddle confronts the small boy who dared to resist his teacher—thrilled and enthralled the children who gathered in small groups to hear this sensational tale.

When recess was over, I marched the students back to the classroom. Mrs. Stockton sat composed and quiet at her big desk in the front of the room. A short distance from her, Reginald stood motionless beside his own desk. He had been crying hard. With both hands clutching the edge of the desk to steady himself, he hung his head and leaned forward, trying to hide his tear-streaked face against his shirt. He was obviously in pain. His classmates quietly stared at him as they entered the room, but he did not look up. Byron walked over and tried to hug him, but with a piercing glare, Mrs. Stockton waved Byron to his seat. She was clearly back in control. Reginald stood, humiliated and completely subdued, quietly enduring the stares of his classmates.

As I watched Mrs. Stockton firmly reestablish her authority in the aftermath of this unexpected rebellion, the submission of her once defiant pupil displayed for all to see, I realized, with a start, that I identified not with the teacher but with the child. As a fourth-grader myself, I had once, like Reginald, wandered off the school grounds during recess. I had been playing with two boys in a small creek at the edge of my elementary school's playground, and the three of us had become so absorbed by our search for minnows and salamanders and frogs that we unthinkingly followed the creek as it wound its way beyond the school property. We did not realize that we had strayed from the school grounds. We did not hear the bell ring. We did not see our classmates line up and follow the teacher into the school building. By the time we became aware that the playground was eerily and utterly silent and frantically raced towards the school, Mrs. Henry had already discovered our absence and was charging out the door to find us. I don't know why Mrs. Henry didn't punish us. She did scold us, and I clearly recall her asking me what I, a *girl*, was doing traipsing off with a couple of boys to play in a muddy creek. What I remember most about that scolding, what has stuck with me through all these years, however, was not her reprimand, but the approving twinkle in her eye and the tone of appreciation in her voice. Something in the way she spoke let me know that, even though I had broken a school rule, she admired my adventuresomeness, understood my inquisitiveness, forgave my transgression.

But for Reginald there was no admiration, no understanding, and no forgiveness. I glanced over at him, his slender body bent over the desk, his dark eyes angry and hurt. I thought about how his mind was always racing ahead of the others, generating questions he wanted answered, ideas he wanted to explore. I understood how bored he was with the tedium of elementary school, how impatient with the pace of the class, how hungry for excitement, and I wanted to celebrate, rather than punish, his bold independence. I even wanted to affirm his defiance, for it seemed to grow out of his impulse to question a world that sought to limit and constrain him. The truth is I liked Reginald for the very traits that were consistently getting him into trouble. I could not see then what now seems to me to be so obvious: had Reginald been a white boy in a suburban, middle-class school, his curiosity would have been nurtured, his leadership potential appreciated, his daring admired. But as a poor African American boy in the rural South in 1970, these very attributes made him terribly, terribly vulnerable. Mrs. Stockton and Mr. Thompson didn't misunderstand Reginald; they were afraid for him. They thought his courage dangerous, his defiance reckless, and his impulse to question everything self-destructive. Every disciplinary measure they took was an effort to teach him to know his place. Reginald, they firmly believed, must learn "to dream not of other worlds."

## Mahahspik?

Early the next Monday morning, I sat at the big, wooden desk in an empty classroom, anxiously waiting for my students to arrive. Mrs. Stockton had said her farewells the previous Friday, and I had spent the weekend carefully, compulsively preparing to take charge of her class. My plan book, outlining the day's lessons in meticulous detail, lay open on the desk, along with the attendance sheet, the lunch and milk order forms, a box of three-cent pencils the school offered for sale, and a stack of textbooks I would be teaching that day: reading, arithmetic, social studies, science, spelling, and handwriting. I greeted my students as they arrived, a few at first from an early bus, and then more and more of them, giggling and squabbling and chattering as they filed into the room. Promptly at 8:15, I quieted the class. Standing at the front of what suddenly seemed to be a vast room, looking out over the rows and rows of children already restless in their seats, I took a deep breath and began the daily routine. As I juggled thirty-eight orders for meal tickets, milk, and pencils, trying to keep straight who owed how much for what, trying to make change while filling out the separate order forms for the office, trying to remember who got free lunches and who paid half price and who promised to pay tomorrow, there was a knock at the door. Upon opening it, I found a little girl of six or seven standing tentatively in the hall. Her neatly braided hair was tied with bright pink and purple and white barrettes, and she wore a pretty, pink-and-white smocked dress.

"Mahahspik?" she asked in a soft whisper, her single-word question foreign-sounding and strange to my ears. She stood, shy but expectant, waiting for my reply. I hadn't a clue what she was saying.

"Pardon?" I responded.

"Mahahspik?" she repeated, drawing the word out a little more slowly, but with no elaboration.

Throughout the previous week, I had struggled to comprehend the rhythms, accents, and idiomatic expressions of my students' rural, black, Virginia dialect. Though I had often failed to grasp particular words, and sometimes even whole sentences, I had been able to get by without understanding everything the students were saying by picking up nonverbal cues—an angry scowl, a playful tone of voice, an inquisitive inflection, an excited gesture—and by paying attention to how others responded to what was being said. As a mere observer in the classroom, I'd been able to cover up the numerous times when I completely failed to understand what someone was saying to me. Now a small child stood at my door with a question I could not comprehend and waited for my answer. Feeling completely foolish, I asked her again what she wanted. "Mahahspik?" was her only, insistent reply. A wave of panic swept over me, the same panic I used to experience during oral exams in college French class when, no matter how hard I tried to decipher the professor's fluent French, the alien words fractured into meaningless sounds. I turned to my students.

They were watching the encounter with curiosity, as puzzled by my behavior as I was by the child's request.

"Can someone please tell me what she wants?" I asked, a little desperately, aware of how helpless I sounded. The class burst into laughter.

"That's Chester's little sister," Matilda volunteered helpfully. "She wants permission to speak to him. He probably has her lunch money." Relieved, I invited the little girl in and pointed the way to Chester's desk.

I quickly learned that the child's question — "May I speak?" — was a ritual utterance, used by almost all the students in the school when they sought permission to speak to someone in another class. But I struggled for weeks before I could comprehend everything my students said, my lack of fluency a constant reminder that I was an outsider, set apart from the students I was teaching and unfamiliar with their world. They seemed to have far less trouble understanding me. But my rapid way of speaking and my own regional dialect — well-known to linguists because it tends to collapse all short vowels into one utilitarian "schwa" sound and fails altogether to recognize diphthongs — must have struck them as odd and confusing, marking me as a stranger.

And I *was* a stranger at Morton Elementary, set apart not just by my accent but by the color of my skin. All but a very small handful of the school's five hundred students were African American, as were its principal, teachers, secretaries, janitors, cafeteria workers, and teachers' aides. All, that is, except me, the school psychologist, and three other classroom teachers, one of whom was a sadistic bully and pariah. Walking through the hall each morning past throngs of students milling about with their friends, I became, for the first time in my life, acutely conscious of myself as a white person, someone with a racial identity. My light skin seemed to call attention to itself, announcing itself as an aberration, making me feel as if I were on display. A few of the younger students, unused to seeing a white person in their school, stared at me the way small children stare at a disabled person in a wheelchair or a homeless person panhandling on the street. Everyone but me, it seemed, belonged, a belonging reinforced by a common dialect, local customs, familiar rituals, and shared memories. I felt completely out of place.

And I knew almost nothing about the world I had entered. My ignorance was a product of the era in which I had grown up. Despite the searing drama of the civil rights movement and the electrifying emergence of the black power movement, most middle-class whites like me knew almost nothing about African American culture. The American history textbooks I had studied in elementary and secondary school had barely acknowledged the presence of African Americans. There was slavery, of course, though that shameful institution was given surprisingly little attention in my schoolbooks, and was rarely, if ever, told from the point of view of the enslaved. Chapters on the Civil War described the courage of white abolitionists, the military exploits of white Yankee and Confederate soldiers, and the leadership of Abraham Lincoln but ignored the contributions of black abolitionists, soldiers, and statesmen. Booker T. Washington and George Washington Carver (never W. E. B. Du Bois) typically made token appearances in the textbooks of those times, but their lives were turned into bland exemplary tales almost guaranteed not to arouse the imaginations — or the questions — of white American schoolchildren. The achievements of most other eminent African Americans went unacknowledged. The America celebrated in the textbooks I had read as a child fully embraced the belief that America had always been the land of "liberty and justice for all"; thus, there was little inclination to discuss the Ku Klux Klan or Jim Crow, or lynchings, race riots, redlining, and poll taxes.

Even at my college, which prided itself in providing a broad education in the liberal arts, African American culture was not a primary object of study in the late 1960s. In addition to the required two-semester Western Civilization history course, I'd taken a number of courses in Asian religions and literatures, studying the cultures of twentieth-century Japan and China, aboriginal Australia, ancient Persia, and medieval Islam; I'd read selected works from Greek, Roman, Italian, French, German, Russian, and Spanish literatures, as well as many of the canonical works of British and American literature; and I'd spent five days with an anthropology class in an isolated and very old Hispanic village in northern New Mexico, participating in the festival of its patron saint and studying its rich culture. But in the three-and-a-half years I was a student there, I never studied a single work by an African American writer, artist, musician, historian, or intellectual. The few books I had read that addressed slavery, race, racial prejudice, and southern culture—Mark Twain's *Huckleberry Finn*, William Faulkner's *Absalom, Absalom*, Harper Lee's *To Kill a Mockingbird*, John Howard Griffin's *Black Like Me*—were all written by white authors.

My ignorance of African American culture was also a reflection of how racially segregated American life in the 1950s and 1960s was, in the North as well as the South. I grew up in a town that included only a handful of black families. Except for the two young African American women who had worked in my home when I was a young child, I had only the most superficial acquaintance with any person of color. There were only five or six African American students in my entire high school, and not one in my class. Nor were there many at my college. I believe only one of the four-hundred-and-fifty students in my college class was black. Perhaps because they had to be truly exceptional to get admitted, the few black students enrolled there tended to be standouts whom I admired from afar: an actress whose charismatic power on stage awed her audiences; a leader and a beauty from Jamaica who was the overwhelming choice for homecoming queen; an extraordinary young man who excelled in everything—academics, student government, sports—and went on to become the first African American attorney general of Colorado. I knew none of these students personally. Before coming to Louisa, I'd never had an African American friend, never been inside the home of an African American family, never spent any time in a black community. I'd never even had a substantial conversation with a black person.

Even at Morton, an invisible color line existed. Because the social life of the school mirrored that of the rigidly segregated town, I found it hard to get to know my African American colleagues. Sometime during those first weeks on the job, each of the three other white female teachers at Morton dropped by my classroom to introduce herself: the pleasant, middle-aged woman who taught the third-grade class across the hall from me; a woman in her early twenties and almost as inexperienced as I, who taught sixth grade; and a psychologist doing graduate studies at the University of Virginia, who worked with troubled students under the supervision of her graduate professor. I did get to know casually one black teacher, Mrs. Perkins, who joined Mrs. Stockton and me for lunch during my first week on the job and who afterwards always greeted me cheerily when I passed her in the hall. But I recall only one other black colleague introducing herself to me, Ramonia's mother, a teacher's aide in a nearby classroom. I would have given anything for an African American colleague to befriend me, invite me to her home, and talk to me about my students, race relations, and Louisa's black and white communities. But in the segregated world of rural Virginia, such acts were hardly imaginable. Nor did I dare cross what I quickly understood to be a rigid racial divide and issue any invitations of my own.

Although I had grown up in a world that was, in effect, a segregated one, I was shocked to find myself in a place where the logic of Jim Crow still dictated the behavior of both whites and blacks. There weren't many African Americans in my hometown or college, it is true, but they had sat in the same classrooms, eaten in the same cafeterias, played on the same teams, performed on the same stages, swum in the same pools, and danced in the same recreation center as me and my white classmates. The only people in the place where I grew up who had lived entirely apart from the rest of the community were the Amish, and they had chosen to do so, a proud minority shunning modern culture and all of us who embraced it. As white ethnic Germans, their segregation had nothing to do with race. And they were poor by choice, for they had renounced all the technologies of the modern age in order to lead a simple life on the land. They had even insisted on maintaining separate schools for their children, successfully procuring, on religious grounds, a special dispensation from the state to allow their children to complete all their formal education by the eighth grade.

Even this relatively benign form of segregation, I knew, had a corrosive effect, creating a barrier between "us" and "them" and encouraging me to view "them" as somehow alien and exotic. Whenever we saw a bearded man in a horse and buggy, a group of bonneted women selling rhubarb and apple pies at a roadside stand, or young girls dressed in long, dark dresses playing in the hot summer sun, we instantly shouted "Amish," reducing these individuals to a single category, distancing ourselves from them. Sometimes we sentimentalized them, becoming attached to men with names like Hosea and Amos who came to our house to paint our barn or shoe our horses and imagining they had a special touch with the paintbrush, a charmed way with horses. Sometimes we stigmatized them, fretting about whether their kitchens were clean, their pies and cinnamon rolls safe to eat. Most of the time we simply regarded them as familiar strangers, a people who inhabited our world but were not of it, perpetual outsiders.

Now, I sensed that many of my African American colleagues and students viewed me in just this way. I wasn't the woman taking over for Mrs. Stockton; I was the *white* woman doing so, and that one adjective seemed to be all that mattered. I felt I had nothing in common with the person they took me to be, a white lady who expected their deference, regarded them with condescension, and elicited their wariness. I wondered whether I would ever be able to convince them to see beyond, beneath my whiteness and to trust me. I began to wonder, too, to what degree my whiteness defined who I was.

I was an outsider in another crucial way, too, for I was a northerner, a Yankee intruder in this southern town and as foreign to the white community as to the black one. Virtually everyone in the school but me, white or black, was a southerner, almost all of them lifelong Virginians with deep, historical ties to Louisa County. I soon recognized that all social interactions were governed by a distinctively southern code of behavior, but I couldn't seem to decipher the code or accustom myself to it. Nor could I fathom the complex set of unwritten rules governing the relations between whites and blacks, the "race etiquette" that required blacks to show deference to whites at all times. My obliviousness to the nuances of this etiquette must have continually created problems for the African Americans I worked with, and particularly for my principal, who, as my immediate superior, had to assert his authority over me while still according me the deferential respect a black man was required to give a white woman in southern society. I didn't understand why Mr. Thompson seemed so uncomfortable in my presence. I couldn't figure out why, when he needed to talk with me, he insisted on standing out in the hall where everybody could see us, rather than calling me into the office to have a heart-to-heart conversation with me.

I was floored when he erupted in fury one day during my first week of teaching after he heard one of my students innocently address me as "teacher." I hadn't minded the child calling me teacher. It seemed a perfectly natural thing to do for a ten-year-old, unsure how to pronounce his new teacher's strange-sounding name. But Mr. Thompson treated this breach of etiquette as a capital offense. Angrily berating the young offender, Mr. Thompson proceeded to lecture the entire class with a great urgency. Never, he told them, had he been so embarrassed by the rudeness this student had shown me. My name, he sarcastically observed, was not "teacher"; it was "Mrs. Hallahan," and they should know to always address me as such. Could they repeat my name after him? Again? And again? The students obligingly chanted "Mrs. Hallahan" on demand. Glaring sternly at them, Mr. Thompson added emphatically that they must also always, always remember to call me "ma'am" whenever they answered me. As in "Yes, ma'am," "No, ma'am." Did they understand? My students nodded soberly. My very presence in the room must have made them anxious. This kind of deference was completely alien to me. By assuming that I required it, Mr. Thompson, I felt, totally misunderstood me.

But the misunderstandings went both ways. One afternoon, a few weeks after I had taken over the class, the sky grew dark and thunder rumbled in the distance. I paid no attention. As the storm grew nearer, however, my students became visibly upset. Some jumped whenever a clap of thunder sounded. Others covered their ears as if the sound were unbearable. None of my students seemed able to concentrate on the lesson I was trying to teach. When an especially bright bolt of lightning slashed through the sky, a couple of girls began to cry. Yet, from my perspective, the storm wasn't particularly threatening or violent. It wasn't even especially close, judging from the gap of time that elapsed between each flash of lightning and the roll of thunder that followed. I tried to calm everyone down, but I couldn't help thinking that they were being superstitious, melodramatic, and unnecessarily emotional.

When the children began to plead with me to turn the classroom lights off, I resisted. If we turned off the lights, I reasoned with them, we wouldn't be able to see to do our work. We'd have to just sit here in the dark with nothing at all to do, and we'd get behind on our lessons. Besides, I assured them, there was absolutely no reason to turn the lights off. The classroom was perfectly safe. I thought my position was entirely rational and completely justified, but they found my refusal to turn out the lights profoundly upsetting. In fact, it made them a little crazed. I had absolutely no idea why they were so terrified, but instead of asking them to explain, I stubbornly tried to soldier on with the lesson. Why, I wonder now, was I so insensitive to their anxiety? I never doubted my own reaction to the storm, never questioned that my response to it was inherently superior to theirs.

After the storm had subsided and the students had filed out of my room to catch their afternoon buses, the third-grade teacher across the hall, who was white, stopped by my room. She wanted to know how my students had responded to the thunderstorm.

"You know," she said, "this was the first really serious thunderstorm we've had since lightning struck the school last fall," her words striking me with no less force than the thunderbolt she was intent on describing. "As soon as I heard the thunder today," she continued,

the memory of that day flooded back. I can't tell you how terrifying that moment was when the lightning hit the building. It blew out all the fluorescent lights on this entire wing of the school building. Made the loudest noise imaginable: first the roar of the thunder and then the lights exploding—pow, pow, pow. We might as well have been in a war zone. Everybody screamed. And then, of course, the building went completely dark. The kids were traumatized. It took us days to calm them down. I didn't realize until this afternoon how much that lightning strike had affected me, too. As soon as I saw that first bolt of lightning, the only thing I could think about was those fluorescent lights exploding in my classroom. My first impulse was to turn off the classroom lights. I didn't care at all about my lesson plans; I figured Social Studies could wait until tomorrow. Maybe you saw us over here, sitting in the dark?

I made a mental note to myself. Listen to the children. Give them permission to speak.

## This Is You Miss Hallanhan

A box of crayons, a pair of scissors, some scotch tape, and a small sheaf of white paper were the only art supplies in my classroom. Mrs. Stockton had carefully conserved these few items, which she had been allocated at the beginning of the school year, permitting only a few of the most talented students to use them, and then only under her careful direction. On the morning after the snowstorm, when I had just begun to observe her classroom, I watched as she hung a large sheet of white paper on the wall at the front of the room. Summoning Reginald, she handed him a box of crayons and told him to draw this month's picture for the classroom calendar. Reginald seemed to understand exactly what was expected of him, and without any further instructions, he diligently began to copy an illustration that appeared on an open page of a small commercial calendar on the teacher's desk. He hadn't gotten very far, however, when Mrs. Stockton intervened and began to berate him for his "carelessness." He had, she scolded, deviated from the original picture, ignoring some of its details, adding flourishes of his own. She ordered him to return to his seat and instructed Cecily to finish the picture, cautioning her not to be careless like Reginald.

I watched as Cecily's picture took shape, noting how carefully and precisely she copied the details of the calendar illustration, sticking closely to the original. She drew a steep, snow-covered hill, a large pine tree, a bright sun. Then she sketched in the figures of four children gleefully sledding down the hill, skillfully coloring their flying hair and smiling faces, their winter jackets, scarves, hats, and mittens with the crayons. The figures she drew so earnestly, I realized with a start as I glanced around the room of tan, brown, and black faces, looked nothing like Cecily or her classmates. Mirroring the children in the calendar picture, the children she drew were all white. She devoted particular attention to the hair of the female figures she was drawing: each of her sledding girls had especially long, straight hair, which she meticulously colored a bright, bright yellow. What was she thinking, I wondered, as she drew the little blonde white girls who looked nothing like herself, nothing like her friends or her family, and who played in a northern winter wonderland that did not resemble in any way the world she inhabited? Looking around, I realized that this classroom filled with black children had not a single picture of an African American on its walls. And virtually none of the images I'd seen in the school's textbooks depicted black people, either.

A few weeks later, I went to the nearest five-and-dime and spent my own money on art supplies for my class. At the time, I naively assumed that the school district was too impoverished to buy crayons and paint and paper and clay for its elementary school students. Eager to give my students the opportunity to create things, I didn't mind at all buying these art supplies for my class. Months later, I would come upon a two-page spread in the local paper, showcasing an ambitious art exhibit produced by the children of Apple Grove Elementary School, one of the county's white grade schools. And I would look wistfully at the photographs of beaming white children standing beside impressive displays of their prize-winning art work: big, splashy posters; bright and colorful pictures made with pastels, watercolors, and poster paint; whimsical papier-mâché animals; sophisticated portraits of nineteenth-century historical figures. But in January, when I purchased these supplies, I had no clue that Louisa's white elementary school had easy access to art materials denied my students. I had no thoughts of art fairs or public exhibits. My goal was far more fundamental: I wanted to get my students to see themselves as appropriate subjects for art.

I would like to tell you that I flooded the room with images of African American art and stocked the shelves with children's literature illustrated by African American artists, but the truth is that in

*1. My friend Mrs. Hallahan. Artist unknown.*

1970 I didn't know anything about African American art or children's literature and I didn't have access to any school materials that featured African American children. But I had an idea. "Draw a friend in this class," I instructed the first time I distributed the newly acquired drawing paper. I imagined them all busily creating portraits of their classmates, so I was surprised to discover that many of their sketches featured a white person: me. One boy even chose to interpret the assignment loosely and copied a portrait of Abraham Lincoln that hung in the room. In our portraits Abe and I command attention. Our images are large, boldly drawn, and centered on the page, our likenesses fleshed out in some detail. Even when a sketch of me is crudely drawn, the artist seems comfortable and assured, employing familiar conventions to capture me and give me a presence (figure 1). Not so the portraits of black classmates, which seem much more timid and tentative. The images in these portraits are typically small, even tiny; some are off center; most are highly schematic, often giving only the bare outline of a face (figure 2). Their creators appear to be struggling

2. *Chester. Used by permission of the artist.*

to find a way to depict the familiar face of a best friend, whose features paradoxically seem more remote to them, less imaginable than those of a white teacher they have known for only a couple of weeks.

I began to connect the difficulty they had visualizing and representing themselves in their drawings with the extraordinary attention many of the girls devoted to my hair in those early weeks. Almost daily, before class began in the morning, the girls crowded around my desk to inspect it, discussing like expert beauticians its texture, its length, its lack of curl.

"Look, Ramonia," Matilda would say, stroking my hair, "can you believe how straight and silky and long it is?"

"Oh, Mrs. Hallahan," Ramonia would sigh, "I wish my hair was as beautiful as yours." And then Cecily and Annie Mae and Jeanine would ask to touch my hair, too, oohing and ahhing as they ran their fingers through it.

Although in the world in which I had grown up there was nothing particularly remarkable about my hair, I had a pretty good understanding of why it held them in its thrall. After all, hadn't my sister helped me iron my wavy hair one summer day to make it look straighter, more stylish, more like the models in *Seventeen*? And hadn't she sat for hours in the sun, her blonde hair anointed with lemon juice, raw egg, and god knows what else, in an effort to make it even lighter, closer in tone to whatever blonde movie star was currently in vogue? If even her straight blonde hair failed to meet some impossible Hollywood standard of sleekness and blondeness that she had fully internalized by age twelve, how did the girls in my class feel when they measured themselves against such an ideal? I wanted them to see that their hair—braided into multiple strands, fastened by brightly colored barrettes, tied back in unruly pony tails, decorated with ribbons, artfully separated into neat cornrows, curling softly around their faces—was beautiful too. I wanted to turn their admiring eyes onto themselves and to see themselves as worthy of representation.

A few weeks later I tried another approach, this time asking my students to draw a picture of their family. But before they began, I encouraged them to tell me what their mothers and fathers, brothers and sisters looked like, and I pushed them to give more and more detailed descriptions. Exactly how small was Emmeline's baby brother? Did he have any teeth yet? Any hair? And Clinton's Dad: Just how tall was he, a foot taller than Clinton? Two feet? What did Linda's mother usually wear to church? Did her hat have a wide brim? Did the color of her purse match her dress? Were Annie Mae's sisters petite like her? Did they fix their hair the same way or style it differently? Was their skin the same shade of brown? I watched as my students began sketching their families, each child hunkered in concentration over a single piece of the cheap white paper I'd distributed. After he had drawn the outline of his family, Reginald suddenly grabbed a brown crayon and quickly colored the faces of the figures he had drawn a dark, rich brown. He glanced furtively up at me, almost as if he were getting away with something, and then he held his picture up for Chester and Harrison to see. They flashed him conspiratorial smiles and immediately rooted around for their own brown and black crayons. Cecily caught on and methodically began adding curly black hair to her figures. A hint of the transgressive accompanied these acts, as if a taboo were being violated. Soon all the students were buzzing with excitement as the images of their families, in all shades of brown and black, took shape. It was as if the students were claiming, collectively, an aspect of their identity that had been denied them. I was thrilled.

I don't know why the girls eventually lost interest in my hair. Probably the novelty of it wore off. I must have come to seem less exotic to them, more complicated, harder to idealize. Nevertheless, I wasn't prepared for the note Jeanine slipped me a few weeks after the drawing exercises. On it she had drawn a striking picture of an African American woman, her hair short and black, her brown face framed by dangling earrings, a brown coat over her bright red dress, black boots pulled up over her checked stockings. Underneath the picture, Jeanine had carefully penned a message: "This is you Miss Hallanhan" (figure 3). The red dress, the brown coat, the black boots and checked stockings were, indeed, faithful renderings of the clothes I wore that day. But my long, brown hair—the object of all that adoration—had been blackened and cropped short, my light skin darkened to a rich, chocolate brown. I viewed Jeanine's picture as an enormous compliment, a precious communication from the quiet little girl with the knowing, observant eyes. And it humbled me, making me realize how little I understood about racial identity, how little any of us really knows about the way others see us.

*3. This is you Miss Hallanhan. Used by permission of the artist.*

Jeanine's picture suggested that at least some of the students were beginning to accept me. But I had in no way overcome the strong, initial suspicion many of the students felt towards me. Most had had little contact with the world outside their close, African American community, few had had any significant interaction with a white adult, and all of them, I was learning, had legitimate reasons to distrust me, a white woman. I could sense their suspicion of me in those early weeks, roiling ominously beneath the surface of our daily interactions. Every so often, it erupted in a sudden, angry remark, an unanticipated resentment, a defiant gesture. Once, when I reprimanded Wendell for misbehaving, he shot back testily, "No white woman's gonna tell me what to do." More often, however, Samuel, the only white child in the room, became the focal point of their distrust.

Samuel was at Morton, along with a handful of other white children, because the school board had assigned all the county's special education students, regardless of race, to the Negro school, and he had been diagnosed with a mental illness. I never knew how my students processed the fact that the white majority had for so long and with such vehemence resisted allowing white and black children to go to school together but seemed to have no qualms about sending the physically handicapped, mentally challenged, and emotionally disturbed white children to the Negro school. But I knew that Samuel's presence in my classroom complicated my efforts to win my students' trust. They tended to view all my interactions with Samuel as inherently biased, projecting onto my relation with him all their anxieties about my racial otherness, all their fears of being mistreated or misunderstood, all their considerable knowledge of white bigotry and discrimination.

Samuel was a very disturbed boy. His mother had died when he was a baby, and he had been abandoned by his father when he was four. A ward of the state, he lived with a foster mother, to whom he was attached. Shortly before I arrived, he had been further traumatized when, in a very unfortunate incident, he overheard his foster mother telling the school psychologist that she couldn't cope with him and didn't feel she could take care of him any longer. Samuel had fully internalized his abandonment and "knew," at some deep level, that he was unlovable. His pale blue eyes cast a perpetually lost, vacant gaze, as if, at his core, there was only a terrible emptiness. He was eerily detached from the world and so vague and unfocused—so "spacey"—that it was easy to forget he was present in the classroom at all. Socially, he was extremely immature. He laughed at inappropriate times, failed to grasp the jokes and stories other kids told, tried with no success to tell his own. Lonely and troubled, Samuel had no friends. Once he told me sadly, "You know, no one wants to play with me; I just get in the way." Much of the time, he lived in a fantasy world. One morning he rushed to my desk to tell me with great excitement that his father had come to his foster mother's house to visit him.

"I was on the front porch, and I looked down the driveway," Samuel told me breathlessly. "And you know what I saw?" he asked, his voice getting louder, more high pitched and excited.

I saw my Daddy walking down that drive! My Daddy! He was walking toward me, in his black jacket and his blue jeans, walking and smiling, and he was carrying an armload of presents, all just for me. I was so glad to see him, I clapped my hands and shouted to him. And then I jumped off the porch and started running out to meet him. I was running and laughing and yelling, 'Daddy! Daddy!' And when I got close, you know what I did? When I got close and he opened his arms to hug me —

here Samuel paused, allowing the suspense to build — "I got out my shotgun and blew his head off."

Although I felt sorry for him, I was never really able to connect with Samuel. He was the only student in my large class with whom I felt no natural rapport, and I had to discipline myself to be patient with him. Nevertheless, many of my students were convinced that I favored Samuel simply because he was white. One day, when I reminded Samuel it was time for his daily appointment with Miss Broderick, the school psychologist, Derrick objected.

"How come Samuel gets to go see Miss Broderick, anyhow?" he asked bitterly. "You're just letting him see her cause he's white."

Derrick's accusation stunned me. Samuel and Marcus had both been seeing Miss Broderick since September, months before I had arrived. Conveniently forgetting this history, Derrick was now accusing me of favoritism. And he wasn't letting up.

"Why don't I get to see Miss Broderick?" he challenged. "You won't let me see her because I'm colored. You just let Samuel go see her 'cause he's white, 'cause he's your white brother."

Some of the other boys started to chime in. "Yeah. Samuel's your brother. That's why he gets to see Miss Broderick. It's because he's your white brother."

I should explain that Miss Broderick sometimes visited my class to observe Samuel and Marcus, and all my students were entranced by her. She was tall and striking, with a calm assurance and a commanding presence, and she had a wonderful rapport with children. It was easy enough to see why Derrick was jealous of Samuel's opportunity to visit her on a daily basis.

I tried to reason with Derrick, but he was growing more and more agitated, and his charges of unfairness seemed contagious. I asked him to step into the hallway with me to talk, even though I was violating the cardinal rule of the school by leaving the room temporarily unattended. As soon as the two of us were alone in the empty hall, I spoke sternly to him, pointing out that I sent Marcus as well as Samuel to see Miss Broderick and that I was simply following the routine that had been established by Mrs. Stockton. Then, hoping to appeal to his kindhearted nature, I confided that Samuel saw Mrs. Broderick because he had problems, serious problems, and she was trained to help him.

I wasn't prepared for Derrick's response. He turned suddenly away from me to hide a flood of tears, then slammed his fist against the wall as hard as he could and sobbed, "But *I've* got problems too." And he was right. I looked at him, his face turned to the wall, his body shaking, and wondered how it felt to be the one child of ten sent to live with grandparents because there wasn't enough room at home; to have to repeat the fourth grade; to find yourself in the same class as your younger brother, the favored one at the home where you no longer lived; to have no textbooks because the school district didn't provide them and your parents couldn't afford them; to be eleven and still struggling to learn to read; to be terrified because your failing grades meant you might be held back once again. Yes, Derrick had problems, too. And nobody was paying any attention.

This incident was not the last time the students accused me of favoring Samuel. Late one afternoon, after a particularly difficult day, I was chiding Ervin about some infraction when he suddenly blurted out,

"You don't love us."

I looked at him in amazement.

"You only love one person in this classroom," he declared dramatically, "and that's Samuel, your brother."

Before I could respond, some of the other boys seconded Ervin's declaration. "Yeah, you only love Samuel, you don't love us. 'Cause

Samuel's your brother. He's your white brother." Soon, every child joined in the chant.

I was too tired to rebut their charge, too frustrated to ignore it, too angry to go on. Their accusations stung, and I could feel my eyes tearing up. I wanted to tell them how infuriating it was to be viewed solely in terms of one's race and not one's actions. I wanted to tell them how annoying it was to be linked to Samuel simply because of our shared racial identity. Instead, I stood in front of my class of thirty-eight ten-year-olds and wept. A hush swept over the room. The children watched me in awed silence. "But I do love you," I finally said. "I love every one of you in this room."

Something important happened in that moment. Maybe my students had been waiting for just such a sign, a declaration, that I cared about them. Maybe they had needed some assurance that, as a white person, I was capable of responding to them without bigotry. Maybe they had misinterpreted my refusal to spank them as an indication that they didn't matter to me. Maybe they hadn't realized that they had the power to hurt me. Whatever the explanation, we bonded in that brief moment when our roles reversed, and I became the powerless, vulnerable one. As they filed out of the room to their buses that afternoon, many of my students pressed notes into my hand. "Mrs. H. is pretty and NICE," read one. "Please don't tell my mother," begged another. "Today I started a new life for my self," announced a third. And my favorite:

My Ashamement.
I'm ashamed of my self. I'm sorry of what I said and did. Please forgive me. I'm very very sorry. I love you very much. I hope you love me.
Love, Ramonia Tirish Jackson

# Concerning This Little Frightened Child

*Concerning this*
*Little frightened child*
*One might make a story*
*Charting tomorrow.*
*—from "Migration" by Langston Hughes*

## I Don't Know How I'll Ever Get Home

At the end of the school day one February afternoon, shortly after my students had filed out of the classroom to catch their buses, Victor reappeared at my door. He had forgotten his math book. After rummaging frantically in his desk, he finally located it and charged back out of the room. A few minutes later, however, he was back and near tears.

"What happened?" I asked, concerned.

"The bus left without me," he said, trying hard not to cry. "I was running after it, but the bus driver didn't see me. He pulled out of the parking lot and drove right off without me. I was running as fast as I could and I was hollering and waving my hands. But the bus driver didn't even slow down." Victor stood in the doorway, trying to catch his breath, still excited by the drama of the chase. Then the full impact of his situation hit him.

"I don't know how I'll ever get home," he wailed.

Though tall and lanky, Victor looked younger than his ten years. With his unruly mop of hair, expressive eyes, and cherubic face, he exuded an innocence that made his sense of abandonment seem all the more poignant. I tried to calm him down. I assured him that a missed bus was not a serious problem. I explained that I would call his mother and let her know what had happened. And with the confident authority of an adult who wants an anxious child to know that everything will be all right, I told him I was sure his mother would pick him up at school as soon as she could. I had ridden a bus to school. I knew all about missing buses.

"But you can't call her," he protested. "We don't have a telephone!"

Taken aback, I suppressed the impulse to blurt out something stupid, like "what do you mean, you don't have a telephone?" Suddenly aware of my own naiveté, I began to see Victor's panic in a new light.

"And anyway there's no car," Victor sobbed. "My Daddy goes to work with my uncle, but they don't get home until way after dark."

I was embarrassed that I had automatically assumed Victor's predicament could be solved with a simple phone call. Although I was well aware that many of my students were poor, I hadn't fully grasped that some of them had no telephone, no car, no way home if the bus left without them. Groping for a solution, I couldn't help resorting to the familiar course of action from my own childhood. Surely, I asked him, there was a neighbor I could call? Or a grandparent? Wasn't there someone I could contact who could drive to school to pick him up? But Victor only shook his head.

"What am I going to do?" he asked, his eyes pleading for help.

I met his gaze. The obvious solution was for me to drive him home myself. I asked him where he lived.

"In the country."

"How far from school?"

"A long ways a way."

"Do you know the way? If I drive you home, can you show me how to get there?

"I think so."

I promised him he'd be home in time for dinner, explaining that we would start out as soon as I could finish up my work at school and meet my husband Bill, who taught at the adjacent junior high. A half hour later, Victor eagerly climbed into our old, white Rambler sedan, his misfortune transformed now into an adventure, his anxiety, if not entirely relieved, superceded by the excitement of going home and the novelty of riding in his teacher's car. We headed out, Bill driving and Victor straining to see over the dash board, his eyes focused on the road ahead, his small body taut, poised to alert us to a sudden turn, an upcoming fork in the road, a landmark. Almost immediately, we left the main road that led to town and drove into the countryside. We navigated a series of secondary roads, passing some prosperous farms, an abandoned house, a row of white clapboard homes. We turned at a cow pasture onto a well-tended gravel road, and after quite a few miles, we turned again, onto a much narrower road bordered by farm fields. Eventually, we entered a dense pine woods. The gravel gave out and the road became dirt. Bill swerved to avoid large potholes. We passed a couple of run-down houses—shacks, really—with tin roofs, unpainted walls, and sagging porches. Smoke curled from their chimneys. In front of one, two young children swung giddily on a tire suspended from a tree. Victor waved. Winding further and further into the thick woods, we could occasionally make out the shape of an isolated cabin hidden among the pine trees. We caught a glimpse of a man chopping wood, heard a dog signaling our presence. But mostly, we were alone in a vast, silent pine forest.

"Are we almost there?" I asked Victor a little anxiously. The woods seemed to grow darker and more impenetrable as we drove on, and now there was only the slightest hint of sunlight filtering through the tall trees. I wasn't at all sure Bill and I would be able to retrace the intricate route we had taken into this remote part of the county, and I began to wonder if we were ever going to find Victor's house. Perhaps we had missed a turn. Perhaps we had taken the wrong dirt road. Then, without any warning, the road gave out, and we were lurching along a narrow lane. We could barely see its outline in the red dirt. Our car dug into deep ruts as we inched our way forward.

"There's my house!" Victor shouted triumphantly, pointing towards a tiny log cabin in a little clearing at the end of the lane. "Right over there."

Dwarfed by the towering pine trees that surrounded it, Victor's house was not much bigger than the log cabins of Virginia's original settlers or of the pioneers who homesteaded on the western frontier. A goat tied beside the cabin bleated at us as we got out of the car. A flock of chickens roamed freely about, scratching in the small dirt yard. The rusting hulk of an old car lay abandoned near a large stack of neatly chopped wood. I smelled the pungent smoke of the wood stove, the inviting aroma of stew cooking, the sweet pitch of the pine woods. Victor's brothers and sisters abandoned their play and gathered curiously around our car, staring solemnly at Bill and me. A couple of dogs circled us, barking furiously. Then Victor's mother rushed out the front door and hugged her missing boy. Victor was home.

Before my visit to Victor's home, I had never suspected that anyone inhabited the vast tracts of pine forests that were owned and logged by a few large and prosperous lumber companies. Nor had I realized just how primitive some of my students' homes were, not houses really, but makeshift huts with no indoor plumbing, electricity, central heat, or telephones. I had from time to time driven past small African American settlements where some of my students lived: four or five simple, one-story frame houses on concrete slabs built in a row along a country road or down a long gravel lane, each with a small plot of land, the red clay gardens awaiting spring planting. But now I understood that these homes, however modest, belonged to my more fortunate students. The poorer ones like Victor lived in far more remote parts of the county, on dirt roads that didn't appear on county maps and weren't maintained by county crews, in ramshackle buildings that were essentially invisible to white outsiders like me.

Until my journey into the pine woods with Victor that February afternoon, I had looked out at my new surroundings—this rural Virginia county where I had temporarily taken up residence—with the eyes of a middle-class, white tourist. I had driven, duly impressed, through the Green Springs district, past the large estates bounded by miles of wooden fences, past fallow fields still bearing the traces of the fall's bountiful harvest, past the Black Angus cattle and Thoroughbred horses grazing in picturesque pastures lined by thick hedgerows. I'd caught glimpses of stately, antebellum houses, hidden down long alleys of enormous old oak trees, graceful and alluring. I'd admired the county's columned and domed courthouse, the quaint buildings lining the courthouse square, and the county seat's large Victorian houses, with their wide porches, bay windows, and fancy gingerbread ornamentation.

And I'd studied, with appropriate awe, the historical markers scattered throughout the county. Here, at Roundabout, Patrick Henry resided when he represented Louisa County in the House of Burgesses. Here, in an eighteenth-century church, the future Presidents Madison and Monroe attended school. Here, at a tavern in the little village of Cuckoo, Jack Jouett Jr.—the South's Paul Revere—overheard the British planning to capture members of the Virginia legislature and set out for Monticello to warn Thomas Jefferson. Here, at Trevilians Station, in one of the largest cavalry battles of the Civil War, Union soldiers led by General Philip Sheridan fought the Confederate troops of General Wade Hampton in an unsuccessful attempt to destroy the Virginia Central Railroad.

I had marveled at this history, its traces still visible in the old planters' homes and sprawling farms, so different from the hardscrabble farms where I had grown up in a forgotten corner of Pennsylvania, where an old home was more likely to be one hundred years old than two hundred and fifty years and no one was particularly wealthy or famous. So little had ever happened in my home county that the historical markers had to resort to marking the passage of people and things from someplace else to someplace beyond: Commodore Perry marched through on his way to the Battle of Lake Erie; escaped slaves desperately seeking freedom in Canada hid in various houses—otherwise unremarkable—that had served as way stations on the Underground Railroad; iron ore was dug out of Lake Erie, forty miles to the north, and shipped on a network of canals and railroads through the region to the Pittsburgh steel mills, seventy miles south; nearly a million soldiers passed through Camp Reynolds, an army transfer station from 1942 to 1945, on their way to the European Theatre in World War II, their temporary stays soon forgotten when the war ended. Louisa, in contrast, boasted a rich and important history, and its lovely antebellum homes stood as romantic remnants of that fascinating past. I didn't, until my visit to Victor's cabin, look beyond their beautiful facades.

Watching Victor hug his worried mother, smelling his dinner cooking on the wood stove, standing in the tiny clearing his father had cut out of the giant pines, I tried to imagine what events in Louisa's past had led his family here, to this isolated and primitive log cabin, and I struggled to comprehend how they managed to survive. I had read the grim statistics concerning the county's rural poor. I had been told that many of Louisa's African American families subsisted on incomes far below the official poverty level. And I had caught telling glimpses of that poverty in my classroom—the anxious look on a child's face, an indirect reference to family troubles, a painful humiliation. Nevertheless, Victor's home, hidden deep in the pine woods, still shocked me. How was it possible, I wondered, that ninety miles from the capital of the richest nation in the world, in a country so technologically advanced that it had recently landed men on the moon, families like Victor's were living in the same conditions as their nineteenth-century ancestors?

I recalled, with a sudden twinge, how much had been made in recent news reports about the impending destruction of some of the area's prized historical estates, casualties of an ambitious project to build a nuclear power plant and dam on the North Anna River in the eastern part of Louisa County. I, too, had mourned the loss of these estates, lamenting along with other angry white citizens over the way the project threatened the beauty and historical integrity of an area a journalist covering the story for a national news magazine likened to the elegant Chateaux region of France. Nowhere, I now realized with chagrin, had I read anything about how the power company's plan to flood thirteen thousand acres would affect the county's poorest families, most of them African American, or where the displaced poor would go, or how they could afford to relocate. And yet, all of the threatened estates had been carved out of the wilderness by African American slaves; their gracious Georgian, Federal, and neoclassical houses had been built, serviced, and maintained by slaves; their owners' wealth had been amassed through the backbreaking labor of slaves who had cleared, plowed, planted, and harvested the fertile tobacco fields.

In 1970 I vaguely understood that my students were the descendants of the slaves who had worked the county's large tobacco plantations from the end of the seventeenth century until the middle of the nineteenth century. Nevertheless, decades later, when I was sitting at a large wooden table in the Special Collections reading room at the University of Virginia, examining an 1814 ledger of a prominent white planter family in Louisa, I was surprised to discover that I recognized most of the surnames of the white planters listed there. They were the very same surnames of my African American students in 1970: Graves, Nelson, Johnson, Pointdexter, Timberlake, Anderson, Desper. The white men named in the ledger had probably owned my students' ancestors. Some of my students were surely blood relatives of these white planters as well, dispossessed descendants of the very planters who had enslaved them.

When I was teaching these students in 1970, I didn't know anything about the history of slavery in Louisa County. I didn't know, for instance, that 62 percent of the people living in Louisa County just before the Civil War—nearly two-thirds of the population—were slaves. Or that slaves were such valuable property that they accounted for more than 50 percent of the county's tax revenues in 1860. Nor did I know that 66 percent of Louisa's white families owned at least one slave and 45 percent owned twenty or more slaves, exceptionally high percentages when compared to the South as a whole, where only 25 percent of white families owned slaves and only 28 percent of those slave owners possessed such a large number of slaves. Caught up in the daily challenges of teaching a large class of ten-year-old children, I didn't ask questions about my students' slave heritage or think very much about the relation between their present lives and a past that the county historical markers presented as venerable and grand.

Coincidentally, at about the same time I was teaching in Louisa, a white University of Virginia graduate student who had grown up poor in neighboring Madison County was asking those very questions. Immersing himself in Louisa County wills, deeds, tax rolls, legal statutes, census figures, plantation ledgers, and other historical documents from the county's nineteenth-century past, he set out to explain the historical relation between poverty and race in this large, rural county. In his doctoral dissertation, which he published in 1982, Crandall Shifflett tells how, soon after the defeat of the Confederacy, the county's white landowners devised a number of strategies to deny the newly freed slaves—my students' ancestors—the political power that their numbers and freedman status should have afforded them. He shows how Louisa's white landowners monopolized the agricultural land, tools, and capital and developed a system of patronage that exploited black workers, in effect, keeping them in a state of peonage not unlike what they had endured under slavery. Black laborers in Louisa County were paid less than white laborers for the same work and provided with lower quality housing and food. They were subject to laws that impeded their mobility and prevented them from leaving their employers. They were taxed at a higher rate than whites (between four and six times the rates of whites) and excluded from the services and benefits those taxes provided. And through gerrymandering and corruption, they had their votes nullified, even before the Virginia state constitution of 1902 disenfranchised black voters.

The success of these strategies, according to Shifflet, "allowed employers to continue to treat their laborers as slaves, call them 'their darkies,' refer to their wages as 'rations,' issue them distinctive clothing (oznaburg), 'settle up' at Christmas time, place them in crude cabins, and label their resistance as laziness and proof of the need for continued white dominance." As a result, Louisa's African Americans were forced to "bargain . . . with patrons for employment, housing, loans, rent, and general access to means of production," all the while having to perform "countless acts of deference" to powerful whites.

Reading Shifflett's history of late-nineteenth-century Louisa County decades after I had lived there, I was struck by how many elements of this patronage system were still in effect when I was teaching in one of Louisa's Negro schools. In 1970, an elite group of white men still controlled the major political offices through the power of appointment. These political appointees still served the interests of large landholders by keeping property taxes low while providing almost no public services for the poor. Whites still expected Louisa's African American citizens to defer to them, negotiate with them according to terms favorable to white interests, refrain from any open political opposition to the status quo, and obey the rigid rules of Jim Crow. African Americans still did not own very much land or have access to much capital, and most of the jobs in the county available to them were still limited mostly to agricultural and domestic jobs. And the policies made and enforced by the white elite still served the landed class at the expense of poor and black citizens. Because of the exceptionally low property taxes, for example, the public schools were chronically underfunded. The sparse funds that were earmarked for education were further diluted by whites' insistence on segregation, which required the maintenance of separate schools for white and African American children and resulted in fewer resources being allocated to the Negro schools. A poorly educated work force, in turn, guaranteed wealthy landowners (some of whom sent their children to private schools) a plentiful supply of agricultural workers who, with little mobility and no other prospects for work, were forced to work for low wages, often in seasonal employment.

By 1970, of course, change was in the air. The Civil Rights Bill of 1964 had made Jim Crow illegal, even though it continued to be practiced, and the Louisa County schools had, under a federal court order, begun to desegregate, sixteen years after the Supreme Court's *Brown* decision. But in 1970 the old order had not yet given way to the new. Familiar customs, time-honored traditions, deeply ingrained patterns of behavior, long-held assumptions—their roots deep in a slaveholding past—still persisted more than a century after Emancipation, haunting race relations, dictating the interactions between whites and blacks, predetermining the future of the county's African American children.

## She Should Have Ate It

As part of my freshman orientation at Colorado College in 1966, I was required to read Michael Harrington's classic book about poverty in the United States, *The Other America*. Discussing this book as we sprawled on the broad lawn of my college's mountain-lined campus, my idealistic classmates and I expressed our outrage at the economic conditions of America's poor and earnestly argued about how their lives might be improved. Most of us had grown up in affluent families during the postwar economic boom, and we were shocked to read about the experiences of America's poorest citizens, who, Harrington told us, went to bed hungry, lived in substandard and unheated homes, had few opportunities to improve their lot, and were deprived of such basic amenities as indoor plumbing, electricity, telephones, cars, standard appliances, and warm clothing. But for all our well-intentioned efforts to come to terms with the presence of poverty in a booming America, the nation's poor remained for us an abstraction. We grappled with the appalling statistics in Harrington's book, considered the feasibility of various kinds of interventions, and examined the politics of Lyndon Johnson's War on Poverty, but in the end, we couldn't really imagine what it might actually feel like to grow up poor in a wealthy nation like ours.

Unlike most of my college classmates, who were raised in homogeneous neighborhoods and sent to elite suburban and private schools, I had attended the public schools of a small town with children from a wide range of socioeconomic backgrounds. This experience provided me fleeting glimpses into the lives of children far less fortunate than I. I remember befriending a classmate in my rural elementary school, a shy little girl named Margaret who wore hand-me-down clothes and lived in a dilapidated old house in the country, its paint peeling, its yard dirt. I invited her to my tenth birthday party. In the midst of the hay rides and pony rides and picnicking on that sunny October day, I realized that Margaret had disappeared, and I went in search of her. I found her in my bedroom, crouched in front of the open door of my closet, staring at my shoes. She was mortified when I discovered her there, gazing in fascination at my black patent-leather Mary Janes, my brown Buster Brown school shoes, my white summer pumps with cloth bows, my red canvas sneakers, my black riding boots. Her face turned bright red, and I intuitively understood that she did not want me to know that the objects on my closet floor, objects I took completely for granted, had the power to mesmerize her. Suddenly embarrassed by the large amount of stuff in my closet, I took her by the hand and gently led her back outside, neither of us speaking a word. The memory of our mutual shame has stuck with me all these years, a frozen moment in time, marking, perhaps, a lost innocence, the sobering recognition that neither worthiness nor virtue, but only an inexplicable stroke of luck, separated me from Margaret and her envy. But such episodes were rare. Growing up, I interacted mostly with other middle-class children. Until I arrived in Louisa, I remained largely ignorant of the tremendous stress children living in poverty endure daily.

Virtually all my students at Morton Elementary were poor. Some were poorer than others, a fact that became apparent to me when I collected lunch money: only a few paid the full twenty cents for a daily lunch; many more paid half that cost, their parents having qualified for the federal government's subsidized lunch program; and the poorest children received free lunches through that same program. To my students, being poor was nothing remarkable. Instead, it was pretty much the norm, a way of life that was familiar, even expected. When two young brothers arrived at Morton with a social worker one February morning, however, my students were as appalled as I at the boys' appearance, for all of us understood that these two little boys were desperately, unimaginably poor. I remember hearing the news of their discovery, the gossip rippling like shock waves through the halls, outraging teachers, upsetting children: how two young boys had been found with their parents in the backwoods; how they had been living in unspeakably primitive conditions, virtually cut off from the rest of the world, barely surviving; how they had never attended a school or been inside a church or set eyes on a town; how no one, neither the county authorities nor the leaders of the African American community nor their nearest neighbors, had known of their existence. But none of this information prepared me for the moment when, on my way to the principal's office one morning, I turned at the top of the stairwell and caught sight of the two brothers walking alone down the long, empty corridor.

The two little boys cautiously made their way towards me. Lit from behind, their small bodies seemed as weightless as the particles of dust that floated above them in the eerie shafts of light. Their gait was slow and unsteady, like an old man's, and as they approached me, I could see that their legs were severely deformed, bowed, I later learned, from rickets, a disease caused by a lack of vitamin D. Their bony arms were impossibly thin, with no more mass than the arms on a stick figure in a child's drawing. Their growth stunted, their bodies ravaged, they seemed at once too young to be in school and old enough to be grandfathers. Deprivation, it appeared, had robbed them of their proper place in time. I had never before met, face-to-face, a severely malnourished child, though I had, of course, seen photographs of Jewish children newly liberated from Nazi concentration camps and television images of starving children in famine-plagued parts of the world. I was shocked to confront these two little boys in the hallway of the very school where I worked. I wanted to cry out in protest. I wanted to embrace and comfort them. I wanted to avert my eyes and flee. I could see as they walked towards me that they were as terrified by my sudden appearance in the hall as I was unsettled by their presence. They must have been bewildered by the turn of events that had brought them to this alien place, confused by the attention of the social workers and teachers and foster parents attempting to help them, overwhelmed by the noise and bustle of the school. Separated from their parents and removed from all that was familiar to them, the two brothers clasped hands in solidarity, as if the presence of the other was all that anchored them in their new world. I can, even now, see the lonely silhouette of these two lost brothers in the empty hall as they walk, hand in hand, bravely, tentatively, into the unknown.

None of my students suffered the extreme deprivation of these two brothers, but some of them didn't get enough to eat. Early one morning as I was taking attendance, I heard a loud commotion in the back of the room. The students sitting near William were snickering, jeering, shouting, and frantically trying to get my attention. Pointing their fingers at William, they yelled out to me, "William is eating his lunch! William is eating his lunch, and it's not even time for school to start!" Their shrieks drew all eyes to the skinny little boy, but their taunts did not stop him from cramming the rest of his peanut butter sandwich into his mouth. He appeared to swallow it in one gulp. An opened lunch pail lay empty on his desk.

Mrs. Stockton had told me to keep an eye on William. "He doesn't get enough to eat at home," she'd explained with a sigh, shaking her head. "And, even though he qualifies for the free lunch program, his parents refuse to sign him up for it. They're too proud to admit they need the help. Sometimes he comes to school hungry."

I asked William to come up to my desk to talk with me. I watched him as he walked up the long aisle. He was small for his age and slight, but he easily made up in personality what he lacked in size. He had an appealing, puckish quality about him, as if he were perpetually imagining ways he could turn work into play, grief into laughter, drudgery into mischief. With his expressive, elastic face and talent for mimicry, he readily assumed the role of the class clown, to the delight of the other students who loved nothing better than to egg him on. But on this morning, William was not clowning. Half expecting me to punish him for eating his lunch at the beginning of the school day, he hung his head in shame. When he arrived at my desk, he managed to smile sheepishly at me. I smiled back.

"William," I asked as gently as I could, "did you have any breakfast this morning?"

"Oh, yes, ma'am," he quickly assured me. Fixing his eyes on the ceiling for inspiration, he began to catalogue all the delicious foods he had heartily devoured at breakfast that morning. "I ate a big stack of pancakes with syrup. And a slab of ham. And some bacon. Lots of bacon. And I ate scrambled eggs and sausage and corn bread—I sure do love corn bread—and . . ." He took his eyes off the ceiling long enough to assess whether I was suitably impressed, then continued quickly, "And I had grits and gravy, a glass of milk, and a whole carton of orange juice." As the menu of his imagined breakfast feast expanded, William grew more and more animated, as though the very thought of such bounty had the magical power to provide him with the energy and sustenance he needed.

Trying to convey my concern without embarrassing him, I observed that, since he had a very big appetite on this particular morning, he would probably want to have some lunch as well. Pointing out that he had already eaten the lunch his mother had packed for him, I offered to order him a hot lunch from the cafeteria and some juice for morning snack, and I assured him that he would not need to repay me.

"Is that O.K. with you?" I asked.

"Oh, yes, ma'am," William nodded, and a huge smile lit up his small, impish face. On that day, at least, he would not go hungry.

Weeks later I assigned a series of exercises in the *Ginn Reader*. They introduced ethical situations that mirrored the one featured in the story the students had studied that day. One read as follows: "Mary caught a wild rabbit. She put it in a cage and brought it food every day. The rabbit ate nothing at all but only tried to escape the cage. After a few days Mary let it go free. Was this wise? Why or why not?" The teacher's manual encourages teachers to use this exercise to engage their students in an ethical discussion, one that focuses on the dilemma a child like Mary would face between wanting to keep the rabbit as a pet and realizing that the rabbit is a wild animal that cannot survive in captivity. There is, from the perspective of the textbook's authors, only one correct answer to this ethical problem: Mary must let the rabbit go.

But the authors did not imagine William. His response was simple, to the point, and, given his circumstances, indisputably correct. "No," he wrote, weighing in against Mary's decision to free the rabbit. And then, to the question "Why or why not?" William answered matter-of-factly: "Because she should have ate it."

William did not just suffer from physical hunger. He had to try to cope with the demands of school when he was too hungry to concentrate. He also had to endure the taunts of classmates when they discovered that he was unfed and ravenous. He was burdened, too, by the fierce obligation he felt to protect his parents from the public humiliation they would experience if their inability to provide enough food for their children became known. He had, after all, gone all year without a subsidized lunch in order to spare them the public shame they believed an official declaration of poverty would bring them. His lapse — when he gave into his hunger and wolfed down the peanut butter sandwich before the morning bell had rung — must have seemed to him like a betrayal of his parents, for he felt compelled to invent his imaginative description of a bountiful breakfast to cover the truth of his family's poverty.

William's effort to spare his parents at his own expense was not atypical. I remember the day Ramonia had such a terrible toothache that she couldn't pay attention in class. Since the school had no nurse, there was little I could do for Ramonia's pain, except to allow her to put her head on her desk and ignore the day's lessons. This coping strategy, I'd learned, was the standard classroom procedure for any illnesses or injuries my students suffered during school hours. I had become accustomed to the toothaches. Most of my students' parents couldn't afford regular dental checkups. To make matters worse, virtually all the qualified dentists practiced thirty-some miles away, in Charlottesville, and many of those dentists didn't accept African American patients. From what I could gather, the only dentist in the entire county of Louisa who treated black children was an old-fashioned country dentist who used the most primitive methods. Rather than drilling out a cavity and filling it with silver, he simply pulled out the decayed tooth, leaving a permanent gap in the child's mouth. The trauma of this procedure only increased my students' resistance to visiting a dentist. Most of the time, a dentist wasn't consulted until a toothache had escalated into a crisis, a crisis that had only one resolution: tooth extraction.

As Ramonia's toothache intensified, I urged her to talk to her mother, a teacher's aide in a nearby classroom. I had great admiration for Ramonia's mother, who was raising her four children on her own while her husband was fighting in Vietnam, and I was confident she would take her daughter to a dentist as soon as she learned about the toothache. Ramonia, however, begged me not to tell her mother. Crying softly, she explained to me that her mother had taken her two little brothers to the dentist a week earlier, but didn't have enough money to take her, too. "Please, don't tell my Mama," she pleaded through her tears. "I don't want her to know about my toothache. It will just upset her, because she can't afford to take me to a dentist and there's nothing at all she can do about my toothache." With that, she lowered her head to her desk and quietly endured her pain.

I honored Ramonia's effort to protect her mother, for I realized that I would only add to her distress if she believed she was imposing yet another burden on her mother. I had recently dealt with a crisis in Sharon's family when a medical emergency made it impossible for Sharon's mother to pay for her daughter's lunch, and I had seen how her mother's anxiety had weighed on Sharon. Sharon had tried at first to handle the situation without letting on how scared she was.

"My mother doesn't have the money to pay for my lunch this week," she explained to me early one Monday morning, trying to sound as if nothing were out of the ordinary. "She wants to know if it's O.K. if she sends it later in the week." Hesitating slightly, she soldiered on. "She's . . . she's sick." And then she faltered. Her eyes filled up with tears. She fought them back. After a long pause, the story she hadn't planned to tell spilled out—how her mother had suddenly become ill, seriously ill; how the pain had become so excruciating that the rescue squad had to be called; how an ambulance had whisked her mother off to the emergency room at a hospital in Charlottesville; how the money originally designated for the family's weekly expenses had been used to pay for the medicine the doctors had said was necessary. Sharon was worried about her mom; she was also worried about how the family could possibly find the money to pay for the doctors, the ambulance, the hospital, the medicine; and she was worried about whether there would be enough money to sustain the family during this crisis. Smart, resourceful, focused on the immediate problem of paying for her lunch, she asked politely whether there was any possibility I could advance her the money until her mother was back on her feet and able to pay me. I assured her that I could loan her the money she needed for her lunches that week, and that her mother could pay me back whenever she was able.

"Thursday," Sharon promised. "She said to tell you she could repay you on Thursday."

But on Thursday morning, Sharon came to my desk with an apologetic note from her mother. It read: "Dear Mrs. Hallahan, I'm so sorry I couldn't keep my promises. I said that I was going to send Sharon's money for lunch today but I'm not able to do so. I'll send it Monday. I was planning on getting her pictures too. But I got sick Sunday and the Rescue Squad took me to Charlottesville and I have been in and out of bed since then. One small bottle of medicine cost $15.00. I have a bad kidney infection. Thank you for being so kind. G. Crawford." I, of course, had no problem with this delay. From my perspective, the money I had loaned her—fifty cents—was insignificant, and I didn't want Sharon's mother to worry at all about paying me back. I certainly didn't want her to feel responsible for being felled by a kidney infection or to feel guilty for choosing to buy expensive medicine essential for her health instead of her children's school lunches. Yet Sharon's mother clearly believed her honor was on the line because she couldn't repay the loan when she promised.

William and Ramonia and Sharon lived with the knowledge that their own physical needs placed a burden on their parents, a burden they sought desperately to alleviate, choosing sometimes to suffer rather than cause the parents they loved to worry. Although they were only ten, they understood that their parents' economic status was extremely precarious and their own well-being therefore uncertain. They and most of the other children in my classroom were growing up without any of the protective illusions that characterized my own childhood: the expectation of sufficiency, the fantasy of invulnerability, the dream of unlimited possibilities. Many of them shouldered adult responsibilities, some missing school to stay home and take care of younger brothers and sisters during a family crisis, others working side-by-side with their fathers in the fields. Although they were remarkably resilient, they had to live with the knowledge that tomorrow's dinner might not materialize, next week's paycheck might not cover the bills, their father's job might not last. For them, the smallest misfortune could have enormous consequences, and the instability of their lives weighed heavily on them.

Even a lost button could feel catastrophic. During recess one day, Cecily suddenly burst into tears. I thought she had been hurt and went running over to find out what had happened. Between sobs, she told me she had lost one of the buttons on her coat. A frantic search involving all her friends failed to turn up the missing button, and Cecily was beside herself. I tried to comfort her, pointing out that a button was not hard to replace and assuring her that her mother could easily sew another button back on the coat. But she was inconsolable.

"Yes," she allowed, "but she'll beat me first."

Scenes like this were common. Minor mishaps that would barely register in the lives of America's affluent children—a lost mitten, a frayed jump rope, a stolen nickel—were profoundly upsetting to my students, who had so little and understood at a very early age the import their carelessness or negligence or bad luck might have on a family battling to stay afloat. A missing button, I quickly learned, can loom large for a child whose mother is struggling to feed her family.

Recalling an incident in his childhood when he incurred his mother's anger by accidently breaking a single egg, the African American writer Gerald Early provides the perspective of a self-reflective adult to the roil of emotions Cecily experienced when she lost her coat button that day. Talking to his teenaged daughter, raised in affluence, after she had accidently ruined the family's fine dining room table while doing a school project, he examines the difference between his measured response to her negligence and his mother's fury when, as a young boy, he accidentally broke an egg after being told not to touch it. "'She slapped my face, hard, two or three times,'" he tells his daughter. "'She called me a name. She was furious with me because it was the last egg in the house, you see.'" As he recalls the incident, the emotional weight of it floods back, and he explains why it was so traumatic for him. "'I was so ashamed, so ashamed.' I was trembling now. 'I was just so ashamed. Not because my mother, you know, was mad. She had a right to be mad. She should have hit me. My mother was very good to me and, you know, I should not have tried to cook that egg. I was so ashamed because I knew, then, at that moment, that I was poor, if one egg meant that much. And I was so ashamed, I mean, that I was poor like that. So damn ashamed of the both of us.'" Reading Early's narrative, I thought of Cecily on that day she lost the button of her coat. Fearing a beating at home, she also must have felt humiliated that her loss weighed so heavily on her and mortified that her friends and I witnessed her desperation. I realized, with a start, that the words I had used to console her—"it's just a little button and easy to replace"—may well have served instead to further humiliate her. My remark must have reminded her just how impoverished her family was, for she faced a beating for losing something I considered to be entirely trivial.

One beautiful spring morning, Cecily arrived in my classroom carrying a large bouquet of purple lilacs, which she ceremoniously presented to me.

"They're for you," she announced with obvious pride, her eyes flashing with pleasure. I made a fuss over the gift of flowers that she had so sweetly bestowed on me that spring morning, telling her how beautiful they were, how they brightened the room, how much I loved lilacs. Cecily beamed. It dawned on me that this young girl, who had so little and wanted so badly to matter, must suffer acutely because she so rarely had things—even small things, like a bouquet of lilacs—to give. I put the lilacs in a glass jar, placed them theatrically on my desk, and smiled at her in appreciation. Flushed with her sense of accomplishment, Cecily announced triumphantly, "I stole them! I stole them just for you!"

## You Can't Trust Anybody

Bill and I were not the only outsiders from our generation living in Louisa County that year. Ten miles or so from the modest, two-bedroom rental house we had made our temporary home, a group of idealistic young people lived together on a commune they had recently established on a former tobacco farm. Radicalized by the Vietnam War, dissatisfied by the excesses and materialism of American middle-class life, and caught up in the headiness and experimentation of a burgeoning counterculture, they had turned their backs on mainstream culture, renounced their material comforts, given up their jobs, dropped out of their degree programs, left their families, and fled the cities where they had grown up, motivated by the dream of creating a utopian community and a permanent home on an isolated farm in a remote part of Virginia. Their commune, Twin Oaks, was inspired by the utopian communities of nineteenth-century America, modeled on the fictional commune in B. F. Skinner's influential *Walden II*, informed by the writings of Thoreau and Marx, and based on the principles of cooperation, egalitarianism, wealth-sharing, and "voluntary simplicity." Curious, Bill and I arranged a visit one sunny Saturday afternoon.

Located on a large tract of farmland, the compound included a small, white clapboard farmhouse with a communal kitchen and dining room; a newly constructed dormitory building with living quarters for most of the members; a barn and a number of outbuildings, some used as workshops; a substantial garden, intended to supply most of the commune's food; and fenced pastures, bright green in the early spring, where a small herd of cows grazed. One of the founding members, from a wealthy family, had bought the farm with money from an inheritance; he had also cashed in an insurance policy to finance the construction of the dormitory building. The people I talked to admitted to me that life at Twin Oaks was often difficult. There had been a series of recent agricultural failures, some due to weather, others to their mistakes as neophyte farmers. They were beginning to see that the farm might not generate any income, contrary to their original hopes. Although they wanted to become self-sufficient, and their hammock-making business was beginning to flourish, they were not able to make ends meet, even with everyone required to perform a set amount of daily labor as well as household chores. To survive, they had decided to send some members out to do salaried factory and construction work, a disappointing development. And, of course, there was the challenge of governing and getting along with the diverse members of a community that had intentionally cut itself off from the outside world. Nevertheless, they insisted they were happier than they had ever been in their lives. Enthusiastic about the future of Twin Oaks (which, remarkably, celebrated its thirtieth anniversary in 1997), they boasted that their communal life in rural Louisa County enabled them to lead more harmonious, satisfying, and meaningful lives, free from the excesses and pressures of the modern, postindustrial world.

At the time of my visit to Twin Oaks, a number of my friends were living in communes and experimental communities in New Mexico, Oregon, and California, and I had anticipated finding among the inhabitants of Twin Oaks kindred spirits, people who might help to alleviate the loneliness I felt living as an outsider in a closed community. So I was surprised, as I listened to the residents I met, that I found myself becoming impatient with their political and philosophical positions and angry at them. I wanted them to know how desperately the children at my school — their near neighbors — needed their skills, training, education, and help. I felt that by isolating themselves from the surrounding community, they were failing society rather than transforming it. They, in turn, questioned what I was doing at Morton Elementary. They didn't believe any meaningful change could be achieved by working within the established system. In fact, they felt that, for all my good intentions, I was helping to perpetuate society's oppression and racism, since, as institutions of the state, public schools served the state's interests. One of their members was a former teacher with a master's degree who had taken a job in the local schools, only to quit after a few weeks when he realized he far preferred to work in a factory than to serve as a "warden" in the public schools. Their criticism stung and made me question whether I was accomplishing anything by teaching in a school that was still segregated by law and under the control of white men who openly expressed their bigotry against blacks. And yet I wondered how the members of the commune could ever practice and test their commitment to tolerance and equality by living in an all-white community that was segregated from the larger world.

Looking back at this encounter, I'm less interested in evaluating the positions we took as idealistic young Americans in 1970 than in thinking about why all of us were gathered on this remote farm having this discussion at all. Why did we all assume we had choices about how to live our lives, confidently debating whether it was better to try to change the system from within or from without, all the while believing that, if we wanted, we could instead choose to be the beneficiaries of the status quo? Why did we take our mobility for granted, picking up stakes on a whim and adventurously moving to an unfamiliar part of the country, to a place where black people had had their mobility restricted for centuries? Why had the dreams of the commune dwellers — children from affluent homes — been fired by the prospect of living on a primitive farm and cultivating the red Virginia clay, a way of life that had defeated the dreams of so many of the local African American farmers? And what intangibles (philosophical and political ideas? a liberal education? a sense of agency? a deeply held conviction of their privileged place in the world?) did those young people bring to the hard life of a subsistence farmer that made their experience qualitatively different from the lives of the poor agricultural workers in Louisa County? Finally, how could a country as prosperous, capacious, and blessed as the United States produce such profound alienation among some of its most fortunate young people and, at the same time, deprive its least fortunate children of their most basic needs? What went so wrong in that era that the U.S. government elicited the trust of neither its privileged nor its underprivileged youth?

My most disadvantaged students had learned at an early age to expect nothing out of life, an expectation all but the most resilient of them would, to their own detriment, carry throughout their lives. They did not believe they had choices, they did not imagine themselves mobile, they had not internalized a sense of their own agency, and they distrusted the outside world. I wondered what would become of children like Donna, a frightened and unhappy girl who lived in a foster home where she received no attention or love. She was always missing school and as a result struggled to do passing work. When I contacted her home to learn the reason for her excessive absences, her foster mother wrote me this note: "Donna hasn't been coming to school because I myself haven't been feeling too well. I just didn't feel up to getting her ready." I had no way of knowing whether this woman was seriously ill, clinically depressed, overwhelmed by her circumstances, or simply negligent. On Donna's fall report card, I saw her foster mother had responded to the low grades Mrs. Stockton had given Donna with a mixture of defiance, distrust, and defensiveness, complaining in a written note: "I think you just grade the children report card anyway you want not by their grades because I no Donna isn't making any F's in spelling nor do she have any business with a D in conduct. I wonder how you would grade your own kids." Cecily confided in me one day that Donna's foster mother refused to let her leave the house and forced her to do all the family's housework. "She can't ever come out and play; she always has to stay home and do chores, like cleaning or cooking," Cecily told me. "Her mother, she's just plain mean to Donna."

What Donna learned from her foster mother's neglect and mistreatment was that she was undeserving, worthless, and unlovable. Resentful and angry, she armored herself against the world. She had no friends, no social skills, and no awareness of how she was driving everyone away from her. A snide comment or a glance of disapproval would set her off, and she would flail at whoever had offended her. Coming to school was, for her, a humiliating experience; she was ashamed of her failing grades, her grungy, secondhand clothes, her meager sack lunch, her sense of not belonging. How mortified and lonely she must have felt that bleak winter morning when a cockroach fell out of her coat as she was hanging it up in the closet and her classmates burst into derisive taunts. "Roaches! Donna's got roaches!" they chanted. "They're in her hair, her blouse, her skirt! She's even got roaches in her underpants! Stay away from Donna. Donna's got cockroaches crawling all over her." Before I could stop them, Donna bolted to the supply closet in the back of the room, slammed the door shut, and wept hysterically. Trying to coax her to come out, I could hear her sobbing plaintively behind the doors, "no . . . no . . . body l-l-loves me." Donna, I knew, was growing up without dreams. She could not imagine herself venturing into the wider world or creating a different sort of life for herself than the one in which she was currently trapped. She didn't even believe she deserved to be happy.

Donna's suffering was complicated, of course, by her court-enforced separation from her biological parents and her unloving and irresponsible foster mother. Unlike her, the majority of my students were deeply attached to their families and homes. Though materially poor, many led emotionally rich lives in families that fostered in them a strong sense of love and belonging. Their home lives were largely invisible to me. But there was obvious passion in the way the boys told stories of hunting squirrel and racoon with their fathers, deep affection in the way the girls recounted stories of caring for their younger siblings. And there was joy and exuberance in their reports of family celebrations and reunions, Sunday school outings and church rituals, pickup baseball games and adventures in creek beds, fields, and woods. Their deep attachments to those closest to them, however, stood in marked contrast to their wariness about anyone outside the charmed circle of their family and church community. I was often troubled by the profound distrust they felt towards the larger world.

Once, in a language arts class devoted to the evocative power of words, the students took turns offering a single word for consideration while the others responded by telling what they associated with that word. Matilda started with the word "home." The children nodded approvingly and entered energetically into the exercise. Their associations flowed: "mama meeting me at the bus," "playing hide-and-seek with my little brothers," "watching my baby sister while my mama cleans the house," "bringing in the wood," "woodsmoke," "papa's pipe," "Mommy's perfume"—a loud chorus of yeahs—"babies crying," "changing diapers," "the smell of baby powder," "the smells of dinner cooking on the stove," "biscuits baking in the oven," "fried chicken," "the hens clucking," "feeding the hogs," "catching frogs down by the creek," "hunting squirrels with Daddy."

But when Emmeline offered the word "friend," the tone of the discussion changed radically and a far more disturbing set of associations emerged. After a short, uncomfortable pause, Annie Mae began: "Someone that pretends to like you, but really doesn't." Some of the girls nodded, sadly, in silent agreement.

"Someone who turns on you," Gloria volunteered knowingly.

"Fist fights," shouted one of the boys.

"Saying mean things just to make you mad," chimed in another.

Suddenly, the children were vying with each other to tell their own painful stories of betrayal and rejection at the hands of "friends," their feelings of hurt and anger and indignation spilling out. I thought perhaps the students had taken a cue from Annie Mae's initial negative association and had focused on the word "betrayal" rather than the word "friend." Hoping to get the students refocused on the exercise and thinking I could redirect the discussion towards more positive aspects of friendship, I decided to intervene and offer a couple of my own associations.

"When I think of the word 'friend,'" I said, "I think of 'sharing.' And 'fun.' And 'trust.'"

The children looked at me blankly.

"You just can't trust anybody, Mrs. Hallahan," Ramonia explained to me sadly, with a sigh.

The deep distrust of others that Annie Mae and Gloria and Ramonia expressed that day extended to the American political system, where it was even more pronounced. One Friday afternoon when we were discussing current events, Clinton said something that startled and alarmed me.

"If Nixon is re-elected, all of us Negro kids are going to starve."

I couldn't figure out what he was talking about, and I must have looked at him strangely.

"We're going to starve to death just like the children on TV," he persisted.

Some of the other students chimed in, voicing their agreement.

"Nixon hates Negroes, and he's already starving little children, and it's just going to get worse and worse."

Shocked by the very real anxieties my students were expressing, I struggled to figure out what, exactly, they were talking about. What starving children? What television program? What Republican policies were they alluding to?

"You know, the Negro children on TV," Clinton reiterated. "They're starving and dying, and it's all Nixon's fault. We're going to be next. If Nixon's reelected, our parents are going to lose their jobs, and there's not going to be any food, and no one is going to care, and we'll just sit around getting hungrier and hungrier. And then we'll die. And Nixon will be happy we're all dead."

Caught up in the fear of this bleak future, a couple of the girls started to cry.

Reeling, I frantically searched my memory for a clue to their distress. And then it hit me: Biafra. My students were identifying with the starving children of Biafra. Famine was threatening the lives of a million or more Igbo tribesmen in the aftermath of a bloody civil war between Nigeria and the breakaway province of Biafra. Wrenching stories in the nightly news told of this mass starvation. Accompanying every story were deeply disturbing images of severely malnourished Biafran children, their ribs protruding, their starving bellies grotesquely distended. The sad-eyed children were too listless, too close to death, to swat the flies that covered their bony faces.

I looked into the anxious faces of the African American children in my classroom and attempted to convince them that the terrible fate of the Biafran children did not await them. I explained that the pictures they had seen on TV were pictures of children in another country on another continent, a country in Africa disrupted by civil war and famine. I explained that though I strongly disagreed with Nixon's policies, the president was not directly responsible for the starving children in Biafra. I explained that the United States had a different government and a different economic system and a different agricultural system than Biafra, and that our country was in no danger of suffering from the kind of devastating famine that was killing children there.

But Clinton and the others weren't buying my explanation. The black children in Biafra resembled their classmates more than any of the other children they saw on television, almost all of whom were white and middle class. The primitive huts where the Biafran children lived and the dirt yards where they sat dying seemed more familiar to them than the affluent, suburban houses of children featured in situation comedies like *The Partridge Family*. And the vulnerability of

Biafran children rang more true to their experience than the cocky self-assurance of Hollywood child actors. In the winter of 1970, in the wealthiest and most powerful country in the world, a class of ten-year-old African American children identified intensely with the most unfortunate children of a tragic, foreign land and feared their own government wished them dead.

# Reach Up Your Hand, Dark Boy, and Take a Star

*Reach up your hand, dark boy, and take a star.*
*Out of the little breath of oblivion*
*That is night,*
*Take just*
*One star.*
—*from "Stars" by Langston Hughes*

## You Think I'm Stupid, Don't You?

Derrick could barely read. Held back the previous year and self-consciously towering over the younger children, he was in danger of failing the fourth grade yet again, and that prospect terrified him. Derrick struggled to master the printed page. Approaching each reading assignment with a gritty determination, he tried valiantly to conquer the letters arrayed against him on the page, willing them to submit to his invading eye. But no matter how hard he fought, he couldn't capture the sounds of the letters or the meaning of the words. As he haltingly struggled to sound out each word, his frustration would build and build, until he erupted into anger or broke down in tears. The first time I tried to help him, he looked at me with wary eyes and said to me, his voice at once accusing and resigned, "You think I'm stupid, don't you?"

Because his reading skills were so rudimentary, Derrick used a beginning reader written for first or second graders that Mrs. Stockton had found among a stack of abandoned books in the supply closet. Its cover was frayed, its pages worn from years of use. Clearly humiliated by it, he complained bitterly that it was a book for babies. His classmates, who generally liked him, nevertheless made fun of his poor reading skills. Many of them were only slightly stronger readers and seemed to feel compelled to mark the distance between Derrick and themselves: they did not read books written for babies. At a second-hand bookstore in Charlottesville, I managed to find a book for older students who needed remedial help in reading. It had stories in very simple prose about famous athletes, musicians, artists, and scientists and was illustrated with vivid, realistic pictures meant to appeal to pre-adolescents. Despite its elementary language, it was designed to look like a book for older students. I brought it into school for Derrick to use, assigning him a story about a baseball player because I knew he was fanatic about the sport. A short while later, he came rushing up to my desk, grinning from ear to ear and bursting with excitement. Holding the book up and waving it exuberantly in front of me, he exclaimed proudly and triumphantly, "This book isn't just for stupid kids, is it?"

"Stupid kids." The words haunted my classroom. Derrick, Louis, Marcus, Donna, Cheryl, Earl, Lillian, Duane, Wendell, Charlie, Adele, Vernice: all firmly believed they were stupid. Many of the other children feared they were as well, an anxiety that undermined every academic task they tackled. Unlike Derrick, many had learned to concede defeat without a fight. For them, school functioned merely to confirm what they already "knew": they were so stupid that trying to learn any academic subject was futile. When a math problem challenged them or a science concept baffled them, they gave up quickly, finding it more comfortable to assume they could never understand than to make any real effort to comprehend. They seemed to prefer the certainty that came from accepting failure to the stress of having to perform. Perhaps, by pre-judging themselves, they achieved a measure of control or protected themselves against disappointment. Perhaps they had already given up on school and were simply marking time until they could drop out. Fewer than half would graduate from high school.

Whenever I gave a test, many of my students panicked. Some carefully copied out the question I had written on the board and then stopped. Some wrote what appeared to be nonsense sentences. Some picked out key words, wrote them clearly, then scribbled wiggly lines that vaguely resembled written words. A few were so sure they would fail that they didn't even try, simply handing in a blank sheet of paper. Math tests revealed that many were hopelessly lost. Spelling tests produced indecipherable writing. Here, for example, are the twenty "words" that one child wrote on his spelling test: bamed, sanemu, sonnem, hamem, canam, balkm, monim, lavele, renlen, falsnu, falem, isarum, canim, gamon, salme, trye, plyll. Even when they were able to complete a task, many of them did so without understanding the basic principles behind it. One of the routine exercises that Mrs. Stockton had assigned required them to copy the week's list of vocabulary words, along with the pronunciation symbols that were printed in the glossary section of the *Ginn Reader*. My students carefully and diligently copied out the words and symbols. But when I asked them what those symbols meant, I discovered most hadn't the foggiest idea.

A standardized reading test administered to my students that spring semester produced sobering results. The highest score in the class was James's. It placed him in the fortieth percentile of all fourth-graders who had taken the test, slightly below the national average. According to the testing agency, James tested in the "average" range and was "able to manage reading at about midyear grade level." But in comparison to the other students in the class, James's score was astronomically high. Ten other students—children I knew to be very bright—were classified as beginning readers for their grade level. Their scores, ranging from the twentieth to the twenty-fifth percentile, indicated that their reading comprehension was below three-quarters of the students their age who had taken the test. They were to be encouraged to read "high-interest material at beginning grade level," and I was advised to monitor their progress and give them individual help. Two-thirds of my students were ranked in the bottom tenth percentile of all fourth graders who had taken the test. "Poor" readers, they were identified as "having serious trouble reading with understanding at this grade level" and singled out as being "in need of individual diagnostic testing with follow-up teaching based on individual needs." Two students, Marcus and Earl, were not even given the test because they were deemed illiterate. There was no individual diagnostic testing available in the school, and with thirty-eight students, I could hardly follow up by designing individual lessons based on the specific needs of each child who had been classified a poor reader, even had I received the training to do so.

Many of my students needed constant, individual attention in order to master the fundamentals I was trying to teach. But if I took the time to sit beside a student having difficulty with a particular problem, twenty or more hands would immediately shoot into the air, nearly every student vying for my attention and begging for help. Whenever I bent down to work with one student, others protested loudly that I was ignoring them. If I didn't reach them quickly enough, some would simply give up, often dramatically announcing defeat. "O.K.," they would declare, throwing down their pencils in frustration, "I just won't do it then."

Louis was one such child. He couldn't sit still. He was impatient, impulsive, and hard to control. He jumped out of his seat, hid in the closet, made faces, threw spitballs, wrote notes, jiggled the desk. Asked to stand in line for a few moments, he would punch his best friend and trip the girl standing next to him. And he had trouble paying attention. Hyperactivity wasn't a syndrome I knew anything about in 1970, but Louis, I see now, fit it to a tee. I discovered that he loved to run errands and do little chores, like carrying messages to the office, moving desks, sharpening pencils, or cleaning the blackboard. I constantly tried to find ways to help him channel his considerable energy, but nothing kept him focused for very long.

In class Louis needed constant encouragement. He would grin brightly when I praised him but collapse the next minute in anger and frustration. If I didn't call on him immediately, he would sob hopelessly, or accuse me of not helping him, or rip his paper to pieces. If I pushed him too hard, he would announce, "I can't do anything right" and stop trying altogether. But Louis had a remarkably lively imagination. Though he sometimes fantasized that his classmates were ganging up on him or that I was going to fail him just for spite, he also drew intricate pictures of racing cars and cartoon characters and imaginary animals. During class discussions, he approached issues from unusual perspectives, often coming up with ideas of striking originality. When I could hold his attention, he was a live wire. At those moments, he would ask question after interesting question, his mind racing. He was, however, always threatening to short circuit, and he would quickly retreat to his conviction that he was stupid, defying me to disagree.

When I tried to convince students like Louis that they were not stupid, they vehemently resisted. They clung to the label; it defined them. Stupid was what you were when you couldn't spell the words on the spelling test, couldn't figure out the math problem, couldn't sound out the long word in the story. Stupid was what teachers determined you were when they mocked your mistakes, chided you for asking questions, or gave you F's on tests without helping you understand your errors. Stupid was what you were—what you must be—when your school district thought so little of you it didn't even bother to provide you with books or certified teachers or specialists trained to help you learn to read. And stupid was what white people assumed you were when they threatened to close all the public schools in Virginia rather than let white children go to school with you. My students had no idea how astute they were. At a very young age they had, in fact, grasped the primary lesson their society had set out to teach them, and they had learned it far, far too well. "I don't expect you to teach *those* children anything," the superintendent of schools had assured me, making it absolutely clear to me that he believed the children he was hiring me to teach were uneducable. This was the lesson that many of my students—so alert and curious, so imaginative, so full of questions and penetrating observations—had learned by heart.

Where could my students find evidence to counter this devastating lesson? Where could they turn to learn about the achievements of black Americans like them? Not the public library. There was none in 1970, and if there had been one, it would almost certainly have been off limits to black children. Not the school library, for, though the nearby white Louisa Elementary School had twenty-seven hundred books in 1967, my school had almost none. Not the county's historical museum. Sponsored by the Daughters of the American Revolution and the Daughters of the Confederacy, it memorialized the accomplishments of Louisa's white planters, soldiers, statesmen, and civic leaders, but was largely silent about the contributions of its African American citizens. Even when I visited this museum in 2001, its version of local history focused almost exclusively on whites. It contained no exhibits, displays, mementoes, or narratives about one of Louisa's most distinguished native sons—John Mercer Langston, for instance. Born in 1829, the son of an emancipated slave and a wealthy Louisa plantation owner, Langston received a B.A. degree from Oberlin College at the age of nineteen and became a famous abolitionist, a spellbinding orator, and an accomplished lawyer and educator. His biographers note that he was "the first black lawyer in the West, the first Afro-American elected to public office . . . the first law dean of Howard University, the U.S. minister to Haiti and Santo

Domingo, the president of the Virginia state college for Negroes at Petersburg, and the first and only black representative of Virginia to Congress." In June 1867 he made a triumphant return to Louisa, where he was cheered by thousands of local citizens—both black and white—who had gathered at the courthouse square to hear him speak. Even a rebel general, initially hostile, welcomed him home after his dazzling speech, telling him, "Langston, you are one of us, and we are proud of you." But a historical marker commemorating John Mercer Langston was not erected in Louisa County until 1995, and then only on the instigation of his alma mater, Oberlin College in Ohio. Until it was erected, there had been no official recognition of John Mercer Langston in the entire Commonwealth of Virginia.

My students certainly couldn't turn to the local newspaper for any affirmation of their intellectual potential or any encouragement to excel in school. In the sixteen years that elapsed between the *Brown* decision and the desegregation of Louisa's public schools, it barely acknowledged that African American students existed at all, as I discovered when I researched the paper's archives in a cozy little room next to its business office. Every September, the *Central Virginian*—Louisa County's only newspaper—marked the beginning of the school year with a charming, front-page story that extended an official welcome to that year's entering class of first graders, listing the names of every newly enrolled six-year-old child. Every *white* six-year-old child, that is. "*The Central Virginian* extends best wishes to all one-hundred-thirty-nine little first graders in the four white elementary schools in Louisa County, and wish the next twelve years to be happy ones, packed with memories of achievements, friendship, and fun," one version of this annual article reads. There is no such welcome for the county's African American first graders. The only initiation into the larger world my students received in the week before they entered the first grade was a Ku Klux Klan rally, staged by outsiders intent on riling up white Louisans against school desegregation and duly reported on the front page of the newspaper.

In the years between the *Brown* decision and the integration of the public schools, this paper prominently featured activities at the county's white schools, covering their sporting events, academic competitions, extracurricular activities, and school programs and touting the accomplishments of their white students. But it paid virtually no attention to any of the activities at the Negro schools. Stories featuring the county's white elementary schools describe a science fair (experiments, posters, and a project on electricity); an Easter celebration (parade, egg hunt, play, and party); an art festival (posters, drawings, paintings, and papier mâché animals); a sixth-grade science field trip to the Louray caverns (adventure, travel, geological studies); a May Day pageant (music, dancing, flowers, fancy clothes, and the crowning of a king and queen); and the activities of white brownie, girl scout, cub scout, boy scout, and 4-H troops (art, music, camping, field trips). Large photographs of smiling white children and their beaming teachers illustrate many of these stories. In contrast, only one story about African American elementary schoolchildren in Louisa County appears around this time. It features a class of special education students at Morton Elementary.

White children, the local newspaper teaches, do scientific projects, make art, perform in plays, go on field trips, practice leadership skills, play sports, and participate in annual school rituals that celebrate their special place in the community. Black children, it implies, do none of these things and apparently have no place at all in the larger community. To some degree, these newspaper stories accurately reflect the limited opportunities at the Negro schools, which did not have the funds to support creative and extracurricular activities that white children routinely enjoyed. But in addition to unintentionally throwing into stark relief the extreme inequalities that existed in schools that were purported to be "separate but equal," this newspaper coverage also conveys the white community's deeply ingrained and profoundly hurtful attitudes toward black children. In contrast to white children, who are regularly depicted as learners, leaders, and achievers, black schoolchildren are portrayed in only one way: as recipients of a federally funded program in special education designed to help them cope with their intellectual deficiencies.

## Schools No Better Than Smokehouses

African American parents, teachers, ministers, and leaders sought to counter these destructive lessons. I found in the newspaper archives plenty of evidence that they actively pressured the county school board to improve the Negro schools in the wake of the 1954 *Brown* decision, appearing repeatedly before the school board to demand that it allocate more money to the Negro schools. Although they did not at first seek the integration of the county's public schools, they pleaded with the board to do something about the unsafe, unsanitary, and unconscionable conditions at the county's black elementary schools. Their anger and frustration at the county officials responsible for providing their children an education equal to white children's are palpable in the paper's reports of these meetings. In January 1958 "a delegation from the Z. C. Morton Negro School in the Town of Louisa"—then housed in buildings constructed in 1921—addressed the board about the "deplorable" conditions of that school. "'Heating is bad, bathrooms are not mentionable, children have to stand in the rain to get their lunch and the lunch room is next to the coal bin,'" Mrs. Susie Hill complained. The school board acknowledged the problems, but claimed they could do nothing unless taxes were raised, something they believed the county's taxpayers would resist so strongly that they felt "it was useless to hold a bond election here." One school board member advised the teachers and parents to "be patient in waiting for improvements." Another pointed out that conditions at the school were so bad that putting resources into it would be tantamount to "throwing money away."

Delegations from other Negro schools appeared at later meetings that year to register similar complaints. They formally asked the board for "sanitary improvements and a better heating system" for the four-room Mt. Garland school; "adequate heat and indoor toilets" for the five-room Ferncliff school; and the replacement of the dilapidated, two-room Shelfar school. Protests like these, along with the county's last-ditch effort to block integration by belatedly improving the Negro schools, led to the construction in 1960 of the school building where I taught. Even as the new Negro elementary school was being built, however, African American parents and teachers continued to lodge complaints about the crowded and deteriorating conditions at other Negro elementary schools, schools that were slated to continue operating even after the new school opened. In 1960 two "colored speakers" from St. Mark's school "told of the poor conditions at that school where 23 children attend in one room, sitting two to a seat." Pleading with the school board, one of them reported, "'We have no lights, window panes are broken, and some of our children have refused to attend school there and we don't blame them. I have seen some smokehouses which were better than St. Mark's School.'" But when the fall semester of 1961 began, there were still eight Negro elementary schools with three or fewer teachers in operation, four of them one-room schoolhouses.

The African American parents and teachers who complained about the appalling conditions of the county's Negro schools at these school board meetings had themselves almost certainly been educated in one of the substandard schools they sought so desperately to improve. They knew firsthand the harm done to children forced to attend schools no better than smokehouses, for they had borne the full brunt of the county's discriminatory practices. They would surely have seen the school board's 1958 refusal to hold a school bond election in the larger context of whites' historic opposition to funding black schools. They may well have been motivated by the example of their own parents and grandparents, many of whom had joined together in the early part of the twentieth century to build and maintain schools for their children in the absence of any funds from the county. These concerned black citizens had used their own money to hire and support teachers and heat and repair the school buildings, and in the 1930s, they had pooled their money to buy a school bus for their children because the county refused to provide one.

I learned more about the hardships they must have endured when I discovered an M.A. thesis, written at the University of Virginia in 1949, that gives a remarkably full account of Louisa's Negro schools immediately after World War II. Written by Paul Everett Behrens, a white man who had taught for three years in one of Louisa County's white schools, it documents the extreme inequalities between Louisa County's white and Negro schools and urgently attempts to address the county's failure to provide adequate education to its African American citizens. As part of his research, Behrens visited the Negro high school and all twenty of the Negro elementary schools in operation in 1948–1949, fourteen of which were one-room schoolhouses. He also interviewed teachers at each of these schools, distributed and analyzed the results of an extensive questionnaire, and photographed many of the schools. He even counted the number of students in each classroom, measured the rooms, and took an inventory of the desks and seating capacity, showing how in one case, for instance, fifty children were crowded into a small classroom with only twenty-two

seats. In addition, he compared the number of volumes in the libraries, the value of the laboratory equipment, the nature of the academic
curriculum, and the range of extracurricular activities in the white
and Negro high schools; the physical plant and playgrounds of the
white and Negro elementary schools; the number and condition of
the buses in the two systems; and the educations and salaries of white
and African American teachers.

Behrens's thesis exposes the enormous disparity between white
and black schools in Louisa County at that time. Describing in detail the dilapidated conditions at Louisa's twenty-one Negro schools,
it also records the county's complete disregard for the welfare and
education of its African American schoolchildren. Only one of the
twenty-one schoolhouses in 1949 had running water, and the water
source for five of these schools was at least a half-mile away. Only five
had electricity. All but one were heated by a wood stove, and many of
those stoves were in poor condition. None had an auditorium. One
school was inaccessible by car for days because of high water. Classes
were overcrowded, often with forty or fifty students of different ages
crammed into a single room. Only about a third of the teachers in the
Negro schools "held collegiate professional certificates." The Negro
elementary schools had virtually no books or maps. At a time when
blacks made up about 40 percent of the population, the Negro high
school had only one-fourth the number of library books, fewer than
half the number of course offerings, and laboratory equipment worth
only 12 percent of that in the white high school. Many African American students, lacking transportation to the only Negro high school in
a county spread over 514 square miles, dropped out at an early age.
Unconcerned by this phenomenon, county officials failed to enforce
Virginia's compulsory attendance law.

The tragic consequences of the county's stubborn refusal to fund
adequately the Negro schools that its Jim Crow policies required were
clearly evident when I lived there in 1970. In that year, according to
the U.S. Census, only 13.4 percent of the county's African American
adult men and 18.9 percent of its African American adult women had
graduated from high school; fewer than 4 percent of all the African
Americans in the county had completed four or more years of higher
education. Even more sobering, the median years of schooling for
black men was only 6.6 years, for black women, 8.0 years. Even as late
as 2000, county officials estimated that 23 percent of Louisa County's

adult population was not fully literate. For many of my students, "getting an education" was not something expected of them. They lacked not just books, fully certified teachers, reading and math specialists, and academic support, but also the role models and mentors, the historical affirmation and familial narratives that middle-class white children in that era took for granted.

When I struggled with a homework assignment as a child, I simply relied on my college-educated parents. When I wanted a good book to read, I casually selected one from the shelves lining the walls of my family's living room or eagerly consulted with Miss Rock, the town librarian, who liked nothing better than to walk with me through the stacks of the public library, personally selecting books for me and passionately recommending them. When I tried to imagine my life as a grown-up, I played hospital with the stethoscope from my father's black leather medical bag or school with the textbooks from the nineteenth-century schoolhouse where my great-grandfather had taught. When I chafed against my society's narrow expectations of women, I automatically looked to my rebellious grandmother, who as a young woman had been officially rebuked (as she loved to tell us) for "ruining the finer fiber of her moral character" by publicly playing basketball in her knickers and who had graduated from the University of Michigan with a degree in physics. How much more difficult it was for the children in my classroom, for whom books were rare objects; libraries, unfamiliar places; intellectual authorities, hostile strangers; professions, distant occupations; and universities, remote institutions.

It is ironic that, in the story of John Mercer Langston and his siblings, Louisa's own history provides a spectacular rebuttal to the destructive and absurd belief held by many of the county's white citizens at that time that African American children were uneducable. And it is even more ironic that a Louisa plantation owner should play a key role in this story by insisting that the children of a former slave — who were also his children — receive an education. Ralph Quarles, Langston's wealthy, slave-owning father, was ostracized from white society for living openly with Langston's mother, a slave named Lucy Jane Langston whom he had emancipated in 1806 after fathering a daughter by her. Defying the mores and conventions of his white planters' class as well as the laws of the state of Virginia, Quarles taught their daughter Maria (and later her husband, who had been a slave on another plantation) to read and write; brought their older two sons, Gideon and Charles, into his library every morning throughout the year "for tutoring and recitations"; and bequeathed the bulk of his estate to his three mulatto sons when he died in 1834, shortly after the death of Lucy Langston. Part black, part Indian, Lucy Langston, a skilled weaver, may herself have come from an educated family; there is speculation that her grandfather was one of eight Indians who attended the College of William and Mary in the mid-eighteenth century.

All three sons left Louisa soon after their father died to seek the educational and professional opportunities denied them as black men in Virginia. Although John Mercer Langston was only four when his father died, and therefore too young to have benefited from his father's formal instruction, his inheritance enabled him to acquire a first-rate education at Oberlin College, an education that helped him realize his ambitious goals even in the face of considerable and persistent discrimination. With his powerful intellect, lively wit, brilliant oratorical skills, and striking charisma, he went on to achieve extraordinary things. His older two brothers also became leaders in their communities, political activists in Ohio and Kansas, and committed abolitionists on the national scene. And the accomplishments of this illustrious family didn't end with the talented sons of Lucy Langston and Ralph Quarles. Charles's grandson was none other than the distinguished American poet, Langston Hughes, whose poems introduce the chapters of this book. I like to think sometimes about the remarkable chain of events that led from Lucy Langston's slave labor on a tobacco plantation in Louisa County, Virginia, to the powerful lyric poetry of Langston Hughes. It is sobering to realize that one fragile link—the early education of Lucy's son Charles in his white father's Virginia library in the 1820s—would never have been forged had the father not defied his southern society's prohibition against educating African Americans.

## Theirs and Ours

I wanted my students to become more adventurous, more willing to explore and take risks, less intimidated by the fear of being wrong or stupid. I wanted them to believe in their own capacity to learn. And I wanted them to discover the pleasure of learning. Early on, I attempted to implement in my crowded classroom some of the experimental practices advocated by the progressive educational theorists I had read in college. Instead of rote memorization and a focus on the correct answer, elements that had characterized Mrs. Stockton's pedagogy, I hoped to get my students more actively involved in the process of learning. But I succeeded primarily in disrupting, disorienting, and destabilizing the children in my classroom.

To combat their fear of failure, I tried to deemphasize grades and get my students to focus on learning. Instead of flunking them on work that was clearly failing, I tried an experiment in which I marked only their correct answers and then handed back their assignments, asking them to continue to work on the problems they hadn't understood and promising to help them. I also enlisted as tutors students who had done well on a particular assignment, pairing them with students having difficulty. I hoped that once my students understood that failing was not an option, the weaker ones would make a greater effort to complete their work and to master the task at hand. I also thought the better students would benefit from their tutoring role, gaining confidence in their academic abilities and reinforcing their own skills while helping their struggling peers.

But my experiment was a disaster. The weaker students clung tenaciously to their conviction that they were stupid, refusing to believe they could figure out what I was asking them to learn. No one had ever before required them to do an assignment until they got it right, and stripped of all their coping strategies—the squiggly lines, the blank pages, the neatly copied reiterations of my directions—they had no idea how to proceed. They were beside themselves when they received their assignments back with no grade; some of them even begged me to give them an F rather than leaving them in limbo. Had the class been a third the size, perhaps I might have succeeded. But without the individual attention they needed, most of the weaker students weren't able to progress. Equally disheartening, the students I drafted to tutor, though willing and eager to help, had no idea how to engage their peers in the process of learning. They seemed to think that helping meant revealing the correct answer. I couldn't convince them that giving an answer without any explanation of how they had arrived at it was not going to help someone learn. "But Mrs. Hallahan," Matilda exclaimed, exasperated, "the right answer to the story problem is forty-two; I don't know how to help without telling Vernice the answer."

Hoping to relieve a near universal dread of math, I also experimented with ways of helping my students visualize abstract mathematical concepts. One day I brought in two large bags of jelly beans and told them one bag was to help them with multiplication during math class and the second bag was for them to eat, after math class was finished. They were nonplussed. What, they wanted to know, did jelly beans have to do with math? But they were also intrigued.

"You mean the jelly beans are for us? And we can eat them?"

"Yes, after we complete our math lesson."

"But when will that be?" a chorus of voices sang out. "How soon will we be done with math? Why can't we eat them now? Does everybody get some? How many do we get?" The appeal of the candy proved wildly distracting, threatening to divert their attention from my carefully planned math lesson. I had not foreseen how exciting, how tempting, a bag of jelly beans would be to children unaccustomed to treats.

I produced a number of empty yogurt cartons I had collected, and I asked for a volunteer. Everyone, of course, wanted to go first. I invited Kevin to come up to my desk and asked him to put four jelly beans in each of five cartons. I intended to ask the students to guess how many jelly beans were in all the cartons combined and to ask each guesser to explain his or her answer. Then I planned to ask Kevin to empty the cartons and count the total. I wanted the students to see that multiplying $4 \times 5$ was equivalent to adding $4 + 4 + 4 + 4 + 4$ and to conceptualize the act of multiplication. But my simple demonstration broke down almost immediately when, as he counted out the jelly beans, Kevin impulsively popped a couple of them into his mouth. The class went crazy. Shouts of "no fair" and "I want some too" erupted. Victor lunged for the bag. William was right behind him. Within seconds the jelly beans were scattered on the floor and the students were on their hands and knees, grabbing them up and devouring them. Nobody was adding or multiplying; nobody was doing any conceptualizing. Instead, children long accustomed to scarcity were gleefully cramming dirty jelly beans into their mouths.

I tried introducing math games. My students were leery. They wanted to know if the losing team would get an F. They wanted to know if playing during math class meant that they would have to stay in at recess and do math. They couldn't imagine a connection between playing and thinking. Games that began with great enthusiasm routinely ended in sudden outbursts, with students breaking down under the pressure of too many frustrated hopes, too many unrealized ambitions. A child would shout out an answer when it was someone else's turn or fight for control of the tape measure or grab some of the marbles we were using for counters, and a promising project would suddenly disintegrate, the class given over to insults, accusations, physical recriminations, and tears. My experiments may have promoted some learning—the better students did become engaged and excited—but they did so at a cost, for they aroused desire in children who had only known deprivation, upsetting a fragile classroom equilibrium that depended on no one having anything at all. Whenever I promoted games in which something was at stake or introduced interesting objects like measuring tapes, beakers, maps, rocks, or postcards, somebody, driven by a maddening fear of insufficiency, a personal history of unfulfilled desires, would explode.

I was continually taken aback by responses I had not anticipated, assumptions I had never considered, each new surprise reminding me of my own failure to imagine the students I was trying to teach. In early April the drama of the crippled *Apollo 13* spacecraft riveted the nation. After an oxygen tank exploded in flight, severely damaging the craft, NASA engineers worked frantically to save the astronauts trapped on board and avert the impending disaster. Each step of their hair-raising and mind-boggling efforts was closely tracked on television, with the news coverage of the event preempting all other scheduled programming. The astronauts' plight held all America in thrall, or so it seemed. This, I thought, was a pedagogical opportunity not to be missed. At the beginning of the class's science period, I checked out the school's only TV (a Title I purchase), wheeled it theatrically into the classroom, and, plugging it in, turned on a newsbreaking update. I assumed that my students would be captivated by the drama, concerned about the fate of the astronauts, intrigued by the technical challenges facing the NASA engineers, interested in learning about the proposed engineering solutions, and curious to know more about this gripping story. I was, to say the least, not prepared for my students' responses to the drama unfolding on board the floundering *Apollo 13* spacecraft.

"They deserve to die," Louis announced emphatically, unmoved by the plight of the astronauts.

Emmeline nodded in assent, adding thoughtfully, "We shouldn't be up there in the first place. God never meant for man to go to the Moon, and this is God's way of telling us that he's angry at the astronauts, and at us, for sending them up there."

"If God had wanted man to go to the Moon," Chester reasoned, "he would have put men there in the first place."

"We've got no business sending people up to the Moon," Clinton agreed. "People are supposed to live on the Earth, not go flying around in outer space like they were some kind of a god."

"It's a sin to try to fly to the Moon," Ervin volunteered. "And this is God's way of punishing the astronauts for not staying on Earth where they belong. God is showing us that man has no right to be up there in space."

"I hope they die," Chester concluded, to a chorus of approval.

Before I had a chance to respond, Lonnie took an altogether different tack. "How do we know they're up there anyway?" he asked skeptically. "Who says we've even landed people on the Moon? *Anybody* can dress up in a space suit and put a silly helmet on his head and pretend he's floating around in space. *Anybody* can gather up some old rocks and tell everybody they're Moon rocks."

"Yeah! There are rocks everywhere. And people pretend to be astronauts on TV all the time," Byron asserted, echoing Lonnie. "Why should we believe there's even been an accident? They could just be faking it. The whole thing could be fake. Maybe they just want to get our attention. Maybe they want to see if they can fool us. Maybe they're laughing right now at how upset everyone is. Maybe they like fooling us."

"Yeahhh," others chimed in, as Byron embraced Lonnie's scenario. "They could be making this all up."

Only Reginald and James, my two budding scientists, held out against these startling views. But their passionate defense of the endangered astronauts did not move their classmates, who were divided between seeing the crisis as an act of God or seeing it as a Hollywood fiction. The science lesson I had imagined teaching was in shambles, and I wasn't at all sure how to proceed. I wanted to engage Emmeline's religious and Lonnie's skeptical perspective on the crisis, but I hadn't in any way anticipated their views, which were so radically different from my own. I had been completely caught up in the drama of the endangered space capsule, in the blurred television images of the three astronauts who had been hurled into space, never, perhaps, to return, in the frantic efforts in the control room in Houston to bring them back.

My expectations on that April morning in 1970—so clear and unproblematic, and so erroneous—were, I realize now, profoundly shaped by my own 1950s childhood in white, middle-class America, and especially by an event that had occurred when I was about my students' age: the 1957 launching of the Soviet satellite *Sputnik*. Early on the October morning it was launched, my father had burst into my bedroom with the exciting news, impressing upon my older sister and me that something amazing and revolutionary, something historic, had occurred. A Soviet satellite the size of a basketball had orbited the earth in ninety-eight minutes. I remember his announcement rousing me from an untroubled sleep, rousing me too from a young child's dreamy inattention to the moral universe. I struggled that day to understand the way my father's unabashed enthusiasm for this astounding engineering feat was darkened, complicated by the fact that the dreaded Soviet state, and not the United States, had accomplished it. After the successful launching of *Sputnik*, I, and virtually all the children I knew, had eagerly followed each new phase of America's space exploration, learning about satellites and booster rockets and gravity as we watched astronauts being catapulted into the atmosphere, blasted into the Earth's orbit, and sent far into space in search of the Moon. Children of the cold war, we were taught to identify with our government's efforts to win the space race, to marvel at the technological discoveries of our country's ingenious engineers, to celebrate the pioneer spirit of NASA astronauts. We grew up believing in scientific progress, trusting in the scientific community, dreaming of becoming astronauts and aeronautical engineers.

My students, I learned that day, inhabited a very different world. Profoundly alienated from their country's governing institutions, which had for so long deprived their people of their rights as citizens, they were inherently suspicious of the government-sponsored space program, seeing it as a white man's enterprise, even dismissing it as a white man's folly. Their heroes were not NASA astronauts and engineers, but an altogether different kind of pioneer, civil rights activists who had made their mark by challenging, not celebrating, their government. Then, too, they lived in a rural county far removed from the urban centers where the aeronautical industry thrived, and the huge amounts of money invested in and generated by that industry did nothing to improve their lot. Indeed, NASA's promise of new technological breakthroughs must have rung hollow to those of them who lived in homes that still lacked the most basic amenities (running water, electricity, telephones, central heat), products of much earlier technological discoveries. Nor did they have much reason to trust in modern science, though they were probably not aware of how some scientists had advanced racist theories to justify their subjugation or used African Americans as unsuspecting subjects in harmful experiments.

Their deep distrust of science was fueled as well by their religious faith, which taught them — as Raphael taught Adam in Milton's *Paradise Lost* — that it was presumptuous to try to know more than God reveals, a grievous sin to seek to penetrate the mystery of the heavens, folly to dream of other worlds. I was reluctant to challenge what their ministers, Sunday school teachers, and parents had taught them. Their discovery earlier in the year that I didn't attend church on Sundays had already elicited a significant amount of concern about the state of my soul. Ramonia had been so troubled by my confession of apostasy that she had urgently invited me to attend her church. "Mrs. Hallhan," she had written me, "would you like to come to The Bible Way Church Sunday. To hear our paster prech. Yes or no Invitation Letter." On questions of faith, I had no credibility.

But I did make an effort to rebut Lonnie's improbable theory that a billion-dollar space program was nothing more than a government hoax. Even as I tried to persuade my students that the *Apollo* 13 capsule was very real and the accident on board life-threatening, I came to see that, without understanding even the most fundamental scientific principles that make space travel possible, they had no basis to judge whether a spaceship was real or fantastic, marooned in space or artfully simulating disaster in a television studio. From their perspective, I had to concede, what I wanted to label as paranoia — the notion that actors were perversely staging a fictional crisis to dupe millions of spectators tuned into national TV — was all too credible.

I don't think I fully understood my students' perspective, however, until many years later, when I read Kristin Hunter Lattany's account of watching a later NASA accident — the explosion of the *Challenger* space shuttle—with her in-laws. A successful African American scholar who was visiting her husband's family in rural Georgia at the time of the *Challenger* disaster, she describes the "blank stares" she received from her husband's family when she expressed her sorrow over the death of the schoolteacher Christa McAuliffe, who was aboard the *Challenger* that fateful day. Initially taken aback by her in-laws' "total indifference" to the accident, which they tended to view as "white folks reaping the consequences of their foolishness," she finds herself reexamining her own response to the disaster. The attitude of her rural Georgia in-laws, she concludes, is an essential aspect of black American identity. "This attitude, the clear distinction between *theirs* and *ours*," she writes, "is a darkly hidden and necessary part of being black in America. Our lives are so hard and our history so wretched that if we identified with everybody's suffering we would never overcome our own for long enough to survive." Standing beside the television screen that April day, a baffled and surprised young teacher, I recognized that my students were making just such a distinction, but I didn't understand why. I only understood that a gulf had opened up between my students and me, a gulf I couldn't bridge.

## We Don't Have Any Films about *Union* Generals

My students had to negotiate the gulf between their rural, southern, black culture and the dominant culture of white America every single school day, for their textbooks were written primarily by white educators for white, middle-class children. They were expected to learn from books that excluded them entirely, rendering their way of life invisible and ignoring their dialect, their history, and their rich cultural heritage. Despite the remarkable achievements of the civil rights movement and the increasing influence of the black power movement, there was virtually no acknowledgment of African Americans in any of the textbooks my students used in 1970, even though most were recent editions from well-known national publishing houses.

Almost all the stories in the *Ginn Reader* were set in middle-class American suburbia. They nearly always featured white children whose fathers set out for work in the morning wearing business suits and carrying briefcases and whose mothers tended spacious houses with modern kitchens, carpeted living rooms, two-car garages, and carefully tended lawns. Occasionally, a face in an illustration that had, in an earlier edition, been white was colored light brown, but this halfhearted gesture towards diversity rang hollow. My students rarely identified with these characters or their comfortable, middle-class lives. What did they know about suburban swim meets or Sunday trips to the city zoo? Good children's literature, of course, often invites its readers to imagine lives that are radically different from their own and to identify with characters who inhabit distant or exotic worlds. But the *Ginn Reader* stories, bland and homogenized, presented these white middle-class characters as a familiar norm, characters who needed no introduction and no explanation. They could only have served to reinforce my students' sense of living outside of mainstream America, of being left out. I hated these textbooks, but I was required to use them. And so, every day I asked the poor, rural, black children in my class to read from textbooks that featured middle-class, suburban, white children living lives of unimaginable luxury and privilege.

The inadequacy of these stories became clear to me when I came upon one that diverged from the formula and described a world that more closely resembled my students'. Set in an isolated part of rural Maine, it featured a young white boy who lived with his family in a log cabin. The boy was responsible for keeping the fire burning in the cabin's wood stove. "That's my job, too," Timothy announced proudly, his eyes lighting up. "My grandpa chops the wood out in our back yard, and I have to carry it in every afternoon and stack it up by the stove. And I have to make sure there's always enough wood in the stove, because if there isn't, the house gets cold. It takes a whole lot of wood to heat our house. A whole lot." I had never seen Timothy so animated during class. He could barely refrain from jumping out of his seat.

I knew that Timothy lived alone with his grandfather in a house without electricity or indoor plumbing. He let me know that he slept on the floor, that his house was cold in the winter, that his grandfather made him do physically demanding chores. His mother was dead, and he often sought from me the maternal attention he didn't get at home. I understood that what he needed from me was a sympathetic ear, a gentle touch, a mother's concern. Sometimes, he would startle me by throwing his arms around my waist and giving me a spontaneous hug, a gesture that none of the other boys in the class would have dreamed of making. But more often, his communications were tinged with sadness.

Since he so often complained about the harsh conditions of his home, I was surprised at the way he brightened when he encountered the fictional white boy in Maine. As he talked about his own cabin in the woods, he pointed in amazement to a picture depicting the boy in Maine carrying an armful of wood towards a small log house. Shaking his head in disbelief, he gazed upon the illustration as if it was somehow miraculous, and then he glanced up at me with a quizzical look, as if he needed some assurance that he was not hallucinating. He must have never before seen a picture of a boy whose world resembled his own, never before read a story about someone who lived a life similar to the one he lived. "He's just like me," he said quietly, his eyes searching the picture for clues to himself. Unlike all the other stories in his textbooks, this simple story magically reflected back to him his own singular image, validating his own rough life in the Virginia woods, and perhaps making him feel as if he had a place in the larger universe.

Mostly, though, the assigned textbooks failed my students. I had been so disturbed by the fourth-grade Virginia history textbook I was required to use in 1970 that I tried to find a copy of it when I began research for this book. Although I didn't remember its title, I managed to track it down with the help of a resourceful young African American woman who worked at the reference desk at the University of Virginia. She was incredulous when I told her that the textbook had championed the Confederate cause and justified slavery as an economic necessity. I began to wonder whether I had misremembered or exaggerated its biases. But when I held it in my hands, I was amazed at how accurately I had recalled its one-sided version of the past. I was surprised, though, to discover that it was written and published in 1956 under the supervision of the Virginia History and Government Textbook Commission. I had always assumed it must have been written in the 1930s or 1940s, not two years after the *Brown* decision, when the modern civil rights movement was seriously challenging Jim Crow.

Leafing through its pages, I quickly confirmed my memory that the only African American named in this textbook is Booker T. Washington, whose accommodationist strategies and emphasis on manual and

vocational training for Negroes made him the darling of white segregationists. Except for him, the existence of Virginia's large African
American population is barely acknowledged. Although illustrations
appear on almost every page, and pictures of Indians—ranging from
friendly and noble to fierce and menacing—are everywhere in the
early part of the book, only two pictures feature blacks: one a portrait
of Booker T. Washington, the other an anonymous blacksmith on the
Mount Vernon plantation. Remarkably, all the other depictions of
plantation life show only white farmhands working the fields.

The history of my students' people had almost no place in this
textbook, which, in effect, erased the contributions African Americans had made, over more than three-hundred years, to the state of
Virginia. As a result, the children in my classroom had no access to
stories about black Virginians, men and women like the clever and
courageous Henry Box Brown, who began life as a slave on a Louisa
plantation and later engineered one of the riskiest and most dramatic
escapes from slavery ever accomplished by arranging to have himself
shipped in a narrow, coffinlike box from Richmond to Philadelphia.
Brown's memories of his life as a slave boy in Louisa County, told
in his autobiography, would surely have intrigued my students, who
would have recognized some of the places he describes. And the narrative of his terrifying escape would almost certainly have sparked
their imaginations. Perhaps, too, his story, and the international fame
he achieved in America and England with his theatrical show, "The
Mirror of Slavery," which used a painted panorama to depict the
evils of slavery, would have inspired them to dream, or instilled in
them a sense of their own agency, or stirred in them an interest in
social justice, or enticed them to venture beyond the farm fields of
Louisa County. But the Virginia History and Government Textbook
Commission, reflecting the racial politics of the time, made sure their
textbook would do none of these things.

When I took over in midyear, my class was studying the period
leading up to the Civil War, or, as it was called in the South, the War
between the States. I was eager to teach this history, a subject bound
to interest my students. But the story of the Civil War my students
were required to read that year was a story that left them out almost
completely. There was no discussion at all of the institution of slavery,
except as it bore on the economic well-being of the South and states'
rights. There was nothing about the *Dred Scott* decision, Nat Turner's

rebellion, the abolitionist movement, the Underground Railroad, John Brown at Harpers Ferry, or African American soldiers fighting for their freedom. The only noneconomic reference to slavery in the chapters on the Civil War and its aftermath, except for a short sentence declaring in the passive voice that "all the slaves were set free," came in a section about the hardships endured by white women and children on the plantations during the war. "Some of the Negro servants left the plantations because they heard that President Lincoln was going to set them free," explain the authors. "But," they add quickly, as if to reassure their young white readers, "most of the Negroes stayed on the plantation and went on with their work. Some of them risked their lives to protect the white people they loved." In this southern version of the War between the States, the only black heroism involved slaves protecting the very people who were enslaving them. What were my students to make of this story?

The rest of this book's Civil War history was devoted to the glory of the Confederacy. My African American students were required to read about the leadership of Robert E. Lee, the valor of Stonewall Jackson, the statesmanship of Jefferson Davis, the ingenuity of J. E. B. Stuart, and the heroism of all the Confederate soldiers "who were proud to wear the gray uniform of the Confederacy" and "proud to follow their new Confederate flag with its stars and bars." The culminating chapter on the Civil War does not discuss the Emancipation of the slaves or Lincoln's Gettysburg Address or the preservation of the Union. Instead, it lauds the bravery of the young Virginia military cadets at the Battle of New Market, making martyrs of the fourteen- and fifteen-year-old boys who were killed and wounded that day. And it tells the story of Lee's surrender at Appomattox as a tragedy in which the better man lost. As "tears rolled down . . . the cheeks" of Lee's troops, Grant and the other Union soldiers took off their hats to Lee, "who because of his greatness as a leader, his bravery, and his love for Virginia, would always be a hero."

Brought up on the other side of the Mason-Dixon Line, I barely recognized this narrative of the Civil War. I understood how crazy, how wrong it was to ask my students to read a history that endorsed the very Confederacy that fought to keep their people enslaved. Yet I was required to submit my course plans to my principal, showing him that, in accordance with the state-sanctioned curriculum, I was dutifully assigning the required chapters of this textbook. I assigned the readings, but I tried to encourage my students to question the book's assumptions. I have my teaching notes from these classes. In one lesson, I began by asking my students whether they knew anything about their ancestors' experiences during the time of slavery and the Civil War. I asked them what they knew about the conditions of slavery, and I tried to get them to imagine the lives of slave children. Did slave children go to school? How old were they when they began working in the fields? What must it have felt like to be owned like a piece of property? How would it feel to be separated from one's family and sold to another plantation? I remember Cecily, in particular, imaginatively entering into this exercise, describing in graphic detail slaves being beaten, threatened, mistreated, wronged, and overworked. I didn't know if she was drawing on family stories, empathetically connecting with unknown ancestors, or projecting her own child's sense of vulnerability and powerlessness onto the slaves of an earlier era. But she had no illusions about happy darkies living contentedly with their loving masters on Louisa's plantations.

I tried, too, to get my students to confront the larger moral questions of slavery. Why is slavery wrong? Can it ever be justified? If a slave master treats his slaves well, should they be grateful? This last question gave my students pause. They looked at me suspiciously, wondering, I guessed, whether, as a white woman, I expected them to say yes. But Sharon wasn't afraid to answer. "No," she argued, "because even a kind slave master was still robbing his slaves of their freedom." I didn't at that time know the story of Henry Box Brown, but I told my students about the Underground Railroad and about how escaped slaves and freedmen joined the Union army and fought to end slavery, and we talked about the desire for freedom that motivated slaves to risk their lives to gain it.

When I visited the county bookmobile that week — accompanied by two of my students — I tried to find supplemental materials about the Civil War that would offer other perspectives. The librarian was a pleasant, middle-aged white woman who seemed eager to help. She wasn't, however, able to find any age-appropriate books on the Civil War in her meager collection, which had more fiction than nonfiction books for children. But she assured me brightly that she had quite a few interesting films that featured important historical figures of the

Civil War. I turned to my students and asked them what famous person from the era they would most like to learn about.

"Abraham Lincoln!" they both shouted in unison, and I immediately concurred.

The librarian looked at me strangely, as if perhaps I should not have endorsed the children's request so enthusiastically. "We don't own any films about Abraham Lincoln," she told me curtly, without apology. Then, turning to my students, she assured them that she nevertheless had "lots of other very good Civil War films," and she encouraged them to make another choice, prompting them by asking, "Who is your favorite Civil War general?"

"How about a film on Ulysses S. Grant?" Byron suggested.

"No," the librarian replied, sounding slightly annoyed. "We don't have a film about Grant either."

"Is there one on Sherman?" Annie Mae asked politely.

The librarian gasped at the mention of Sherman's name, as if Annie Mae had just asked for a film on a serial killer or a child molester. "No, we certainly don't own any films about Sherman," she barked, adding pointedly, "We don't have any films about *union* generals."

Exacerbated, I asked the librarian to tell me exactly what films were in the Civil War series she was recommending. By then, I had already anticipated her reply: Jefferson Davis, Robert E. Lee, Stonewall Jackson, J. E. B. Stuart. I looked over at my two disappointed students. After a thoughtful pause, Byron shrugged. "Well," he conceded, "Stonewall is a pretty cool name." And on that basis Byron and Annie Mae carried back a film celebrating the military feats of the Confederate general Stonewall Jackson to show to their African American classmates.

## Pleces Sint Us More Books

When a friend of my mother learned that I was teaching in an impoverished school with no books, she organized a book drive at her church. Galvanizing the local community, she collected boxes and boxes of used books for my students. I brought them to school early one Monday morning and arranged them in neat rows on the empty shelves below the windows in my classroom. My students were astonished when I told them the books were for them and that they could take them home to read. How, they wanted to know, would I keep track of all the books? What if they lost one of them? What if their little sister or brother scribbled in one? Suppose someone kept one and didn't return it? Suppose someone on the bus stole the book from them? But when they realized I really was going to let them take the books home, they were beside themselves with excitement. They would show the books to their parents, read them to their little brothers and sisters, share them with their cousins. When they lined up for the bus to go home that afternoon, they cradled those books as carefully as they might a baby sister, and with as much fierce pride.

The notes they wrote to thank the stranger in Pennsylvania who had sent the books capture something of the pleasure they derived from the books. Annie Mae's note was typical: "Thank you very much for the books. I like them. I carry some of them home. I glad you gave them to us to use. And you gave a lot of them. truly yours, Annie Mae Davis." Like Annie Mae, many singled out the act of carrying the books home as particularly significant. "I took some home," Howard wrote, giving that fact equal weight to "the books was good to read." Others focused on the people who had donated the books: "I don't no you but I think you is good," Byron declared, while Sharon acknowledged that "I have never seen you before, but I think you are a very nice woman." Some identified their favorite book: "Hello Mrs. Koller. Thank you for senting our hold class all of the books. I injoy the books very much. I especial like the book about the 'Little Ballerina.' I think it is a very groovy groovy book. I really like all of the books. I have to close now. Specially yours. Ramonia Tirish Jackson." Matilda was clearly impressed, and a little taken aback, by the length of her favorite book, noting that "I like the book about the Bobbsey Twins in the Country. It was a good book but I have not finish reading it. It is a very long book. 22 stories and 282 pages. I like all of the 4 Bobbsey Twins. They are all very good." And Sharon, one of the most avid readers in the class, gave an overall assessment of the books: "How are you? Fine I hope. I really love the books you sent us. I have read most all of them. I have one now that is called — 'Alice in Wonderland.' I love them very much. They are very special to me. . . . The two best books are 'Cinderella' and 'Alice in Wonderland.' Thank you very, very much. Thank you. Your's Sincerely and Truly loving friend, Sharon Crawford. P.S. My teacher's name is Mrs. Hallahan. I think you know her." Perhaps the most touching note was Ervin's. Using his thank you note to ask for more books, he wrote simply: "Thank you for the books you sint me plesces sint me more books. Plecess. I will close now, love, Ervin."

"Plesces sint me more books": these are not the words of a child who cannot be educated. Ervin's modest plea for more books is a poignant rebuke to the county superintendent, who expected nothing of African American children; to the county supervisors, who refused to adequately fund the Negro schools; to the county school board members, who neglected to allocate money for books or libraries or laboratories at the Negro schools; and to the white citizens of Louisa County who, without acknowledging that they were responsible for creating the segregated and underfunded Negro schools that produced low test scores and high dropout rates, pointed to those deficiencies to confirm their belief that African Americans were uneducable. The children in my class were not "stupid kids"; they were kids who had been systematically denied access to a quality education.

Only once in the five months I taught at Morton did I encounter a white person who shared my belief in the intellectual potential of my students. Mr. Drumheller was an education professor at the University of Virginia, serving that year as a consultant to the school district as it began the process of integration. He observed my class one afternoon at the request of my principal, who hoped he could help me solve my chronic disciplinary problems. His arrival, just as we were beginning to discuss a story the students had read, caught everyone's attention. Even though he took a seat in the very back of the room, where he could observe the class without calling attention to himself, my students were highly conscious that an important person was watching them, and they behaved accordingly. Needless to say, Mr. Drumheller did not witness any acts of defiance or misbehavior that day. His mere presence in the back of the room was enough to bring the kind of order I'd been striving all semester to achieve.

Freed from the pressure of maintaining order, I could concentrate on the lesson at hand. Our story was about a goblin. Louis thought a goblin was a turkey; Chester, a large cup. I wrote "goblin," "gobbler," and "goblet" on the board to help the students sort through the confusion, then asked Reginald to look up all three words in the dictionary. He read the definition of "goblin" aloud: "an evil or mischievous sprite, ugly or misshapen in form." Immediately, hands shot into the air as children eagerly vied to tell their stories about goblins, each one more imaginative and scarier than the one before. Nearly everyone, it turned out, had had a personal and frightening encounter with a goblin. They lived under children's beds, in the back of closets, out in the dark woods. They haunted grandparents' houses, disrupted funerals, terrified whole communities. Then Sharon, frowning the way she always did when she was thinking hard, intervened. "But if goblins are so scary and bad," she wondered aloud, "then how come Mr. Penny believes they've been helping him out?" Her question brought the students back to the story. Could there be a nice goblin, one that does good deeds? Is Mr. Penny correct in thinking a goblin haunts his house? Are there other possible explanations for the unseen help Mr. Penny is receiving? Everyone had an opinion, and soon the children were arguing passionately with each other, pointing to a detail here, a passage there that might support their particular interpretation, the room crackling with energy.

When I talked to Mr. Drumheller after school that day, he wasn't interested in talking about my students' behavioral problems, though he acknowledged that keeping such a large class of energetic children focused was a challenge. What he wanted to talk about was how smart my students were. "You certainly have your hands full," he conceded. "Thirty-eight students! And *so bright.* I couldn't stop smiling when they told their goblin stories. They really know how to tell a good story. What active imaginations! I was astounded by their insights into the story. And the questions they raised were fascinating. Some of those kids — whew — they're really sharp. Very, very sharp."

"Yes, I know," I told him, beaming. "They're very smart."

# Larger Than Truth Can Be

Emancipation: *1865*
*Sighted through the*
*Telescope of dreams*
*Looms larger,*
*So much larger,*
*So it seems,*
*Than truth can be.*

*But turn the telescope around,*
*Look through the larger end—*
*And wonder why*
*What was so large*
*Becomes so small*
*Again.*
— *"Long View: Negro," Langston Hughes*

## You Couldn't Separate Us

Early one Saturday in March, Bill and I visited a nineteenth-century mill near where we lived. I have photographs we took of the mill that day. A barnlike structure with a high-pitched roof, it juts out over a turbulent river, anchored by massive stone pylons. Traces of snow still cover the north side of the roof in my photo, but spring has clearly arrived, and the river is swollen from rain and melting snow. A bright March sun illuminates the rough texture of the old wooden boards; the wavy glass in the eight-paned, recessed windows; the distinct marks of the hand-cut nails; and the long, wooden loading plank leading up to a second-story door. Swiftly moving water pours over the adjacent dam, spewing white foam and churning dangerously in the pool below the falls. River water floods the nearby trees. Arriving at this mill on the bright March day in 1970 when my photograph was taken, we met the mill's owner, a white man about my grandfather's age. A long-time Louisa County resident, he immediately knew we were "outsiders." After we had introduced ourselves as teachers in the local schools, he sold us a bag of flour, ground on the premises, and cordially answered our questions. Flattered by our interest in the old building, he soon launched into a series of stories about its history, all told with the colloquial speech and lilting drawl of a gifted southern storyteller.

One story, prompted by my question about the high level of the water that day, recalled a time when he was a boy and almost drowned in the river. He had been playing with Dexter, his "good pal, a colored boy who lived over yonder in a log cabin. It's gone now. Been gone for years. Dexter and I, we did everything together when we were boys. You couldn't separate us." The river had flooded that spring, the water had risen to a record height—"a couple feet higher than it is now, I reckon"—and he and Dexter, each goading the other, had daringly attempted to cross the river above the dam in a tiny rowboat. In their struggle to fight the powerful current, their boat capsized, and they were thrown violently into the river. As they clung desperately to the overturned boat, the relentless current pulled them towards the top of the dam. Just as they were about to be swept over the falls, their boat caught on a small snag in the river, a snag that, though it held them and their capsized boat precariously above the dam, threatened to give way at any moment.

Sure they were about to drown, he and Dexter locked eyes. At that instant, the old man told us, the experience still vivid in his memory, he recognized his own terror perfectly mirrored in his friend's terrified face. "I figured then," he said, "that it was all over for the two of us. I thought we were gonna go over the falls, and I knew we couldn't last but a few minutes in the water below. My only comfort was knowing we were going down together, knowing we'd have each other right up to the very end."

But they didn't drown that day. Somehow, the two boys, frantically working together to save themselves, managed to reach the shore unharmed. I can't remember any of the details of their miraculous escape from the floodwaters. That part of his story, oddly enough, didn't stay with me. What I remember instead was the mill owner's portrayal of his relationship with his "colored" boyhood friend: the warmth in his voice when he described the boy's cleverness and mischievousness and sense of adventure; the deep, nearly mystical camaraderie he still felt between them, sixty-odd years later; the well of emotion as he recalled that defining moment when he and his black friend faced death together on the roiling river.

Minutes after he finished his tale, as we were saying our good-byes, the mill owner casually inquired where I was teaching. As soon as the words "Morton Elementary" crossed my lips, his eyes went cold.

"I don't see why you even bother trying to teach those negra children," he snorted in disgust. "You're just wasting your time." He made this pronouncement dismissively, as if his point were entirely self-evident. And then he added in an aggrieved tone: "That school never should have been built. It's a terrible waste of taxpayers' money. A terrible waste. There's no good reason for the county to throw away taxpayers' money on a big, fancy school for colored children. Everyone knows they can't learn much more than to write their own names."

"Everyone knows." The year was 1970, but this man, standing beside the old mill where he still ground flour, seemed stuck in a past when "everyone" commonly referred only to white people, a past when what white people "knew," what they stubbornly refused to question, was a doctrine of white supremacy that declared all people of African descent members of an inferior race. Having embraced this doctrine, he could not imagine Louisa's African American children wanting, needing, or acquiring an education.

The mill owner must have been around seventy when I met him. He was born, then, at the turn of the last century, around the time states in the South began codifying their Jim Crow customs in the wake of a series of Supreme Court decisions signaling the legality of racial segregation in public transportation, public schools, and public accommodations. He had, it appeared, fully absorbed the segregationist beliefs of those times. In the face of more recent court rulings and the Civil Rights Act of 1964 outlawing segregation, he held stubbornly to his conviction that African American children did not deserve—and had no use for—an education equal to white children's. Indeed, at the very moment when the county was under a federal court order to integrate its public schools, he was still voicing opposition to the county's belated efforts in the 1950s to improve the chronically underfunded

Negro schools, efforts initially undertaken to prevent integration. Unwilling to accept the impending desegregation of the county schools, he could only meet its inevitability with a steely resistance.

Decades after this encounter, I still puzzle about how this man—capable, it seemed, of feeling a deep attachment to his black childhood friend—could hold such a profoundly racist belief with unwavering conviction, professing it openly, shamelessly, and uncritically. And he was no anomaly. In fact, his words eerily echoed those of the county's superintendent of schools on the day he hired me. A cultured man with a bachelor's degree from the University of Virginia and an EdD from New York University, Dr. Martin had made no effort that day to hide from me his contempt for the intellectual potential of the county's African American students. He clearly assumed I shared his racist views. Dr. Martin appeared to see no contradiction in declaring uneducable nearly 40 percent of the county's students he was responsible for educating or in asserting that the black children he was hiring me to teach were unteachable.

Both Dr. Martin and the mill owner were voicing deep and historic racial prejudices that the state of Virginia itself invoked when it presented its arguments against implementation of the *Brown* decision of 1954 to the Supreme Court in the proceedings leading up to the second *Brown* decision (May 31, 1955). Arguing that Virginia was "unalterably opposed to the operation of nonsegregated public schools in the Commonwealth of Virginia" and vowing that the state would use "its power, authority and efforts to insure a continuation of a segregated school system," Archibald Robertson, one of the attorneys for the state, relied on a series of overtly racist stereotypes to portray African Americans as inherently inferior to whites. In addition to depicting blacks in the most insulting terms possible, describing them as diseased, promiscuous, and immoral, he contrasted "the general level of educational capacity and attainment" of whites and blacks to suggest that black children were intellectually inferior to whites and thus unworthy to share classrooms with white children. Robertson apparently saw no irony in his casting aspersions on the intelligence of African Americans during legal arguments in which the opposing legal team, already victorious in *Brown*, included such brilliant African American lawyers as Thurgood Marshall, Spottswood Robinson, and James Nabrit.

In his argument to the court, Robertson adamantly denied that the state had any responsibility for black children's low levels of educational achievement, as measured by standardized tests. And yet he insisted that any implementation of *Brown*—that is, any integration of the state's public schools—would be an unacceptable and intolerable violation of Virginia's "traditions." Those traditions, he surely knew, had unilaterally denied African Americans access to even a rudimentary education in the eighteenth and nineteenth centuries and had systematically deprived them of public schools equal to those of whites in the twentieth. Choosing to ignore these facts, Robertson characterized the white people in his state as emotionally traumatized by the sudden disruption of their long-held and cherished traditions. The majority of Virginians, he told the court, "feel a sense of bewilderment that traditions and systems that have operated with judicial approval since 1870, and, in fact, since 1619, can be so readily swept away." By invoking "tradition," he was clearly appealing to earlier judicial opinions that had permitted segregated practices, including the operation of separate schools for whites and blacks, on the basis of "the established usages, customs and traditions of the people." Yet Robertson could not assert the sanctity of Virginia's traditions without identifying those traditions with the state's slaveholding past. Simply by reminding the court that these cherished traditions traced all the way back to 1619, he identified them (accurately, if inadvertently) with the institution of slavery, and the Virginia state laws that made it illegal to teach a Negro to read or write, forbade "slaves or free Negroes" to assemble "for the purpose of instruction in reading or writing," and barred "any free person of color . . . who shall for the purpose of being educated be sent from the state" from ever again residing in Virginia. His outrageous assertion that "we are not aware of any unfairness or inequality, and we are not responsible for" the low level of educational achievement attained by black children in Virginia is thus contradicted by his own appeal to traditions that were by their very nature inherently unfair and predicated on extreme inequalities between the races.

Reinforcing Robertson's appeal to tradition in these oral arguments, Lindsay Almond, then the attorney general of Virginia and soon to be the governor, made a fiery speech to the court in an effort to prevent it from ordering any quick implementation of *Brown*. Indeed, it is clear that he sought to prevent any implementation of *Brown*, ever, confidently asserting at one point that there "will not in my judgment in the lifetime of those of us hale and hearty here, be enforced integration of the races in the public schools" of the Virginia county he was representing. Almond predicted that the 1954 *Brown* decision would have a "crushing impact" upon public education in Virginia, and, cunningly appropriating the language of *Brown*, he sought to focus the court's attention on the impact that decision would have on the "hearts and minds" of white southerners who were devoted to their customary way of life. His argument seemed calculated to arouse an emotional response by portraying *Brown* as a direct and unconscionable attack on the South's venerable traditions. He spoke of "the sudden shock entailed by the uprooting and demolishing of a way of life enshrined and institutionalized in the hearts and minds of the overwhelming majority of millions of law-abiding citizens, their fierce and deep-seated devotion to their customs and traditions composing as they do, the warp and woof of their mores of life."

But, like Robertson, Almond refused to acknowledge that the customs and traditions he defended so passionately were rooted in the institution of slavery and the economics of the plantation, instead elevating them to a quasi-religious and legal status. And he adamantly denied that whites' resistance to school integration had anything to do with racism. "On the surface the problems confronting us do not stem from racial antipathies," he confidently asserted. "Those who spout that propaganda are either abysmally ignorant of the facts of life or are as reckless with truth as Sherman was with fire in some parts of our country." Incredibly, shortly after denying that white Virginians were motivated by any "racial antipathies," Almond went on to lament the "damage" that would be done to the "hearts and minds" of white children if they had to share "the same drinking fountain, the same toilets" with black children.

By invoking cherished southern traditions while categorically denying the terrible consequences those traditions wrought, both these attorneys, who represented the state of Virginia and articulated the beliefs of a majority of its white citizens, sought to preserve the status quo through a willful obfuscation of the historical record. Unwavering in their conviction that, to quote my own superintendent, "you can't teach *those* children anything," they conveniently forgot the countless ways they and their ancestors had actively sought to prevent or subvert the education of African American children.

Oral histories recording the experiences of African Americans during Reconstruction and the Jim Crow era serve as crucial reminders of what so many white southerners in those days chose to "forget." Such histories recall, for instance, the way white authorities in Virginia threatened a white, female teacher from the North because she "communicate[d] to the colored people ideas of social equality with whites"; the way a white store owner in Alabama confronted a northern white man sent by the Lutherans to help start a school for black children, telling him, "You going to teach these niggers to read? . . . some of the white folks back at home are afraid ya'll are going to teach them to read and that's going to ruin them"; and the way a white missionary who came to Alabama to minister to the African American community was told by local whites that "she had to go" because of her efforts to teach black children to read and was summarily removed from the school, taken to the airport, and sent home. These oral histories also tell the stories of white supervisors of black schools who "didn't worry about the children learning because they didn't want anybody that asked a lot for your kids"; who "didn't want the black schools to have anything. . . . You got the leavings"; and who "never picked the blacks who he thought would do a good job of teaching and educating the black kids. He got the ones who were strong and ugly, who he thought would keep the kids in place. . . . He'd look at them, how they walk and how big and burly they were, and he'd pick them out from there. . . . Didn't worry about any brains. He just wanted somebody, just a person there. . . . We had no voice in choosing the teachers."

Letters and newspaper articles written by African Americans corroborate these memories. For example, a black journalist in late-nineteenth-century Georgia reported that the schoolhouse which he and other freedmen had built was burned down by whites. And another freedman wrote to a Union general during Reconstruction to complain that "our teacher whom we have employed here was shot down by a crowd of Rebel Ruffians for no other cause than teaching School. . . . This is the second teacher that has been assaulted. The Rebels make their brags to kill every Yankee teacher that they find." If, before the war, laws in states like Virginia prohibited the education of slaves and free blacks (and punished the few who defied them, like

Margaret Douglass of Norfolk, with jail terms), these reports indicate that after the war many southerners took it upon themselves to prevent blacks from going to school.

In his argument against the implementation of *Brown*, Almond sought to portray that momentous 1954 decision outlawing segregation in the public schools as a decision to sacrifice southern white culture and Virginia's public school system to a "noble" but unrealizable principle, one he likened, incredibly, to the ideal of temperance. Thus equating the forced segregation of black school children in inferior schools with the social vice of drinking, he predicted that *Brown* would, like Prohibition, prove a disastrous social experiment, one that would inevitably be rescinded because human nature—which he believed abhorred any race mixing—can never be changed. Almond ended his argument by melodramatically begging the court not to "press this crown of thorns upon our brow and hold the hemlock up to our lips." But the African American men and women I quote above tell a very different story, one in which white southerners in a position of power had, over the course of more than three hundred years, ruthlessly sacrificed the education of black children to the ignoble cause of white supremacy.

## Mourning's Children

In Louisa County, the traditions Almond and Robertson fought so fiercely to retain were firmly rooted in plantation culture. While Louisa's planters went to considerable effort to assure that their own sons acquired an education, they had enormous economic and political interests in keeping their slaves (and poor whites) ignorant. For them, education was a prerogative of the elite, one that helped them consolidate and perpetuate their power. By singling out their sons as alone worthy of educating, they were able to distinguish their heirs from everyone else and thus solidify their social position. The account book that the Louisa planter David Watson kept from 1813 to 1830, for example, demonstrates how seriously Virginia planters took the responsibility of educating their sons. In addition to recording the costs of operating his large plantations, Watson, himself a learned and highly literate man, lists the expenses incurred for the education of the sons of two deceased planters. As an administrator of their father's estate, Watson allocates considerable sums of money between 1813 and 1818 to educate William and Walter Dabney, first hiring and boarding resident schoolmasters, then paying tuition and board for a private school, and finally sending Walter "to school over the mountains." In 1819 Watson is again put in charge of a child's education when Dr. William Wardlaw dies. Wardlaw requests in his will that Watson supervise his son's education, directing that "His son William is to be afforded the best opportunity to acquire a good education, & his expenses to be paid out of the general estate, till he arrives at the age of 21 years." Watson immediately begins allocating $150 per year "for this boy's schooling in Richmond," as well as money for books and other educational fees. Watson's records indicate that Louisa's planter class highly valued formal education and took pains to assure that its sons—who were to inherit the property, wealth, and privilege of their fathers—were properly educated. Education clearly served an important function in shaping and perpetuating the planter class.

But while David Watson sees to it that these sons of white planters are nurtured with books, tutors, schoolmasters, boarding schools, and universities, the slave children on his farms make do with the essentials for survival. In preparation for the cold and wet winter weather, for instance, Watson distributes blankets in 1828 to his slaves, including "1 to Mournings children Henry & Sam." All the slave children on his plantations were, in a sense, "Mourning's children," born in captivity, bought and sold as commodities, forced to work at an early age, and allocated just enough material resources to keep them fit to work his tobacco fields and maintain his household. Their intellectual potential is of no interest to Watson, who views their worth in terms of the future physical labor they can provide him and compares the inflated "price of a good crop negro man" with the price of "good riding horses." His account book meticulously tracks the production of wealth based on the labor of his slaves. The blankets he distributes annually to his slaves constitute one of the costs of owning human property. The education he helps to provide for the sons of the oligarchy can be seen as another such cost, for these sons must learn to manage and conserve their families' wealth — much of it residing in the bodies of slaves — in order to preserve their privileged class and racial status.

When his father dies in 1825, David Watson records an appraisal of his father's slaves, who constitute a significant portion of the property

to be distributed among the heirs. The eighty-four slaves in his father's estate include approximately forty-five children eighteen years
old and younger. In his elegant handwriting Watson estimates each
slave's relative value based on his or her capacity to do hard physical
labor, as well as their future potential earning power: $150–250 for
6-to-8-year olds, $275–300 for children between the ages of 9 and
12, peaking at $400–500 for boys 16–18 who are old enough to do
the work of a mature man. To assure a fair monetary division among
the heirs of his father's estate, Watson systematically breaks up slave
families: Nanny's 4 children (ages 6–16) are divided among 3 different heirs, as are Mima's 6 children (ages 6–14) and Reuben's 3 children (ages 6–18); Lucy's 3 children (ages 7–12) are divided between 2
heirs. Watson even uses one slave child—"Patsy/Nanny's girl about
8 years old"—to seal the final distribution, reassigning her "to [his]
sister Nancy to make her [portion] equal to what had been given to
the other children [of his deceased father] before the division." As
this account book reminds us, African American children under slavery were viewed as property, treated as commodities, and separated
from their families in order to achieve a notion of fair and "equal"
distribution of property among family members of the plantocracy.

Slave children learned, at a very young age, that their place was in
the fields or the kitchen, not the schoolroom. Quoting a former slave,
the editor of an oral history project undertaken in Virginia during the
Great Depression explains that "the use of children in the field was,
according to ex-slaves, a part of the 'discipline' of the slave system.
Horace Muse, who thinks he is 112 years old, declares: 'Children had
to go to de fiel' at six [years of age] on our place. Maybe dey don't do
nothin' but pick up stones or tote water, but dey got to get used to
bein' dere. Uncle Zack [who was an elderly, disabled slave] . . . Used
to set in de shade lookin' at de chillun goin' to d fiel' an' mutter, 'Slave
young, slave long.'"

The assumption among white planters that black children were
an abundant source of cheap labor—and one they were entitled
to exploit—carried over after Emancipation. In his book on late-
nineteenth-century Louisa, Crandall A. Sifflett observes that "Louisa farmers who had once owned slaves never quite rid themselves
of the idea that black labor was theirs." The account books of Thomas
Watson bear out his assertion. Shortly before the war, this member of
Louisa's Watson family records small sums of money that he gave to

slave children as "harvest money" to acknowledge their unsalaried labor in the fields that growing season. He notes, for instance, that he allocated twenty-five cents each to "Lavinia (girl) water-toater" and "Caleb (boy 11 or 12 years old)." After the war African American children like Lavinia and Caleb were no longer officially slaves, compelled by their masters to work on their farms without pay. But Watson's account books indicate that they were hardly free to go to school. In fact, their lives did not change very much, despite their legal emancipation. As a system of peonage replaced slavery in this agricultural county, most black children in Louisa County continued to work in the fields or households of white farmers, receiving very low wages for their efforts.

Some were even forced to work in order to help their fathers fulfill their contractual obligations to their former slave masters. According to the detailed Freedman Accounts which he kept after the war, Thomas Watson enters into various contractual arrangements with former slaves who quickly find themselves bound to him through financial loans they cannot repay. He leases old slave cabins on his plantations to freedmen, many of whom were his former slaves, charging them a significant amount of rent for primitive structures like "the house (or rather the room) which is the western one of the double cabin in the southern row, at Chestnut forest." He lends them money at interest. And he pays them very low wages (six to eight dollars per month for an adult male farm worker, three to four dollars a month for a female domestic worker, one dollar per month in the case of one young boy). These financial arrangements make it virtually impossible for the freedmen ever to pay back their debts or to escape Watson's control.

By the 1880s, some of these contractual workers have acquired so much debt they have to resort to lending Watson their sons to help work it off. Owing Watson $440.05 in the form of a bond plus a yearly interest and earning only 40 cents a day from him, Richard Wheeler, for example, sends his son Moses to work for Watson, with the understanding that all the boy's wages will go to Watson to help pay down the father's debt. In another case, a father sends his son to work to help pay off a debt incurred by the boy's grandfather. Explaining this arrangement, Watson writes: "And I bargained with Harry [Quarles] to have his son, Sam for this year to be paid quarterly at the rate of three &

half dolls. Per month. And Harry expressly promised that Sam's wages shall go to pay an old debt Harry owes me — now amounting to over twenty dollars — being on account of money advanced & paid for land bought for Harry's father — amongst my papers may be found one giving a statement of this transaction." And when Sam Quarles has children of his own, the cycle is repeated. Sam hires out his own children — a boy of about 11 and a girl of about 9 — to Watson, asking that they be employed "'in labor suited to their ages.'"

Needless to say, these children had little opportunity to go to school. Despite Emancipation, they were still bound economically to their father's or grandfather's former slave master and, like earlier generations of slave children, expected to go to work at a young age in preparation for a lifetime of menial labor. And the whites who exploited these African American children — hiring them at very low wages, requiring them to work to help repay family debts, keeping them out of school so that they could fulfill their work obligations — continued to treat them as members of a subservient caste.

Although they had lost the right to own slaves, former members of the planter class continued to assert power over the county's African American laborers and to perpetuate both the hierarchy and the racist stereotypes of the plantation. These stereotypes were typical of many white Virginians in positions of power after the Civil War. The Virginia commissioner of agriculture, for example, argued in 1877 that black laborers were in fact preferable to white laborers because they could be treated more like slaves. Pointing out that farmers would have to pay white farm workers "double what we have to pay the negro" and would be obligated "to give them flour in place of cornmeal," he warned that white laborers were far more difficult to control because they were more educated and thus less accustomed to being obedient and subservient. "'It is a disadvantage for a farmer to have a laborer who thinks he knows more than his employer," the commissioner observed in explaining the problem white workers pose. "The farmer must be able to direct the movements of the laborer. The negro has been raised to obey. Not so with the white man.'"

This line of reasoning led directly to the conclusion that African Americans should not, in fact, be educated, for education threatened to undermine their usefulness to white farmers as cheap, pliant, and dependent farm laborers. An eminent Virginia professor, speaking as chairman of the faculty at the University of Virginia, made this precise argument at the Southern Education Association meeting in Richmond in 1900. Asserting confidently that African Americans' central purpose in life was as a "'source of cheap labor for a warm climate,'" this man—an educator by profession—declared that Negro education should consist of nothing more than "'Sunday-school training,'" adding that in everything else but menial labor the black man "'is a foreordained failure, and as he knows this he despises his own color.'"

Virginia's white elite also had political reasons for denying the state's black citizens an education. An active black electorate was threatening to whites who held political power in Virginia, especially in those counties with sizable black populations—the very agricultural counties that had imported large numbers of slaves to work sprawling plantations in the antebellum period. Intent on disenfranchising African Americans, white Virginia politicians rewrote the state constitution in 1901–1902 in an effort to exclude black voters. These legislators exploited the fact that most blacks in the state had been denied access to an education by making a literacy test, as well as a poll tax, a requirement to vote. Boasting at the Virginia State Convention of 1902 that "'this plan will eliminate the darkey as a political factor in this State in less than 5 years,'" Carter Glass told an approving audience of legislators that "there stands out the uncontroverted fact that the article of suffrage which the Convention will today adopt does not necessarily deprive a single white man of the ballot, but will inevitably cut from the existing electorate four-fifths of the negro voters.'" Although poor whites, too, were disenfranchised by this act, Glass's gleeful prediction about the effect of this plan on black voters was accurate. The new state constitution effectively silenced the black electorate. By 1940 "fewer than 10 of every 1000 Virginians" voted in state elections, as "compared with 147" in 1900, before the state's constitution was revised. In the mid-1950s, when the issue of school desegregation dominated state and local elections in Virginia, less than 25 percent of African American adults were registered to vote in Virginia. Furthermore, in many rural counties in the 1950s, even blacks who were fully literate and had paid the poll tax did not vote under pressure from their white bosses. Denied access to the ballot box and shut out of county governments that relied almost entirely on appointive positions, African Americans in rural counties like Louisa thus lacked the political power to demand better schools for their children. And without better schools many could not escape the illiteracy and poverty that denied them their voting rights.

The logic of the Virginia commissioner of agriculture, writing in 1877, the University of Virginia professor, speaking in 1900, and the state legislator, addressing the Constitutional Convention in 1902, deeply informs the traditions of Louisa County and the state of Virginia, traditions that Almond and Robertson sought with such passion to preserve in 1955. Those traditions, which benefited a white elite class at the expense of African Americans, worked to deny black children access to education, thus assuring white landowners yet another generation of laborers too poor, illiterate, unskilled, and dependent (they hoped) to leave, organize, vote, or protest. As late as the 1940s, the future civil rights leader and congressman, John Lewis, then a poor boy in rural Alabama attending a segregated, one-room elementary school he describes as "just a shack really," was forced to skip school in order to work in the fields. "This was true for almost every child in our school," he writes. "It was a Southern tradition, just part of the way of life, that a black child's school year was dictated by the farm rhythms of planting and harvesting. You went to school when you could."

Indeed, the logic that dictated that a bright African American boy like the young John Lewis annually abandon his studies in order to work in the fields still governed the thinking of many whites, northern as well as southern, even in 1970. This became clear to me when, during a visit with my husband's family in an affluent suburb of Philadelphia in the spring I lived in Louisa, I encountered a distinguished Philadelphia doctor who wanted to know all about my experience teaching in the "Negro school" in Virginia. Encouraged by his interest, I began to tell him about my students. I told him about Derrick's struggles learning to read, Reginald's rebelliousness, James's intellectual curiosity. Then I told him about Sharon. I described to him how very, very smart she was and explained how her insights often challenged me to reexamine my own assumptions. Singing her praises, I declared that I had never known a child who was as perceptive, thoughtful, or wise. He listened attentively, nodding his head, responsive, I thought, to my praise and admiration of Sharon. Then he said enthusiastically—and I will never forget his words—"She sounds quite exceptional. Maybe, when she's a little older, you can arrange for her to come to Philadelphia to work as a maid. I know lots of people who are looking for reliable maids. It's very hard to find good help these days." I imagined my star pupil becoming a lawyer, a teacher, a psychologist, but this man, who expected all his own children to earn advanced degrees and enter the professions, could, solely because Sharon was black, only think of her as a future maid.

## Do We Have to Sacrifice Our Children?

In his 1955 legal argument against the implementation of *Brown*, Lindsay Almond rhapsodized about Virginians' "devout and firm conviction as to the legal and moral soundness of their public school system which they have maintained for generations and into which they have poured their souls, their substance and their sacrifice." But, in fact, in much of Virginia, public schools had historically received very little support, financial or otherwise, from the white citizens whose cause Almond championed. In the antebellum years, Richard Kluger points out, "education, which the North and West saw early on as a vital requirement, was of small concern to those in control of the Old Dominion of Virginia." Citing tensions between planters and poor whites, Kluger observes that

> proper Virginians were understandably unenthusiastic about the spread of learning among the rabble. Publicly supported schools to teach pauper children to read, write, and count were opened in scattered locations, but by 1845 there were no more than 10,000 children attending public schools in Virginia; that year in Massachusetts, which had a population slightly smaller than Virginia's, the total attending public schools was 158,000. By the middle of the [nineteenth] century, the percentage of native whites of eligible age attending school in Virginia—12.26—was the lowest in the nation except for California and Florida, which were frontier societies.

In antebellum Virginia, then, education was for the most part viewed as a privilege of the propertied classes—most of whom owned property in slaves—and not a public service that the state should provide to its citizens. There was scant support for educating whites of the lower class. After the Civil War, this historic resistance to public education intensified, for the defeated Confederates were even more hostile to educating the emancipated slaves than they were poor whites, and they viewed "universal public education . . . as a carpetbagger invention, and taxes to support it . . . as socialistic."

In the years following the war, whites in Louisa County adamantly opposed the Free School movement, refusing to fund public schools with tax dollars in large part because they did not want to educate or pay for the education of African American children. A historical essay printed in the local paper, the *Central Virginian*, in 1957, documents the intensity of white opposition to the establishment of a public school system after the Civil War. Titled "Louisa County Struggle for Free Schools, 1868–1878," it explains that "the Free Schools . . . were opened in November 1870" and then reports that "there was much opposition. The people [meaning, of course, white people] generally did not like the free school idea and were unwilling to send their children to them or to be taxed to support them." Citing a telling diary entry made by the county's newly appointed superintendent of schools, the Reverend L. J. Haley, after the defeat in 1872 of a tax levy targeted for the public schools, this newspaper article identifies the very problem—voters' resistance to increasing taxes to support public education—still plaguing the county schools when it was written in 1957. "'I learn from all quarters,' writes Haley in 1872, 'that the people of Louisa County are violently opposed to the School Law, and the whites generally will not vote an increase in taxes for school purposes.'" As a result of this opposition, the few schools in Louisa that did exist for African American children in the late nineteenth and early twentieth centuries were almost all sponsored "by churches, northern whites, and individual philanthropists."

It is interesting to speculate why this newspaper article, describing "the great unwillingness of people of Louisa County to support their public schools even at this early date of 1872," was published in 1957, at a time when there was not only increasing pressure from African American parents to improve the county's Negro schools but also mounting white opposition to federally mandated integration of the public schools. The year this article appeared in the local newspaper, the Democratic candidate for governor, Lindsay Almond, who hailed from adjacent Orange County, declared that integration of the public schools "'would lead to mongrelization and hybridization of each race to the destruction of Virginia.'" Adopting a strategy of unified defiance known as Massive Resistance, Almond—the same man who as the state attorney general had argued against the implementation of *Brown*—vowed to close the public schools in Virginia rather than to comply with court-ordered integration. He endorsed a plan that had been adopted by the state legislature the year before, authorizing the governor to close any school operating with state funds rather than allow it to be integrated. This plan, known as the Stanley plan, relied on a system of pupil placement, understood by its supporters to be the "'first defensive outpost in the anti-integration network," since "'pupils would be assigned to preserve complete segregation." Should the federal courts order the enrollment of even one African American student in a white public school, the governor would under this plan intervene and close the school. As part of his campaign stump speech, Almond "would raise his right arm and proclaim that he would lose this limb before a single black child entered a white school," eliciting wild cheers from his audiences.

The official platform of the Democratic Party of Virginia that year took a similarly militant stand against integration, proclaiming "'we will oppose with every facility at our command, and with every ounce of our energy, the attempt being made to mix the white and Negro races in our classrooms. Let there be no misunderstanding, no weasel words, on this point: We dedicate our every capacity to preserve segregation in the schools.'" Although a few whites spoke out in favor of integrating the public schools of Virginia and some supported a less draconian plan that would have allowed a limited amount of integration in a few receptive districts, "the overwhelming majority of white Virginians, by perhaps as much as a 3 to 1 margin, supported" Almond's candidacy, strongly endorsing his promise to close the public schools rather than integrate even one of them. As in the 1870s, "free schools" aroused fears of race mixing and revealed the deep resistance of whites to providing African American students with an education equal to that of white students.

Soon after becoming governor in 1958, Almond did in fact defy the federal courts by shutting down public schools in Charlottesville, Norfolk, and Warren Counties rather than permitting them to comply with federal court orders to enroll black students. This action left "approximately 13,000 pupils . . . with no public school to attend." Though the bulk of these students enrolled in private schools or resorted to attending makeshift classes in homes and churches, "several thousand students received no formal education at all." Only after both the Virginia Supreme Court of Appeals and a federal district court ruled the school closings unconstitutional in January 1959 did Almond relent. After initially delivering a defiant speech in which he attacked "'those who would overthrow the customs, morals and traditions of a way of life which has endured in honor and decency for centuries'" and vowed not to give up the cause of segregation, he called a special session of the General Assembly, where he announced that the state was powerless to resist the federal courts and advocated the repeal of the school closing law. His about-face infuriated the most rigid segregationists who had hoped to prevent the integration of even a single school. But, in fact, it signaled only a moderate shift in Almond's position away from massive resistance to what some historians have dubbed "passive resistance," or tokenism. In place of such radical tactics as school closures, Almond endorsed a series of recommendations — described by supporters as a "containment policy" — intended to keep public school integration at an absolute minimum. These recommendations, made by a commission of "moderate" legislators appointed by Almond and adopted as law in 1959, embraced the notion of "freedom of choice" and included a provision for public tuition grants to support children attending private schools.

A white boycott continued to disrupt the Warren County schools even after Almond rescinded his school closure order, and a local version of massive resistance continued to plague the Prince Edward County schools, shutting down all the public schools there from 1959 to 1964 while allocating public money, in the form of tuition grants for white students, to maintain "private" schools for those pupils. The black students in this district were left with no schools to attend for much of this period. Norfolk and Arlington schools, however, began to admit some black students in the winter of 1959, and Charlottesville complied with court-ordered integration in the fall of 1959. But the Pupil Placement Board continued to assign black students to segregated Negro schools unless they actively sought to transfer to a white school, could prove that they lived closer to a white school than a Negro school, and could meet certain academic standards set by the board. As a result, the percentage of African American students enrolled in integrated schools in Virginia was less than 1 percent in 1962 and about 5 percent in 1964. Significant school integration in Virginia did not begin to be achieved until around 1968.

No schools were closed in Louisa County, though a local chapter of the segregationist Defenders of State Sovereignty and Individual Liberties initiated a private fund drive to "help educate children in areas where schools have been closed by court order," an act of solidarity with supporters of Massive Resistance. But in all matters concerning the integration of the schools, county officials dragged their heels. Three days after the *Brown* decision in 1954, the local paper reported that school officials were "sitting tight on the new school problems that will come from the Supreme Court's decision regarding segregation of white and colored students in public schools." The school board agreed to take "no action," preferring instead to wait for guidance from the state. Meanwhile, the county supervisors steadfastly refused to increase Louisa's historically low tax assessments (based on only 25 percent of the true value of property) or levy new school taxes, though they did allocate money in the late 1950s to build the Negro elementary school where I taught. In 1960 these supervisors turned back the school board's request for more funds, even as the county's citizens — white and black — publicly complained about "low teacher salaries, unsafe buses, [and] poor schools" and resentfully denounced "the land hogs of this county, who buy every piece of land they can get" while keeping property taxes low and refusing to support public education. Beholden to large landholders, the supervisors ignored these citizens' complaints. They seemed far more concerned about maintaining the county's low property taxes, and retaining their hold on power, than in addressing problems in the public schools.

Writing about the eventual desegregation of the Louisa County schools in 1992, a local historian chose to downplay the conflict, anger, and unrest of this period. Noting only that "the 1960's ushered in decided change" in Louisa County, she asserts that "desegregation [of the county schools] mandated by the Civil Rights Act of 1964 was carried out with dispatch." But her curiously truncated narrative is a seriously distorted history, one that ignores the way powerful county officials openly defied the 1954 *Brown* decision and vigorously sought to avoid, obstruct, and delay school integration. In fact, even though the "freedom of choice" policy instituted under Almond allowed a handful of black students to be admitted to Louisa's white schools, the dual-school system continued virtually intact until the 1969–1970 school year. In 1967 the county school superintendent, seeking to address problems ranging from overcrowding (especially in the Negro schools) and inadequate space to the need for vocational training, special education, elementary school libraries and librarians, kindergartens, and elementary specialists, proposed three radically different plans for consideration. Neither the school board nor the board of supervisors chose the obvious option, Plan C, which called for the elimination of the dual-school system. Even after the Department of Health, Education, and Welfare (HEW) threatened in 1968 to cut off all federal funds to the school district because the board "had not taken sufficient steps to integrate the Louisa County public school system," county officials chose to take "no action." In the face of this threat, the superintendent of schools announced that the county's Freedom of Choice plan—the very plan that the HEW officials had deemed deficient—would once again be in effect for the coming year.

By this time, however, many white parents and teachers had become persuaded that school integration, once unimaginable, was now not only inevitable but desirable. Concerned about the threatened loss of federal aid, anxious about the expense of impending court battles, fed up with the public schools' chronic funding crises, cognizant of the wasteful costs of maintaining a dual school system, and tired of the crippling uncertainty produced by the county's efforts to resist the federal laws, a significant number of whites began to speak up in favor of integrating the public schools. Publicly breaking ranks with county officials—who, it is important to remember, held their positions by appointment, not popular election—they began to openly support Plan C, which called for the building of a comprehensive high school and the complete integration of the public schools. In February 1968 the white Green Springs Elementary School PTA came out in support of Plan C and the white Louisa County Education Association voted unanimously to support it as well. In March, the *Central Virginian* ran an editorial in support of Plan C, regarding it as the best "long-term solution" to the problems plaguing the schools. In April the white Apple Grove Elementary School PTA and the white Buckner Elementary School faculty and staff followed suit. And by May of that year, the Green Springs PTA proposed unifying all the county PTAs in order "to work in a united effort to more effectively deal with the school problem." All these groups had come to view integration as a way of saving and improving the public schools. While the local paper continued to print letters from farmers and businessmen who opposed a new tax levy and from die-hard segregationists who advocated the defiance of the court order—one complaining that "control of education usually precedes the takeover of nations by dictators"—white proponents of integration seemed to have the momentum.

But the school board continued to stall. When the superintendent asked for more time to implement the changes, fearing that there would otherwise be "chaos," the board voted to delay answering HEW. Then a divided board voted to consult a Richmond lawyer because, as the board chairman, R. J. Fisher, explained, "I don't go along with all of the HEW practices. In all of the readings of news items the courts have not upheld the freedom of choice-procedure in the school systems. I think this is contrary to most of our beliefs in democratic principles." By May 1969, however, the school board, "fearful of the loss of Federal funds," finally voted to implement "total integration for 1969–70." School integration, finally, was a fait accompli.

Or so the people of Louisa County thought. A week later, the school board suddenly and unexpectedly rescinded its original vote. "School Board Votes Return to Freedom of Choice Due to Proposed Budget Cuts," the headline of the *Central Virginian* shouted in huge black type, as if war had just been declared. This reversal, which appeared to be one final attempt by county officials to avoid the integration that a majority of parents and teachers—both white and black—wanted, proved incendiary. The very next week, at an emergency meeting of the PTA Executive Council, "700 Aroused Citizens" showed up to protest the board's decision. A picture in the paper shows hundreds of concerned citizens crowded into a large room to protest the board's action. The accompanying story records their communal anger and disbelief. Blacks and whites alike spoke passionately in favor of integrating the public schools. They expressed their fear that the board's action would result in the loss of much-needed federal funds, and they wanted to know why the board assumed that an integrated school system would cost more than a segregated one. Ominously, the superintendent explained that he would need extra money in order to create additional special education classes, presumably implying that he planned to subvert integration by using special education assignments to continue to segregate black children. One parent asked plaintively, "Do we have to sacrifice our children while you play with the Federal Government?"

The meeting was historic. Not only did it bring whites and African Americans in the county together, championing the cause of public school integration, but it pitted them against the small clique of powerful white men who had, until then, run the county virtually unchallenged, making decisions that served their self-interest at the expense of public education. One of the most remarkable moments in this dramatic meeting occurred when a participant stood up and publicly asserted that a particular school board member who favored integration had been the victim of intimidation. "It is a well known fact," this man stated, "that an attempt has been made to intimidate a member of the School Board for his position, and I think that this School Board member should be given an opportunity to state where he stands." Turning to the school board member who had been intimidated, the speaker called on him by name, "Mr. Rogers." At that moment, B. V. Rogers stood up in front of seven hundred fellow citizens and declared openly that he was for total integration. Explaining that he had, in fact, voted for integration in the last school board meeting, he then told the crowd exactly why he supported it. This public declaration was clearly in bold defiance of the kind of intimidation that powerful whites had been using against African Americans and whites who supported black causes since the time of Reconstruction. By revealing, naming, and defying this intimidation in so public and so integrated a forum, these citizens challenged the old racist way of doing things. They seemed intent on embracing a more open, a more democratic process that evening.

A week later, hundreds of angry citizens attended a school board meeting to protest its decision to retain the Freedom of Choice plan. They demanded that the board members explain their decision, the role the board of supervisors had played in it, and the impact it would have on their children. Reporting on that meeting, the local newspaper

declared that "the Louisa County School Board was placed on the firing line." One board member, Mr. Harkrader, defended the county's
Freedom of Choice plan, under which, he claimed, "Louisa County has
moved ahead very effectively . . . with the amount of integration determined by the school the parents choose to send their children." But
those in attendance were not mollified. They wanted to know whether
the cuts that the board of supervisors had made in the school budget
had foiled the original plan to integrate the schools, and they sought
to determine whether the school board or the county board of supervisors was calling the shots. Noting that the school board claimed its
decision was based on the budget cuts while the supervisors claimed
they had allocated enough money for the school to operate under
either plan, an exasperated Oliver Harris argued, "Somebody has to
be wrong somewhere." Another parent expressed "a growing lack of
confidence in the ability of the school administration."

That same week the county board of supervisors held a public hearing on the budget that drew more than five hundred citizens. At that
hearing Dr. Martin, the superintendent of schools, pleaded for the
supervisors to restore the $330,113 it had cut from the school budget.
A number of people representing the African American community
pointed out that they had repeatedly appeared before the board of
supervisors, detailing the substandard nature and overcrowded conditions of some of the smaller Negro schools, but that nothing had
been done. Many people voiced concern about the impending loss
of federal funds in the wake of the decision not to integrate the public schools. Mrs. Shirley Winn, for instance, "wanted to know how
the schools will survive if this money is not received." But the supervisors deflected these concerns, insisting that "this was a School
Board question and not one for the Board of Supervisors." Speaking
in support of the supervisors, W. W. Whitlock asserted "the fairness
of the freedom of choice plan," adding in the patronizing voice of
the traditional white southerner that he had many "colored friends"
and proclaiming "his love for the colored people." But Whitlock was
clearly in the minority, and his position, which had a few years earlier been held by a majority of white citizens in the county, had little
support. In response to his defense of Freedom of Choice, an African American minister, the Reverend Hayes, pointed out that the
Supreme Court had ruled for integration and against the Freedom of

Choice plan. Another man, J. B. Harris, "rose to inform the gathering that he had been in contact with the HEW office both in Charlottesville and Washington and was advised by them that if Louisa County did not comply with the HEW directive, the federal funds would be lost." Others stood up to say that they would be willing to pay higher taxes to pay for improving the education of their children. William Palmore, for example, identified himself as "a taxpaying dirt farmer" and then announced that he "wouldn't mind paying more taxes for education. His investment was in his children." Finally, a man named Otho L. Jackson declared how important it was that "all stand together and love one another. He desired that all children, whether white or colored, have a good education." The paper concludes its coverage of this meeting by noting that it "was generally orderly, but boos, hisses, jeers, laughter and applause were sprinkled throughout the speeches."

In the end HEW officials met with Louisa County school administrators and school board members and denied their request to continue with the Freedom of Choice plan, instead directing them to carry out "total integration." HEW did, however, allow the county to postpone the integration of the elementary schools for one more year. At a special meeting, the school board voted, four to one, to integrate grades 8–12 in the fall of 1969 and to integrate the elementary schools in the fall of 1970.

And so, in the winter of 1970, sixteen years after the Supreme Court declared school segregation illegal, my ten-year-old students were still sitting in a segregated classroom in a segregated elementary school in Louisa, Virginia. The following year, they would enter the newly integrated elementary schools as fifth graders. But after four years at Morton, the Negro school had come to feel like home to them, and they anticipated the impending integration with a mixture of excitement and dread. Even though they understood why their parents had opposed segregation, many were leery about attending an integrated school. They were reluctant to leave the familiarity and comfort of "their" school, and they were anxious about how they would fare in schools with white children and teachers.

When I talked to them about their anxieties, some children expressed the desire to stay together with their classmates. "Who wants to be mixed up with a bunch of white kids, anyway?" Matilda asked. "I've got all the friends I need right here in this room." Others voiced fears that white students and teachers would mistreat them. "My cousin is in a white school now," Cecily confided, "and she says everybody picks on her, even the teacher." Clinton offered a story to corroborate Cecily's. "My cousin had a white teacher who beat him and yelled at him and gave him bad marks and then he got a Negro teacher who helped him and never got mad at him." But others countered these fears with reports of friends and relatives who had had very positive experiences in integrated schools. "My cousin lives in Washington, D.C.," Emmeline explained, "and she had a Negro teacher that beat her all the time, but the next year she got a white teacher who was so good to her and taught her all kinds of interesting things. I think it doesn't matter what color a teacher is; what matters is who she is." Wendell was not so optimistic. He found the idea of integration threatening, and he predicted that there would be racial hostilities in the newly integrated schools: "My mother says just wait till next year and then white teachers will find out how bad Negro kids can be." Mostly, though, my students viewed the upcoming changes primarily in terms of loss. "I don't see why we have to go to any old white school, ever," Reginald lamented. "We're going to lose all our friends. We're going to have to sit in class with strangers. Besides this is the best school. I don't want to go to a different school." Louis nodded in agreement, then announced defiantly, "I won't go."

I understood their ambivalence. I had only to look at the way desegregation was being implemented in the senior and junior high schools in Louisa that year to see that integration, even though it represented a major civil rights victory for African Americans, also came at a cost to them. In dismantling the dual school system, the School Board demoted African American administrators, making them assistants to whites or moving them from the high school to the junior high. Black teachers who were not fully credentialed were also demoted; some may have lost their jobs. Initially, the school board canceled many extracurricular activities and dances, fearing interracial dating. Events associated with the Negro schools were abolished. And the board made no attempt to change the Confederate nickname of the newly integrated high school. African American athletes found themselves playing for the Rebels and budding African American journalists wrote for a school newspaper called *The Rebel*.

Even more troubling was the willingness of white school administrators to give up on the African American students who were, after years in overcrowded, underfunded classrooms, performing well below grade level. A report in October 1969 found that approximately 170 students in the integrated junior and senior high schools were "three or more years below their grade level." Forced for the first time to deal with the full consequences of its dual school system, white administrators appeared all too eager to write off these students, most of them from the underfunded Negro schools, rather than devote more funds to remedial education. Perpetuating the belief that black students were uneducable, one stated that these students "have reached their learning ability and the school has nothing to offer them."

In his memoir about coming of age in the 1950s and 1960s, Henry Louis Gates addresses the sense of loss that many blacks in his small West Virginia community felt when the schools were desegregated soon after the *Brown* decision. Having himself begun elementary school a year after his town's schools were integrated, he writes that he did not realize until much later "that for many of the colored people in Piedmont . . . integration was experienced as a loss. The warmth and nurturance of the womblike colored world was slowly and inevitably disappearing, in a process that really began on the day they closed the door for the last time at Howard School [the Negro school], back in 1956." But he also speculates that his own self-assurance, independence, and youthful political activism were in part products of his integrated education. The children I taught in 1970 were about to venture out from the "warmth and nurturance of the womblike colored world" that the Negro school had provided them and enter integrated schools where they would be in the minority. I could only guess at the time how they would be changed by that experience.

# Where Is the Jim Crow Section on This Merry-Go-Round?

*Where is the Jim Crow section*
*On this merry-go-round,*
*Mister, cause I want to ride?*
*Down South where I come from*
*White and colored*
*Can't sit side by side.*
*Down South on the train*
*There's a Jim Crow car.*
*On the bus we're put in the back—*
*But there ain't no back*
*To a merry-go-round!*
*Where's the horse*
*For a kid that's black?*
*— "Merry-Go-Round," Langston Hughes*

## We're All Colored

"**B**LACK AMERICANS MAKE PROGRESS," the headline of the *Weekly Reader* announced in large block letters. I smiled to myself as I picked up the parcel of newspapers reserved for my class in the main office. I had been teaching at Morton Elementary for more than a month, and I had been searching for instructional materials on African American culture with little luck. Here, at last, was a story guaranteed to engage my students. Photographs of African American students in integrated classrooms. Graphs showing a steady rise in the incomes and educational levels of black Americans. An entire front page devoted to the impact of the civil rights movement and the Civil Rights Act. I couldn't wait to distribute the newspapers and present my fourth-grade students with this report on the lives of black Americans like them.

As soon as my students caught sight of the headlines of their *Weekly Reader*s that afternoon, however, I sensed that something was terribly, terribly wrong. Instead of the sea of waving hands that usually greeted my opening question, "Who would like to read?" I looked out over an eerily still classroom of scowling children, their bodies tense, their eyes on high alert. No one volunteered to read. Instead, my students sat warily at their desks and glared at me. A storm was brewing, but I—a twenty-one-year-old white woman who had never before lived in the South—had no idea what was wrong, no clue why they had suddenly turned angry and sullen. I called on Ramonia, someone I could count on to read well and one of the class's acknowledged leaders. But she refused to read. I called on Clinton, another leader. He shook his head. I called on polite and dependable Emmeline. She looked away from me. And then, much to my relief, Matilda raised her hand.

"I'll read," she volunteered. Some of the children gasped out loud at Matilda's offer, and others shot her accusatory looks, as if she had somehow betrayed them. But the tone of her voice was not conciliatory. It was defiant. Matilda smiled mysteriously at her classmates, taking the time to meet their disbelieving stares. "Watch me," her flashing eyes seemed to say. And then, in a perfectly composed voice, she began to read: "NEGRO AMERICANS MAKE PROGRESS." As she read on, she pointedly substituted the term "Negro" every time the word "black" appeared in print. At once, the tension in the room lifted. Now everyone wanted to read. Chester and Emmeline followed Matilda's lead, using "Negro" in place of the adjective "black." Annie Mae and William substituted "colored" instead. Gloria alternated indiscriminately between the two terms. No one uttered the word "black." Inspired by Matilda, the class collectively conspired to banish that word, refusing its power to define them, keeping at bay whatever demons it conjured up in their minds.

I didn't say anything about this communal act of censorship and revision until the class had finished reading the lead story. Then, I intervened. I told them we needed to talk about their reaction to the author's use of the term "black." I explained that many African Americans, including influential writers, important civil rights activists, and well-known entertainers preferred to use the word "black" to describe themselves rather than words like "Negro" and "colored." I tried to explain the thinking behind this preference. I told them about the black power movement, the popular slogan "black is beautiful," and the efforts of prominent African Americans to instill racial pride in their people by embracing the term "black." And I assured them that the author of the *Weekly Reader* article had in no way intended to insult them when he chose to refer to them as black. My students found none of my explanations persuasive. Nothing I said altered their conviction that "black" was one of the worst things you could call somebody. Eight years later these same children would pose for their senior class photographs in magnificent Afros worthy of Bobby Seale and Angela Davis, but on this February day in 1970 they adamantly refused to be identified as black, a word they understood to be a racial epithet, a threat to their integrity, a mean-spirited charge leveled at them by white people in their hometown.

"But calling someone black *is* an insult," Chester insisted. "White people are always calling us black, just to make us feel like we're no good. They think they have the right to lord it over us, just because of the color of our skin. When someone calls me black, I want to fight him."

A chorus of emphatic yeahs reinforced Chester's position.

"Colored," Annie Mae suggested, "is a better word for describing us. It's not upsetting to be called colored, 'cause that's what we are. We're all colored."

"But Negro is the best word to use," Reginald weighed in. "That's the proper name to use to describe our people. It says we're all brothers." Everyone, including the girls, nodded.

"I don't think this writer has any business calling us black," Clinton complained. "He should know that it's a put-down. He should know he's insulting the people he's writing about."

"The problem," explained Sharon with her usual thoughtfulness, "is that white people call us 'black' to make themselves feel superior. They want us to believe we're beneath them just because we're colored." Then she recounted her defiant response to a white teenager who had humiliated her by deploying the demeaning words "black girl" to enforce the customs of Jim Crow.

"When I first moved back to Louisa from New York City," she recounted, "I put a penny in a gum-ball machine downtown. A real big white boy came up to me. He was wearing a varsity football jacket, and he was very tall, and his neck and shoulders were huge." She stretched out her arms to emphasize just how huge.

> He was acting like I had done something terrible by putting a penny in the gum-ball machine. He walked right up to where I was standing, got in my face, and stared at me, hard. I could tell he was mad, really mad. 'Black girl,' he said to me, like I was dirt, 'Black girl, you can't use this gum-ball machine. You're black.' I was so scared, I wanted to run. I was afraid he was going to hurt me. But do you know what I told him? I told him, 'You see my shoes? They're black. You see my face? It's brown. My name is Sharon and I can buy gum from any machine I want to.' And then I got my gum and walked away. And he just stood there, staring at me.

Listening to the way my students sought to preserve their dignity by repudiating their "blackness," I began to realize how complicated and confusing—how messy—the task of defining a self was for the thirty-seven African American children sitting in my classroom. They were only ten years old. Born in 1960, six years after the *Brown v. Board of Education* decision, they were three when Martin Luther King delivered his "I Have a Dream" speech, four when the Civil Rights Act was signed into law, five when the Voting Rights Act was passed, six when Huey Newton and Bobby Seale founded the Black Panthers, eight when King was assassinated in Memphis. Yet they still lived in a segregated town reluctant to end its enforcement of Jim Crow laws that systematically excluded, subordinated, and disenfranchised people like them, people, that is, who had even "one drop" of "black blood" in them. How, I wondered, did they manage to sustain their fierce pride in their "Negro" and "colored" identity while recoiling in horror at the thought of being "black"? Was their response to the black power movement's defiant appropriation of the word "black" a reactionary one, evidence of their traditional rural upbringing, or was it a radical and heroic form of resistance to the racism they encountered daily? Could it be both? Had they unconsciously internalized white culture's color prejudice, tragically preferring brown skin to black (and white to brown), or had they penetrated the secret of America's "miscegenated heart"?

Sharon's anecdote opened a floodgate, and the stories spilled out. Reginald told how, whenever he went into a store, clerks always followed him around, watching his every move, sure he was going to misbehave or shoplift. "It makes me so mad," he confessed, "I want to steal something just to get back at them." Ramonia told how her father routinely encountered discrimination at a PX store on the Air Force base where he was stationed. "Why," she asked plaintively, "can't they just treat him like all the other soldiers?" Annie Mae told how once, at a store counter, some white kids had intentionally knocked the candy she had selected onto the floor. "I just don't understand why they are so mean to us," she confided quietly. "Do you think," she asked, her dark eyes solemn, "there will ever be a war between colored people and white people?" Compelled to defend themselves against what they understood to be the taint of blackness, these children sought mightily to ward off the ugly, alien images of themselves they discovered in the suspicious eyes of Louisa's storekeepers, the contemptuous eyes of adolescent bullies, the mocking eyes of white children who cruelly knocked their candy on the floor.

Confiding in me about the many times they had been wounded by the hateful or demeaning actions of white people, my students seemed, for a moment, to forget that I was white. Then Lonnie, who sat in the very back of the class, suddenly shot up his hand.

"What color do you think I am?" he asked. His was no curious or casual query. It was a challenge, and I could feel all eyes watching me to see if I would pick up the gauntlet. I looked carefully at Lonnie before answering. I studied the color of his face, his neck, his arms. I compared the color of his skin to the children sitting near him, noting in a way I hadn't really registered before the wide range of skin tones, the multiple shades of brown and black among the students sitting before me.

"Lonnie," I said at last, "I'd say you're a very light brown—tan maybe, or beige."

Lonnie nodded his head in satisfaction. "Right," he declared. I could tell that he was proud of his light skin, that he wanted me to acknowledge that he was not, in any literal sense of the word, black. But my interrogation was not over.

"And what color do you think you are?" he asked, challenging me again.

I was surprised by Lonnie's question, surprised and disconcerted, for it forced me to examine the set of neat racial categories I had always taken for granted. I realized that I had never really thought about being any color at all, had always simply accepted the premise that I was white. I realized, too, with a sharp stab of shame, that I had allowed the racial categories of white and black to separate me from my students by unthinkingly accepting them as valid and natural. Unconsciously, I'd based my identity on being "white." Worse, I had enjoyed the power and status my whiteness conferred upon me without ever questioning their legitimacy. I began to see that this persistent little boy questioning me from the back of the room understood far better than I how the privileges I enjoyed as a "white" person derived from an utterly absurd set of assumptions.

I held out my arm and observed it closely. Although my ancestors were German and Scots Irish, I am not fair skinned. During the summers of my childhood, I used to get so dark from long days in the sun that my grandfather affectionately called me his little brown bear. As a teenager, I proudly sported a fashionable, bronze suntan. Looking down at my arm that day, I realized what Lonnie had obviously known all along: my skin was not much lighter than his light brown skin. Indeed, after a week or so in the summer sun, it would surely darken into a deeper shade of brown.

"I'm tan, too, Lonnie," I told him. "I'm almost exactly the same color as you." Lonnie smiled broadly at my admission. I hadn't fully understood how much status he derived from his light skin or considered the implications of that status for his darker-skinned classmates.

Then, noticing the veins on the underside of my forearm, I added as a playful afterthought, "And I'm even a little bit blue, too."

Lonnie bolted out of his seat. Charging up to the front of the room, he grabbed my right hand and inspected it carefully, staring with a scientist's interest at the blue veins running in distinct lines from my palm to my wrist, the streaks of blue crisscrossing the back of my hand. Then he turned around to face the class and announced theatrically: "She's blue."

The class went wild.

"She's blue! She's blue!" my students shouted triumphantly. Pounding their fists on the desk, stomping their feet, they joined together in a gleeful chant: "Mrs. Hallahan's blue!"

I can't explain the giddiness of that moment. Did my students want to bring me inside their colored world, claim me as their own? Or did the prominence of my blue veins somehow mark my "white" body as aberrant, monstrous even, ridiculous and strange? Did they need some release from the seriousness of our discussion, the weight of the insults and color prejudices that the *Weekly Reader* article had dredged up from their past? Or did they seek to express the absurdity of their society's racial classifications by embracing an upside down world—the teacher is not white but blue and her "black" students have the power to make her so? I joined in their giddy laughter. I did not mind at all being colored blue that Friday afternoon. Released from the tidy categories of white and black, I reveled in my messy, multicolored, mongrel self.

## White-Washing Mo

Unlike my African American students, who daily grappled with the indignities of Jim Crow, I had little reason to question the dominant social and racial hierarchy when I was a child, growing up white and affluent in a small, predominantly white Pennsylvania town in the 1950s. I was, after all, a direct beneficiary of that hierarchy. It bestowed on me a unified sense of self, assuring me of my inherent worth, protecting me from external threats to my integrity, conferring on me an enviable status in the world. But it also blinded me to the racial inequalities all around me.

The only African American I knew intimately when I was a child was my family's live-in housekeeper. Tall and reed-thin, with flawless coffee-colored skin, an elegant beauty, and a fierce intelligence, Alberta Sherwood supported herself and her invalid father by washing, ironing, scrubbing, dusting, and vacuuming my family house and caring for my two sisters and me. Despite my strong attachment to her, I never questioned why she was the servant, I the served. I devoured the rich chocolate cakes Alberta baked especially for me—the quick "one-egg" cake sometimes deployed to coax me out of a sulk, and the more elaborate "ultra cake," made with sour cream and butter, layered with chocolate custard, topped with a dark chocolate glaze, and offered up for my birthday celebrations. But though our mutual love of chocolate was a bond that connected us, and we playfully conspired together to find ways to eat it, I never once questioned why Alberta ate alone in the kitchen while the family gathered around the dining room table. I was grateful for the way her affectionate nickname for me—Messy Bessy—legitimized and even honored my natural propensity to spill milk on the counter, dribble spaghetti sauce over the tablecloth, cover the floor in glue and glitter, and splatter my clothes with mud and finger paint. But although I had been taught to address all adults in a formal manner, I was oblivious to the way my affectionate name for her (I—we all—called her Alberta) demeaned her, denying to her the dignity and status I automatically accorded all white adults. I admired this young African American woman who loved books even more than I did, retreating to the family room on her breaks with a cup of coffee and a hefty novel where she became completely absorbed in her reading. But I never asked why someone of her intellect and curiosity was ironing my clothes and making my bed. I was incapable of imagining how trapped she must have felt, cut off from her community, isolated from people her own age, living in someone else's house with little privacy, dependent on others for all her transportation, and saddled with the tedious work of cleaning house and caring for someone else's three young children.

There is a glimpse of Alberta in a home movie of my sixth birthday party. She is shy about having her picture taken and tries at first to turn away from the camera. Yet even in her self-effacement, she is radiant. Just as she begins to smile, I appear suddenly from out of nowhere, hurl myself onto her lap, pretend for just a few seconds that I am blissfully asleep on her shoulder, then dart away. Whatever inarticulate longing—for intimacy, nurture, comfort—my playacting expresses, it has the effect of deflecting attention away from the complicated woman my father is trying to capture on film and focusing it instead on her role as my caregiver, a role that limits and constrains her. As a six-year-old child, I see, I was already adept at laying claim to her, a claim that bears the taint of ownership.

Yet I could not always suppress the troubling contradictions that threatened my tidy and smug sense of self, contradictions that Alberta's presence in my family home made visible. Alberta closely followed the activities of the civil rights movement in the early 1950s—she was working for us when the *Brown* decision was handed down—and she was passionate about blacks' struggle to attain equal treatment under the law. I was too young to comprehend her commitment to civil rights, yet it had an impact on me in ways I could not understand at the time. I will never forget arriving at my grandparents' place one sunny summer day and discovering, to my dismay, that my grandmother had painted the black face of the hitching post white. I have no idea how long this hitching post—a stock figure of a slave jockey—had stood there or who had installed it, an improbable icon on this fifty-five acres of fallow land (a child's paradise) in northwestern Pennsylvania, far from the imposing plantations of the American South and the wealth that slavery had made possible. I can only guess at what symbolic import it was originally meant to carry, standing as it did by the stone steps to my grandmother's garden, greeting visitors as they drove down the long gravel driveway to the modest, clapboard house. But in my childish ignorance it had delighted me, especially when my grandfather Sporty tied up his horse, Lady Grey, to the jockey's ring in order to boost me into the saddle. Until that morning, I had never questioned why the face of the little jockey we called "Mo" was coal black, never thought about why a statue of a Negro jockey stood on my white grandparents' property. It had never occurred to me that this figure, with its jaunty cap, white breeches, and bright red coat, helpfully holding out its arm to receive the reins of a horse, might be offensive.

I was shocked that day to discover the statue with its freshly painted white face. It looked completely ridiculous, bizarrely defaced, and I found its newly assigned racial identity strangely upsetting. Why, oh why, had my grandmother done something so odd? I could only gather from a brief exchange among the grownups that something Alberta had said about the hitching post when she accompanied the family on a previous visit had so mortified Gram that she had dug out an old can of white paint from the basement and set about earnestly attempting to turn Mo into a white man. The little figure that had always delighted me, I vaguely understood, had fallen into disgrace. By whitening its face, my grandmother sought to remove some deep shame she felt at its presence in her garden. Her gesture was my first inkling that an insidious serpent haunted my Eden.

My grandmother's impulse to tidy things up after the sting of Alberta's remark may have been born of repentance, but it was also an act of erasure, distancing my family from America's long history of racism, denying our complicity. It didn't so much engage issues of race as protect me from them, driving all the difficult and troubling questions underground. What was I to make of a bigoted remark, spoken by a family friend, at a party my parents hosted? How was I to reconcile my town's widely embraced civic ethos of fairness and tolerance with the fact that the few black citizens in my community lived in a single neighborhood in the poorer section of town and were primarily employed as janitors, cooks, bartenders, handymen, and domestics, never as teachers, doctors, lawyers, or businessmen? How was I to make sense of the fact that the first genuine intellectual I had ever known was my family's black housekeeper? For all my grandmother's good intentions, Mo's white face kept all these questions at bay.

But if Gram's gesture helped to preserve my tidy sense of self by assuring me that my family and I could not possibly be racists, that tidiness, like the thin layer of white paint covering Mo's blackness, was a veneer. Underneath was muddle and confusion. The messiness of my childish efforts to make sense of racial—and class—identity is evident in my complicated response to Alberta's departure. When her father died, Alberta was finally free to pursue her ambitions. She quit her job with my family, moved to Washington, D.C., and began a lifelong job at a city bookstore. Stubbornly loyal to her, I was not about to accept the new cleaning lady, a white woman named Thelma Howsare. Mrs. Howsare, as I was instructed to call her, had grown up in the Appalachian Mountains, the child of barely literate parents, and she had been forced to quit school after the eighth grade to help care for her younger siblings during the Depression. She spoke in a thick, colorful, and to my child's ears, comical, Appalachian dialect, nothing like any kind of dialect I'd heard before, and I was immediately suspicious of her. Never mind that Mrs. Howsare would go on to work for my parents for more than thirty years, timing her homemade bread to come out of the oven when I arrived home from school, bringing us fruit and vegetables and flowers from her abundant garden, and teaching me with her mental astuteness that intelligence is not the sole possession of the formally educated. When she was newly hired, I was dead set against her. And, improbable as it now sounds, I disapproved of her on the grounds that she was white.

Race became a crucial factor in my resistance to Mrs. Howsare the night I learned about the theft at Mamie Snyder's house. Mamie was a good friend of my older sister Debbie, who, whispering conspiratorially in our bedroom late one night, after the lights were out, told me about the theft: how the Snyders' new cleaning lady—the *white* cleaning lady—had been caught with valuables she had stolen from Mamie's mother. The story shocked us, not only because a crime like this was almost unheard of in our small town, but because it involved, in some deeply personal way, a violation of family and home. In the dark that night, the crime seemed bigger and scarier than it was, the threat more general and pervasive. Surely, we thought, it was significant that the thief was white. Nothing had ever been stolen from the Snyders when they had employed a black housekeeper. Were we, then, vulnerable, now that our beloved Alberta had been replaced by a white cleaning woman? We moved swiftly, relentlessly, from the particular to the general. Maybe white cleaning ladies were inherently untrustworthy; maybe they were all potential thieves: sneaky, cunning, dishonest, unreliable, disloyal, and greedy. Spinning our paranoid theory in the dark, we frightened ourselves, for soon we were projecting our evil stereotype onto the innocent Mrs. Howsare, fanning our childish fears by imagining her a sinister intruder in our home.

The next morning I acted out my fear. Attempting to befriend me, Mrs. Howsare asked me to demonstrate my little sister's new, plastic toy cash register. I set the register up on the kitchen counter and banged fiercely on its keys. The cash drawer shot open with a forceful ping, and I scooped up twenty dollars in play money. Slapping the cash into her hand, I looked Mrs. Howsare directly in the eyes and declared, coldly, mercilessly, "Here's your week's pay; you're fired." I knew immediately that I had made a mistake, for she winced, an emotional reaction that shattered the demonic image of her I had foolishly concocted in the night. I could tell that my cruel remark had hurt her, and I was sorry. Recalling this story now, I see that I had as a young child already internalized my family's class position, already imagined myself the boss with power over the hardworking adult hired to care for me.

I still wonder, though, why my sister and I—white children living in a largely white community—were so quick to mistrust a cleaning woman because she was white. Did we fear something dangerous or unreliable buried in our own white bodies? Or, more likely, did we need to distance ourselves, as privileged, middle-class white children, from white women who scrubbed floors, cleaned toilets, and addressed people as "you'uns"? And why did we draw such a sharp distinction between black and white domestic workers? Did we assume

African American housekeepers were more trustworthy simply because that was all we had ever known, or because, in our grief over Alberta's departure, we idealized what we had lost? Or did we prefer our black caretaker because we intuitively recognized that she, like us, was of a higher class than the Appalachian white woman? Or, even more troubling, had we fully internalized the racist assumption that blacks are inferior to whites and belong in the kind of menial jobs white people shun? Is it possible that we suspected our white cleaning lady because we thought a respectable white person would not take such a menial job, a black person's job?

## Drenched to the Skin

Like my sister and me, my Louisa students were sometimes unable to sort out the tangled categories of race and class. One morning Emmeline told me about a disturbing episode that had occurred the night before, when she accompanied her mother to a white neighbor's house to help with a medical emergency. While her mother rushed the ill neighbor into the car, she told Emmeline to go into the house to retrieve the youngest child. "The house was filthy," Emmeline told me as she described her shock at seeing a sink full of unwashed dishes, moldy food on the counter, a table strewn with garbage, the baby crawling on a floor soiled with dog excrement, old newspapers piled to the ceiling, cupboard doors made of cardboard. "And it smelled so bad, I thought I was going to throw up. It was so dirty, I just couldn't make myself go in there," she confessed. "I tried to, but I just couldn't do it," she shrugged apologetically. Shaken by her realization that some white people lived in abject poverty, Emmeline was confused. "No Negro I know lives like that," she declared indignantly, unsure how to process the fact that this particular white family was far more destitute than anyone she associated with in her black community. Well aware that the white people in her town looked on all Negroes as inferior to them, yet feeling superior to these particular white neighbors, she was unable to grasp how her own class position factored into her response to their grim situation.

I watched her as she told me this story. She was a large girl with a pleasant round face and intelligent eyes. She wore a crisply pressed, white cotton blouse with a Peter Pan collar, a light blue cardigan sweater, and a matching, pleated skirt. Her shining black hair was carefully combed and braided, with neatly cut bangs over her broad forehead. I tried to imagine her, so immaculately groomed, so meticulous in all she did, peering in horror into the filthy house of her white neighbors, struggling to comprehend how anyone could live like that. Her glimpse into the squalid interior of their house profoundly unsettled her, not only because it brought her face-to-face with extreme poverty, but also because it brought home to her the fact that as a black person in her rigidly segregated southern town, she was viewed by whites as inferior even to these poor white neighbors whose house she found too disgusting to enter.

What made no sense to Emmeline—what could only be incomprehensible to a black child—was the doctrine of white supremacy that informed nearly all interactions between blacks and whites in her community. People who openly espouse white supremacy today tend to be dangerous fanatics or disaffected loners who join hate-mongering organizations like the Ku Klux Klan. But in those days the majority of white southerners (and many northerners as well), most of them law-abiding, nonviolent, and respectable people, simply accepted its premises without question. "White supremacy was like water," Timothy B. Tyson, born the same year as my students, writes of growing up white in a small North Carolina town a few hundred miles from Louisa, "and we were like fish, and of course we were all drenched to the skin. All the social signposts of American life taught me that white people were superior in some vague and undefined way." Testifying to the power of this doctrine back then, Tyson tells how he found himself as a young schoolboy recoiling from the prospect of drinking from a water fountain immediately after an African American child—one of only two in his recently "integrated" school—had done so. Even though he was raised by open-minded parents who actively supported the civil rights movement and taught him to respect black people, and even though he knew his response was irrational and wrong, he felt repulsion at the prospect of sharing the fountain with a black child. "Deep down," he writes, "I did not want to drink after him. Without really understanding why, and even though I knew better, somewhere inside I had accepted white supremacy. The world had kenneled a vicious lie in my brain, at the core of the lie a crucial silence, since there was no *why*. Black was filthy, black was bad, I had somehow managed to learn."

The ten-year-old African American children in my class had been taunted and bullied by white children who, like the young Tyson, had at a very young age internalized a belief that "black was filthy." To defend themselves, my students sought to trouble the simple alternatives of white and black and unsettle fixed racial categories, for their dignity depended on their ability to subvert or refute the doctrine of white supremacy. They taught me to see the messy and contradictory assumptions about race all of us secretly harbor. White supremacy, however, acknowledges no such messiness, insisting instead on imposing clearly defined and rigidly policed racial categories and reducing everything, in the most literal way possible, to black and white.

I knew that white supremacy had served as a justification for slavery and was itself a lasting product of that institution. I knew as well that, after Emancipation, members of the white elite had strategically used it to forge a solidarity between them and working-class and poor whites who might otherwise have built alliances with black workers. I suspected, too, that it had been invoked to ward off white anxieties about the complexity—the messiness—of racial identity, thus allowing whites of all classes to deny or repress some of their society's most profound contradictions. Hoping to recover some individual voices from Louisa's past that might shed light on how this system of belief had structured the relations between whites and blacks in Louisa County over the years, I turned to the rich archives of the University of Virginia Library in Charlottesville.

There, I discovered a recently published book containing the names and legal descriptions—transcribed from antebellum court records—of every slave who had been freed in Louisa County prior to Emancipation. Sitting beneath the skylights of the library's sparkling new reading room, poring over the nineteenth-century legal documents that this odd little book had unearthed, I tried to imagine the stories behind the names of the hundreds of Louisa slaves manumitted by their masters in the years leading up to the Civil War. A significant number of those freed in 1834, I later learned, were the slaves of a planter named John Poindexter, who, after his religious conversion to Baptism, denounced slavery as an evil, lamented his sinful participation in it, and granted all his slaves their freedom;

he later bought more slaves in order to free them, too. Some of the others were granted freedom when their owners died. A few even inherited property, an act that suggests their white masters were also their fathers, anxious in the face of death to own up to their paternity and provide for their illegitimate children. "A yellow boy James," for instance, was freed, along with his mother, by John Boswell, who bequeathed him "the tract I bought of John Goodmen" and instructed the estate's executors "to give the said James a horse and saddle with Mine bonds and a cow and calf and a tolerable education." But for most of the entries, the slaves' names were followed only by detailed physical descriptions, so essential if whites were going to be able to distinguish the free blacks from the slaves still in their possession.

Using an elaborately constructed terminology to draw fine distinctions regarding a person's racial features, these descriptions reveal that many of the slaves who gained their freedom in Louisa County in the first part of the nineteenth century were of mixed race: Edward Poindexter had a "light yellow complexion"; Sarah had a "bright complexion, nearly white" and "straight hair"; James Minor Poindexter had a "light complexion approaching nearly white"; Huldah was "a bright mulatto" with "long straight hair"; Edward Harris was "nearly white" with "straight light hair" and "hazel eyes." These freed men and women were obviously the children or the descendants of whites, most probably of wealthy planters or their sons and male relatives. Whether their white fathers and grandfathers had been motivated by lust, power, and aggression, by the perverse need to humiliate their male slaves, by loneliness and longing, or, in the very rare case of a couple like Ralph Quarles and Lucy Langston, by defiant love that was apparently mutual, these men who by day were "drenched to the skin" in white supremacy had sought out black women at night for sex and, perhaps, comfort and companionship. As the property of those men, the female slaves had little choice but to comply; many were forcibly raped. The lighter-skinned offspring of these liaisons were often the beneficiaries of their white fathers, more likely to be brought into the household to do the less onerous work of house slaves, more likely to be taught valuable skills, more likely to be freed, and more likely to be given a bit of money or property when their father and master died.

As a result, even within the African American community, color and class became closely associated, as my light-skinned student

Lonnie understood so well in 1970. The clerks who entered these legal descriptions of Louisa's newly freed slaves made their own color prejudices known, judging one "very black" woman with "thick lips" to be "homely," for instance, while noting that a man with a "rather yellowish complexion" had a "good countenance" and calling another "a very likely bright mulatto man." Yet even the lightest-skinned men and women in these court records were, according to the doctrine of white supremacy, still "black," and thus believed to be inherently inferior to the white clerks who duly recorded, and sometimes praised, their Caucasian features.

What were these clerks thinking, I wondered, as they carefully described the variety of skin colors among the newly freed slaves, colors that ranged from "very black" and "dark" to "gingerbread" and "a shade between yellow and black" to "light" and "nearly white"? They must have realized how inadequate their society's rigid racial categories of Negro and white were, how absurd its efforts to maintain a clear-cut distinction between two "separate" races. And they must have understood that intraracial relations were far more complicated, and messy, than the doctrine of white supremacy ever admitted. Surely they knew that a freed black whose "light" hair "was inclined to be straight," whose skin was "nearly white," and whose eyes were "hazel" could easily slip out of the county and pass as a white person somewhere else. They must have also had a sense—from rumor, family resemblance, or open acknowledgment—who among the newly freed were the children of white planters, half-siblings to people in their community who were privileged, educated, and wealthy. Perhaps they themselves were kin to some of the free blacks whose names they recorded in the county courthouse.

But despite the large number of slaves and free blacks in Louisa County who bore the physical traits of their white fathers or ancestors, most whites refused to acknowledge their essential relatedness to African Americans. In fact, the reality of widespread miscegenation seems to have intensified their need to insist on racial differences. This fact became clear to me when I read the letter a daughter of Thomas Watson wrote to her mother in 1884. I was shocked to see how vehemently this woman, a member of Louisa's white elite, expressed her contempt for "the colored race," a people who, she fumed, "disgusted" her. She complained to her mother that "my cook now is a stupid *animal* and I have her girl, 12 years old, for nurse and house maid . . . both have the coarsest African cast of features and manners. The real *savage* comes out all the time." Her savage remark suggests just how fiercely members of Louisa's ruling white elite sought to distance themselves from free blacks after the Civil War had put an end to slavery, and how stubbornly they clung to the notion of white supremacy. Twenty years after Emancipation, this planter's daughter feels compelled to maintain a clear demarcation between herself and the black laborers she employs in her household, declaring them stupid, coarse, uncivilized, and bestial so that she can see herself as intelligent, refined, civilized, and human. But the intensity with which she asserts these differences betrays a fear that the distinctions she insists on drawing are in danger of collapsing. Included in her rant against the "colored race" is a scornful and cryptic reference to blacks as "Father's pets!" Might her need to assert her superiority over these African American women be driven by jealousy, resentment, or rivalry towards them or revulsion at her father's promiscuous sexual behavior? If her racist remarks are elicited by a fear of miscegenation in her own family, they may reveal how fully she has embraced the notion that southern white women were supposed to be the guardians of racial "purity," charged with assuring the legitimacy of the patriarchal inheritance. Underlying her need to distance herself from the black women who cook and clean for her may be the anxiety that she is, in fact, closely related to the "savages" she disparages with such passion. White supremacy may be for her a form of denial, providing her with a tidier version of reality than she knows to be true, allowing her to avoid confronting the fact that racial purity is a fiction.

Under the institution of slavery, white supremacy had permitted her father, Thomas Watson, to assume a paternalistic stance towards his slaves and to imagine himself a benevolent master even as he casually bought and sold the human beings on his plantation. In his account books, he attends closely to the personal needs of his slaves, giving $2.50 to his gardener, for instance, because "his family was sick," $4.00 to a slave named Solomon because "he is going to be married," and a $5.00 gold piece to Dolly because "she is in the family way" and "her husband lives off this plantation . . . and she has one young child already." His antebellum ledger entries include a remarkable number of details about individual slaves on his plantations and paint a portrait of a man keenly interested in their lives and observant of their habits. Yet for all his apparent concern for the well-being of his slaves, Watson coldly records how he "swapped Davy" for a female slave and her infant "giving $108.50 *to boot*" and "bought a child of Mimy's, named Eli, about 5 years of age from Jno:Barker."

White supremacy also allows Watson to distance himself from his own complex feelings for his slaves. He sentimentalizes "Old Cupid—the oldest negro I have," noting with awe and pride that "he tells my children that they are the 5$^{th}$ generation of Watson's that he has seen!" while remaining impervious to the reality that, for Old Cupid, those many years of loyal service were spent in enslavement. He acknowledges his profound gratitude towards his slave Eliza, who nursed his dying mother-in-law "with a fidelity & tenderness really touching" when he "was absent on a trip to Arkansas." But his response to Eliza's generosity is to give his young son one dollar to reward Eliza, as if a token amount of money might relieve him of his emotional debt to her while conveniently serving to initiate his son into the psychic economy of slavery. Most astonishingly, white supremacy enables him to believe wholeheartedly that his land puts him "constantly in the presence of God, and of his power," even though that land turns him into a slave owner who actively buys, sells, and swaps human beings.

After slavery is abolished, Watson relies on white supremacy to reestablish his position of power in a society ravaged by war, humiliated by military defeat, and disrupted by the abolition of slavery and the presence of an occupying army. No longer able to construct himself as a benevolent master, handing out Christmas money and dispensing small amounts of spending cash to his slaves, as he did before the war, he begins to drive hard bargains with his black laborers, seeking, always, for economic advantage over them. He complains about their inadequacies, pays them begrudgingly, uses what he considers to be their faults and failings to justify giving them low salaries, docks their pay for illnesses and infractions, reduces their salaries over the winter months, and charges them high prices for their basic necessities. When Jacob Ragland, one of his tenant farmers, "left my service—dissatisfied about his accommodations" in one of the former slave cabins, Watson figures, somewhat vindictively and without any evidence, that "I scarcely owe him anything—especially as he left me when *thrashing wheat*; and short of hands." Not at all inclined to remember his former slaves' past service or to invoke the values of fidelity, loyalty, and tenderness, he is ruthless in his dealings with them, demanding, for instance, that Ragland's "family must vacate the house from today." Perhaps because of his own precarious economic status in the aftermath of the war, perhaps because free blacks are no longer his property but instead potential competitors, the end of slavery intensifies and makes more visible his adherence to white supremacy. Unable to accept the freed blacks as equal to him or even as independent of him, he can be charitable to them — as he is in the 1880s when he gives food and clothing to two old women who had once belonged to his wife — only when they are destitute and entirely dependent on him.

By the end of the nineteenth century, white supremacy was being widely invoked to justify the establishment of Jim Crow laws, the disenfranchisement of black voters, and the inherent "logic" of the status quo. Even the southern branch of the very Baptist Church that had persuaded John Poindexter in 1834 to renounce the "sin" of slavery and to free all his slaves publicly embraced this doctrine, issuing a statement in 1891 insisting that Negroes were meant to occupy "'a subordinate position to whites'" and blithely asserting that "'whenever [the Negro race] shall understandingly and cheerfully accept this condition, the race problem is settled forever.'"

But white supremacy was not just a belief held by southern slave owners and their descendants. It also informed the thinking of ardent abolitionists from the North, men like Marcus Sterling Hopkins, the Freedmen's Bureau agent sent to Louisa County to oversee the education of blacks during Reconstruction. In his diary Hopkins describes some of the ways the local whites abused and took advantage of the newly freed blacks, and he objects to the violence and "brutal prejudice" he witnesses against the freedmen, noting with disgust "the meanness of the prejudice against the Negro in this country." Yet the abuses he records with such disapproval also served to confirm his belief in the inferiority of blacks. "The freedmen are being outraged and swindled," he writes in his diary, "to about the extent that such an ignorant stupid yielding subservient class would be anywhere else — and a little more on account of political feeling."

Hopkins never wavers in his passionate commitment to his educational mission, insisting that "we must have good schools for all" and working diligently to establish schools for freed blacks. He is proud of the colored schools he supervises, observing that "I never saw teachers or scholars take more interest in school" and declaring an exhibition he attended at the "colored" school "very creditable." Yet he clearly views the freedmen he has come to help as his racial inferiors, observing in 1868 that "with our Negroes I fear we can never have a really high state of civilization." He thinks nothing of relating how, at the Republican Convention for the Third Congressional District, he and his fellow white, educated Republicans "would all laugh at the occasional display of ignorance on the part of an Irishman or some of the darkies." White supremacy even served as a bond between this Freedmen's Bureau agent from the North and the former slaveholders he got to know in Louisa County. Although they had been his enemies during the war and held views on slavery, politics, and Reconstruction that were antithetical to his own, he and they could agree on one thing: white supremacy. After a visit from one planter, Hopkins writes in his diary: "Mr. Page called and I discussed Slavery and 'Niggers' with him. We agree on 'Niggers' but not on Slavery."

Marcus Sterling Hopkins entered this comment in his personal diary in 1868, little knowing that it would survive to trouble and disturb twenty-first-century readers like me, who prefer to believe that nineteenth-century abolitionists and Freedmen's Bureau agents were innocent of racial prejudice and white supremacist beliefs. Rife with contradictions, his diary undermines any tidy narrative we might wish to tell celebrating the northern opponents of slavery.

One hundred and two years later, while I was living in Louisa, a journalist wrote an editorial in the local Louisa County paper endorsing integration. Like Hopkins's diary entries, it is full of internal contradictions regarding the principle of racial equality. Reflecting on the long history of segregation in the south, H. D. N. Hill attempts to persuade his readers that integration is inevitable and even desirable. Yet, like Hopkins, he cannot free himself of white supremacist assumptions. Janus-like, Hill attempts to look ahead to a society that embraces "equality of opportunity" and "non-exclusion," even as he feels compelled to look back to—and to defend—a society built on segregation. His thinking is not that of a mean-spirited racist, the kind of violent, ignorant redneck that Hollywood loves to portray in melodramatic films about the South, but rather that of a well-meaning, thoughtful, and educated white man who senses that the entire edifice of Jim Crow—an edifice in which he has comfortably dwelled all his life—is crumbling around him. He grapples openly with social issues that are clearly painful for him to address, endorses the integration of public places, and projects a temperate voice at a time when most voices around him were shrill and loud. Nevertheless, he feels the need to rationalize, justify, and naturalize segregation.

Posing the question, "What is a segregationist?" he writes: "It is basically human to like some of your fellows and dislike others. . . . In a way all of us are segregationists. We like some people, dislike others. We don't want to associate with some and enjoy the association of others." Arguing that the segregationist impulse "seems very natural . . . and in no way wrong," he conveniently ignores the terror, violence, humiliation, degradation, poverty, and illiteracy caused by the particular segregationist policies of Jim Crow, a tyrannical system that civilized countries all around the globe hardly considered "very natural" or "in no way wrong." In addition, he attempts to rewrite the virulent racism of his society by imagining that blacks were equally responsible for and equally desirous of segregation: "Likes and dislikes, of course, work in reverse. The people we don't like, don't like us. Whites tend to want to be segregated from Negroes, and the Blacks in turn prefer to be segregated from Whites." In his revisionist history, he portrays African Americans as willing participants in Jim Crow, choosing to live apart from whites because they share with them a mutual dislike of people of a different race.

Segregation, for Hill, is primarily about freedom of choice, and he emphatically asserts that "the freedom to choose one's friends and acquaintances seems as normal, natural and basic as freedom of speech and assembly and the right to life, liberty, and the pursuit of happiness." He does not acknowledge here the harsh (and sometimes capital) punishments southern white racists inflicted on those blacks and whites who chose to socialize with, marry, work with, or even simply converse with people of the opposite race. He thus obscures the fact that segregationists systematically denied these people their freedom to choose their friends and acquaintances, and they did so because they believed and taught that blacks were inherently inferior to whites.

Striving to strike a balance between the old ideology and the new, Hill grants that "equality of opportunity for each to utilize his abilities to the fullest extent and equality under the law are certainly also basic," adding, rather remarkably given the history of Jim Crow in the South, "I believe no one would deny these as essential." But the pull of the old causes him to immediately qualify this statement. "But equality of opportunity . . . and freedom of choice seem in no way related and should not be confused," he writes, implying, I gather, that an African American's right to equal opportunity should not interfere with a white person's freedom to choose his associates and thus to reject any involuntary association with a black person. Hill allows for the integration of public schools, public restaurants, and public recreation, and I am sure that these allowances must have seemed to him at the time enormous concessions. But he then goes on to oppose "unrealistic means to force unnatural integration," giving the example of "busing school children long distances to achieve racial integration," an example that seems especially peculiar, given that black and white students in his own county had for years been bused long distances to achieve racial segregation. His essay reveals how much harder it is to alter, fundamentally, the structure of one's thinking than to adapt to new laws. At some deep level, Hill still believes segregation is "natural"; integration, "unnatural."

Despite all his considerable efforts to stake out a moderate and conciliatory position on race, Hill shies away from addressing the wrongs that white segregationists have committed against African Americans, asserting instead that because older white southerners were brought up "naturally, understandably, and unashamedly" to be segregationists, it would now be "unfair to accuse Southerners of racism and being segregationists. Certainly they were—how else could they have lived in their society?" His question is rhetorical. But in presuming that all his readers would agree with him that older white southerners could not have lived in their society without being racists and segregationists, he unintentionally reveals just how steadfastly he still clings to the old ways of thinking. His question fails to admit that some white southerners broke ranks with their segregationist neighbors, often suffering ostracism and harassment for doing so. It fails to acknowledge the crucial role segregationists played in creating "their society" by assuring that most blacks would never attain the education or status that would make them social equals while treating even the most educated, prosperous, and accomplished African Americans as if they were inferior, subservient, and unequal to even the lowliest white person. And it fails to hold the old segregationists accountable for the ethical choices they made when they exercised their precious freedom to choose. Urging his readers not to judge people on the basis of their past racism, he seeks as well to wipe away blame for these injuries and deny all responsibility for them. Indeed, he never even acknowledges them. Rather than confront the past, he gets out the can of paint and whitewashes it.

## Soul Power

"We cannot address the place we find ourselves," Timothy Tyson writes, "because we will not acknowledge the road that brought us here." He is specifically referring to the way "the nation has comforted itself by sanitizing the civil rights movement, commemorating it as a civic celebration that no one ever opposed" when, in fact, "most whites—and many middle-class blacks—recoiled in fear of these changes and huddled in the suburbs of their own indifference." Hill's editorial participates in this process of sanitization, for even as it accepts the end of segregation in public places, it rewrites the story about how that end was achieved. Making no mention of the courageous and arduous struggle of African Americans to exercise the basic rights of citizenship granted them in the Fourteenth Amendment and ignoring the fierce resistance of most white Virginians to any form of desegregation, Hill presents "equality of opportunity" as a gift whites have chosen to bestow on blacks. His view of African Americans is no less patronizing than that of the nineteenth-century planter Thomas Watson or the Freedmen's Bureau agent Marcus Sterling Hopkins. By declaring segregation natural, insisting that segregationists have nothing to be ashamed of, and refusing even to acknowledge the terrible consequences of Jim Crow, Hill averts his eyes from the history that would help him come to terms with the changes roiling his present-day world.

I knew very little about that history when I was teaching in Hill's Louisa County in 1970, and as a result, I didn't understand very much about the place I found myself. Luckily for me, I had thirty-eight students to educate me. I still have a plastic bag filled with the pictures my students brought to class to illustrate their oral reports during Negro

History Week, pictures that provide a window into what they tried to teach me about their culture and its heroes back in 1970. There was, of course, nothing in the required curriculum that called for a study of African American history. At the time Virginia didn't even celebrate Lincoln's birthday, dismissing it as a Yankee holiday and commemorating Robert E. Lee's birthday on February 19 instead. A newspaper editorial in the local paper that year boasted about the state's refusal to honor the president who had emancipated the slaves. But I'd read in *Time* or *Newsweek* about a recent campaign to get schools to set aside a week in February as Negro History Week in order to introduce America's schoolchildren to the achievements of African Americans, and this seemed like an obvious way of supplementing my class's required textbook, with its narrow, all-white version of Virginia history.

I didn't know at the time that Negro History Week was already a well-established tradition in many black schools in the South, the brainchild of Carter G. Woodson, an African American scholar and educator. He had created it in 1926 to counter the damage he believed was done when black children learned about the world only from books written by whites, books he believed gave the false impression that the white man "has accomplished everything worthwhile," thus "making [the Negro child] feel that his race does not amount to much and never will measure up to the standards of other peoples." My students didn't seem to be aware of this tradition either, for when I proposed the idea, they were surprised. When I asked each of them to choose an important African American to learn more about, they eagerly began to shout out the names of popular entertainers and well-known civil rights leaders.

Opening the bag that I have kept all these years, I discover random photos of TV stars, gospel and soul singers, and civil rights leaders cut out from magazines and newspapers. There are glamour shots of Diana Ross and Aretha Franklin, an advertisement for "The Best of Bill Cosby," a photo of Flip Wilson in the middle of a comic routine, and six different pictures of Diahann Carroll in her TV role as the nurse Julia, a particular favorite of the girls because of the allure of a brown-skinned doll in her image, an African American Barbie outfitted, these pictures show, in a prim white nurse's uniform and a sparkling gold and silver evening gown. Mixed with these promotional and commercial images from 1970 popular culture are some more sober ones that capture something of the political turmoil of the civil rights movement: numerous portraits of Martin Luther King; a snapshot of a ceremony honoring Rosa Parks; and a disturbing closeup of a black man's corpse, its youthful but lifeless face bathed in an eerie light, a fallen hero, I presume, of the civil rights movement.

Among these scraps, remnants of another era, James's contribution stands out. It is a collage commemorating Martin Luther King, and it is filled with the language of black power that my students, in their angry response to the *Weekly Reader* article, resisted so strenuously. "Black is beautiful," proclaims a caption in the lower right corner, making me wonder how James—who often withdrew from the noisy hubbub of the classroom, burying his head in a book—viewed his classmates' adamant resistance to the term "black." His collage is a testament to the changing times, for even as it displays multiple images of King, the advocate of nonviolent protest, it features an excerpt from a magazine article that describes, and implicitly endorses, the violence that erupted when "in the end, the black man said, with bitterness, 'Burn, baby, burn.'"

The central theme of James's collage, however, is not violence, but agency, black agency. According to the magazine excerpt pasted at the top, the 1960s "will be remembered as the time in history when the black man in America drew himself up to his full height, looked the white man in the eye, and said, 'We are equal, man.'" James's collage is a rebuke to moderate whites like Hill who imagined themselves benevolently granting blacks equality. It celebrates the civil rights movement as an essentially African American achievement, and it presents King as the very embodiment of black agency. Beneath a photo that shows King energetically speaking into a microphone, his right hand raised and extended towards his audience, James has added emphatically: "Help! Was his name! Black help!" To illustrate his assertion that King "died with Soul," he has drawn a rocket ship, labeled *Soul Power*, its engines firing it dramatically, forcefully into space. Looking at this collage today, I can't help wondering if James was thinking of me when he clipped and pasted the sentence lamenting the difficulty of "educating the whites to recognize their own unawareness." Thirty-four years after he presented me with this collage, I hope I may finally be beginning to understand what James was trying to tell me.

# The Too-Rough Fingers of the World

*Bring me all of your dreams,*
*You dreamers,*
*Bring me all of your*
*Heart melodies*
*That I may wrap them*
*In a blue cloud-cloth*
*Away from the too-rough fingers*
*Of the world.*
*— "Dream Keeper," by Langston Hughes*

## There's Your Problem

"There's your problem," Mrs. Stockton warned me during my first week at Morton, pointing to a good-looking boy seated in the back right-hand corner of the room. Marcus wasn't from Louisa County. He had grown up in an impoverished section of Alexandria, Virginia, one of eight children. His mother was a prostitute and an alcoholic. His father had long ago vanished from his life. Instead of attending school, Marcus had taken to roaming the streets with some of the tougher, older boys in his neighborhood. As a nine-year-old, he had been caught stealing, not his first offense, and the state had removed him from his home and sent him to live with foster parents in Louisa.

As I write this, I wonder how I know these facts and whether they are all true. I must have heard them from Miss Broderick, the young school psychologist who worked with Marcus daily in individual therapy sessions. She had access to his personal files, and when she talked to me about his problems, sometimes referred to his past life in Alexandria. Still, I wonder whether, in my memory, the real little boy named Marcus has hardened into the familiar stereotype of the urban, African American boy who is abandoned by his father, raised by an addicted and promiscuous mother, and enticed by the lure of the streets into a life of violence and crime. That stereotype fails to convey the psychological complexity of the troubled child in my class, the boy whose bravado and defiance masked, but could never entirely suppress, the fear and vulnerability that threatened to overwhelm him. All I know for sure is this: Marcus was a ten-year-old boy from a blighted, urban neighborhood in northern Virginia. He had gotten into serious enough trouble with the law that he had been removed from his mother and sent to live with strangers in the rural county of Louisa, a hundred and some miles from all that was familiar to him. He was functionally illiterate. He was homesick. And he was very, very angry.

During the few months I taught his class, Marcus knocked over desks, stole money, ripped pictures off the bulletin board, urinated into a jar, and put his hands up a girl's skirt. He bullied the weaker boys, terrified the girls, tried to blackmail his friends, made violent threats to anyone who annoyed him, and got into numerous fistfights, most of which he started by taunting other boys. "Your father is a god damn black mother fucker," I once heard him whisper to a classmate quietly working at a nearby desk, and the two of them were quickly exchanging blows. Once he threw a pair of blunt-edged scissors at another boy, who ducked. The scissors were hurled with such force that they stuck in a bulletin board on the back wall. Worst of all, though, were the times when Marcus disassociated from the world around him and, utterly possessed by his inner demons, exploded in fits of uncontrollable rage. I learned to recognize the early signs: the low muttering to himself, slowly rising in pitch; the glazed eyes that no longer seemed aware of the rest of us in the room; the trancelike state. But I could never prevent that frightening moment when he gave into his madness. I couldn't reach him then; I could only try to keep him from harming the other students by removing him from the class or sending for help.

Even though they were understandably leery of him, some of the other children in my class were drawn to Marcus. This was especially true of the more adventurous boys. They admired his swagger and risk taking, and they recognized that he knew more than they did about the larger world beyond their isolated community. "That's the Washington Monument!" he shouted one day when a picture of the Mall appeared in the *Weekly Reader.* "That's right near where I live." And immediately he was the center of attention, spewing facts about the nation's capital, describing its monuments, and telling what it was like to live in a big and important city. He also knew all about the latest top-forty hits, the hottest Hollywood stars, the hippest fashions and fads, and he liked to hold forth before a rapt audience of his less-informed classmates who had had far less exposure to popular culture. He knew, too, about all kinds of forbidden things that they, as country kids, had never heard of. Something we were discussing in class one day prompted him to give, in a rush of excitement, detailed instructions about how to sniff glue. Before I could stop him, he had piqued the curiosity of the entire class. Cocky, mercurial, street-smart, and glib, despite the fact that he couldn't read a word, Marcus had the kind of charisma that attracts followers. Unfortunately, he only knew how to lead his disciples into trouble.

That trouble eventually led to a conference with his foster parents. An African American couple in their sixties, with grown children of their own, they were of a class and generation of southern blacks who valued propriety and decorum, conducted themselves with a hard-earned dignity, and interacted with white professionals like me with a polite and practiced formality. Kind, caring, and generous, they took their responsibility to Marcus very seriously. But they were completely baffled by him. Mr. Cook told me how shocked he had been when he took his new foster child to church for the first time. Marcus, he recalled, pulled his shirt tail out of his pants, elbowed the person sitting beside him, tore up the church bulletin, and paid no attention at all to the service. Shaking his head in disbelief as he related this story, Mr. Cook told me how appalled he had been when he realized that his new charge had no clue how to behave in church. "No one," he confided in me sadly, "has ever taught this boy about right and wrong."

The Cooks had Marcus's best interests at heart. Yet neither they nor I considered how disoriented Marcus must have been by the strange place where he found himself, a place so different and so far from his home, a place where he had been sent against his will. We didn't ask whether this city child might find the silence and darkness of a country night terrifying. Or whether this neglected boy might find our constant attention intrusive, our high expectations anxiety producing. Nor did we take into account how confusing our imposition of a complex set of rules must have been to this streetwise boy who, before his arrival in Louisa, had hung out on the concrete playgrounds of an urban neighborhood, unsupervised and on his own. Focusing instead on the problems he was causing us, we were bent on reforming him.

So was my principal, Mr. Thompson. A hard-line disciplinarian with an authoritarian style, he demanded, and usually got, absolute obedience from Morton's students. His oversized wooden paddle loomed large in the imagination of the children in my class, who dreaded being sent to his office for misbehaving and sometimes burst into tears at his mere appearance in my classroom. I didn't believe in corporal punishment, and I didn't think spanking a boy with severe emotional problems was an appropriate course of action. But I was always sending Marcus to Mr. Thompson. I didn't know what else to do. I was thus a reluctant collaborator in what became increasingly harsh punishments inflicted on Marcus. I remember one particularly disturbing episode when Marcus disrupted the class and I sent for Mr. Thompson. When the principal attempted to remove him from the classroom, Marcus physically resisted, startling us all by suddenly pushing aside this very large man and bolting impetuously into the hall. A furious Mr. Thompson set out in hot pursuit. We could hear the two of them struggling outside the classroom door: Mr. Thompson's commanding voice as he heaved Marcus to the floor; the thud of the boy's body as it hit the linoleum; Marcus's plaintive cries as he realized he could not escape; then the echo of receding footsteps in the long, cinder-block hall as the principal marched the captured student to the office to be punished—beaten—for such a brazen act of defiance. Not long afterwards, Mr. Thompson returned with a chastened Marcus. Grasping the sobbing boy firmly by the collar, he threatened the entire class with the most dire punishments should they, like Marcus, ever defy him.

Marcus, as Mrs. Stockton had warned me, was a problem child. But he was not, as she had suggested, my primary problem. My problem was much, much larger than Marcus. I struggled to assert my authority in the classroom, but I never succeeded, and my class was always on the verge of a meltdown. I didn't just have trouble controlling Marcus. I had trouble controlling the majority of my students, especially the boys. Most of them were normal kids from close, intact, churchgoing families that made a point of teaching them all about right and wrong. My difficulties stemmed in part from my lack of experience and training. I didn't have even the most rudimentary notion of how to keep thirty-eight children quiet, focused, and in their seats, and I was familiar with none of the behavioral strategies that a certified teacher would have learned in a teacher-training program. I was also temperamentally unsuited to the role of disciplinarian, being by nature more playful than stern, more easygoing than strict. My impulse when confronted with disobedience was to negotiate, not to assert my power or to intimidate. Only twenty-one, I didn't easily or automatically assume the role of the adult. In fact, I often found myself identifying with my erring students, an identification that made it hard to judge or punish them. Furthermore, as a child of the 1960s, I didn't really see myself as an authority figure at all, but rather as someone who questioned authority.

My students, in contrast, had been taught all their lives never to question authority. They knew that the giant wooden paddle in Mr. Thompson's office, a tree switch, leather belt, hairbrush, or the bare hand of an angry parent at home awaited any child foolhardy enough to transgress that fundamental rule. But I couldn't imagine hitting a child. Unfortunately, once my students realized I had no intention of ever spanking them, many of them felt under no constraint to obey me. Absent the threat of physical force, I couldn't convince them I had any real authority over them. I tried, without much success, to find an effective substitute for the palm slappings, spankings, and whippings to which my students were accustomed. Adopting a punishment that had worked well for Mrs. Stockton, I began ordering unruly students to remain in the classroom with me during the lunch period instead of joining their friends in the cafeteria. Under Mrs. Stockton, this punishment had had a chilling effect, humiliating the transgressor, who glumly ate alone under her disapproving glare, desperately missing the banter and camaraderie of the lunchroom. But when I tried this tactic, my students immediately began competing to eat with me, finding my "punishment" a welcome opportunity to escape the noisy cafeteria and enjoy my company. Humiliation, it turned out, wasn't part of my repertoire. I also tried taking away privileges — recess, morning fruit break, trips to the Bookmobile — but I had a hard time keeping track of the various sentences I had imposed on all the infractions my thirty-eight students were committing. In my worst moments, I resorted to yelling at the kids. Even then, my voice failed to communicate any real authority, losing its power as it grew more shrill. Ultimately, my own incompetence put me in an impossible bind. Confronted with an intractable or disruptive student I could not control, I sent him to the office, where Mr. Thompson carried out on my behalf the very kind of corporal punishment I opposed on principle.

Mr. Thompson became alarmed by the number of students I was sending to him to punish. He and I both knew that I couldn't keep relying on him to do my job for me, but I adamantly resisted what he believed was the obvious, the only solution: I needed to administer my own spankings. He couldn't comprehend my resistance. "How," I remember him asking me, "did your parents punish you when you disobeyed?" When I explained to him that I had never, ever been spanked, slapped, whipped, or beaten, he was incredulous. At first, I think, he thought I was lying to him. Even after I persuaded him that I had in fact lived twenty-one years without anyone ever laying a hand on me, he couldn't fathom my upbringing. "But how on earth did your parents and teachers make you behave?" he asked, staring at me as if I were an exotic creature in a zoo, its colors too flamboyant, its movements too bizarre to be from the same planet he inhabited. I could sense the cultural gulf between us widening. I thought his punishments—however standard in Negro schools at that time—were unnecessarily severe and sometimes abusive. But he thought sparing the rod was an indulgence only privileged, white families like mine—people whose status and wealth protected them from the harsh realities of the world—could afford.

"Negro children," this African American man patiently explained to me, "are different. They need to be kept in line. They need to know who's the boss. You have to be very strict with them, or they'll give you trouble. You have to come down hard on them. They only understand you mean business when you have a paddle in your hands." Corporal punishment, he insisted, was not only necessary, but expected, a routine part of school and family life in the African American community. Most of the parents of my students agreed with Mr. Thompson. Whenever I consulted them, they urged me to use physical force on their misbehaving children. "Hit him until he listens," Wendell's mother told me in exasperation during one parent-teacher conference. "It's your job to make him work." Louis's father issued similar instructions. "Make him behave," he ordered, adding confidently, "hit him; he'll do what you say." These parents expected their children to obey me, but that obedience, they were convinced, had to be coerced. Because they did not believe in sparing the rod, they made a point of telling me when they had used it on their errant children so I would know that they were fulfilling their parental responsibilities. Ervin's mother, for instance, once sent me a note meant to reassure me that she was addressing Ervin's most recent transgression. "When I heard what Ervin said to you," she wrote, "I took off all his clothes and whipped him good." From her, I learned that the dreaded spankings that Mr. Thompson administered in his office were routinely repeated at home when parents learned that a child had gotten in trouble.

One day I held a class meeting to discuss the escalating problem. Some of the boys told me bluntly that they thought I was afraid to hit them. Most of the students agreed with their parents and Mr. Thompson; I needed to be much more severe with them when they were bad. "You have to be meaner," they told me earnestly. Cecily suggested I adopt the strategies that her first-grade teacher had used. "Mrs. Jones was really mean," she explained. "If she caught you talking out of turn, she taped your mouth shut. If she caught you acting up or running in the halls, she tied you to your chair, so you couldn't move. You didn't want to get into any trouble with Mrs. Jones." Chester recommended the punishments his third-grade teacher had used. "She made you stay in at recess and write, over and over, that you wouldn't get in trouble again, a hundred times or more on the blackboard, until your hand felt like it was going to fall right off. And if that didn't work, she beat you. Man," he sighed, recalling the force of her paddle, "she could really hit." Quite a few students pointed out that Mr. Snead, the other fourth-grade teacher at Morton—the white man who had been sent to Morton after breaking the arm of a child at a white elementary school—was an especially effective disciplinarian. "He raps his students on their knuckles with a ruler," Clinton informed me. "And he pinches them until they squeal. And he makes them stand on one leg in the corner of the room until they're about ready to faint." William nodded, clearly in awe of Mr. Snead and his harsh punishments. "He's always beating his students," he added. "He hits them hard, with a big board, five to ten whops at a time." I was stunned. Were my students really suggesting I adopt the sadistic methods of a man like Mr. Snead, a man who terrified them?

Although I tacitly violated my "principled" stand against corporal punishment every time I sent a misbehaving child to Mr. Thompson, I was never convinced that spanking was the answer, and I desperately wanted to find an alternative way of keeping my class under control. Since most of the African American teachers at Morton, like my students' parents, believed in corporal punishment, I sought out advice from the three white, female teachers in the school. One, Mrs. McPhearson, was, like me, a first-year teacher and a recent college graduate. She confided that she had originally been opposed to corporal punishment, but after struggling all fall to maintain order in her sixth-grade class, she had come to see "how necessary it is" in order to control "these children." Mr. Thompson had persuaded her that the African American children in her class were different from the white children she had taught as a student teacher in Charlottesville and, unlike those white students, had to be spanked in order to be controlled. Another, Mrs. Cox, taught third grade in the classroom across the hall. A supporter of school integration and an experienced teacher, she had volunteered to transfer to Morton from one of the county's white elementary schools. Like me, she was philosophically opposed to corporal punishment. Knowing that it was used widely at Morton, she had brought a large paddle into the classroom at the beginning of the school year and displayed it prominently at the front of her room. The first time one of her students disobeyed her, she told me, she ordered him to the front of the room and gave him a severe spanking as the rest of her class watched. "I tried to make this spanking as dramatic and frightening as possible," she explained. "I wanted to make it absolutely clear that I was willing to use that paddle. It's still there, where they can all see it. But I've never had to use it again." From what I could gather from across the hall, her classroom, with its largely symbolic paddle propped on the ledge of the blackboard, was a model of order and calm. Only Miss Broderick, the school psychologist, eschewed corporal punishment altogether. When she visited my class, I envied her ability to command my students' attention without ever raising her voice or threatening punishment, and she gave me some hope that I could learn to assert my authority without resorting to physical punishment.

But one day in mid-February, when I sent Marcus to the office for yet another major transgression, Mr. Thompson decided he'd had enough. He showed up at my classroom door carrying his enormous paddle, Marcus in tow. Calling me out into the hall, he handed me the paddle.

"Hit him," he ordered.

I protested at first. Holding the paddle awkwardly in my right hand, surprised by the weight and heft of it, I reiterated my objections to corporal punishment. But my principal was not about to back down.

"It's time for you to take charge," he announced. "Your students need to know you'll spank them when they misbehave. They need to learn to be afraid of you. You have to get over your reluctance to hit them or they're never going to listen to you. YOU must punish Marcus for what he did today. I'm going to stand right here until I see you spank him. Go on now. Hit him."

I hesitated initially. I didn't want to prolong this showdown, but I didn't want to give in, either. I could see Marcus from the corner of my eye, watching intently as I futilely tried to face down Mr. Thompson. Did this troubled boy sense that I was as helpless before the authoritarian figure of Mr. Thompson as he? Did he realize how ridiculous I felt? Did he understand what was at stake? Finally, I gave in. Telling Marcus to bend over, I grasped the heavy, wooden paddle in both hands and swung it, without conviction, at his rear end. After taking the blow, Marcus straightened up, then quickly turned away from me. He was not hiding tears. He was not seething in anger or burning with humiliation. Instead, he was trying, quite unsuccessfully, to suppress a smile. Mr. Thompson looked at me in disgust. Spanking, it turns out, has no sting if the person administering it doubts its efficacy. I never picked up a paddle again.

## Dat's What You Git Effen You Sass Me

Mr. Thompson cared about the students at Morton Elementary School, and he sincerely believed he had their best interests at heart when he spanked them. His heavy reliance on corporal punishment was not at all unusual in the Negro schools of that era. Charlayne Hunter-Gault remembers the way the teachers in her segregated black elementary school in rural Georgia routinely reinforced their lessons with physical force. "Repetition and memorization were the hallmarks of education at Washington Street School," she writes of her school days in the early 1950s. "And if you got it wrong there would be hell to pay. 'Hold out your hand, miss,' I can still remember Miss Mary Wright saying sternly. I would hold out my hand and that stinging old brown leather strap would come crashing down onto it." One of her friends, she recalls, got "four licks . . . for missing 'piano' in the spelling bee." Gerald Early describes similar memories at his urban elementary school in Philadelphia in the 1950s, telling his young daughter:

> When I was in grade school . . . the teachers didn't mind roughing you up if you didn't learn your lessons. Most of the teachers I had were black and at that time it was considered appropriate to spank kids, to whip them, especially black kids, in order to keep them in line. You know the old saying, "Spare the rod and spoil the child." So I grew up in that. When I had to learn my multiplication tables in the fourth grade, the teacher would have us sit in a circle and she would drill us with flash cards. If you didn't know the answer, you were smacked on the hand with a ruler. I was terribly afraid, so I memorized these tables as if my life depended on it.

Horace Porter, a contemporary of Early's but brought up in the rural South, recalls the "whippings" he and his classmates received at their black elementary school in Columbus, Georgia, in the late 1950s and early 1960s. Describing them as "strikes (usually on the hand but sometimes on the backside) given with a leather strap," he notes that "a few teachers were well known for their severity. Their licks were essentially lashes." And Debra Dickerson, who was born in 1959, just a year before my students, tells how spankings were standard fare for even minor infractions at her segregated elementary school in East St. Louis in the late 1960s. "Passing notes or talking in class? A minimum of three lashes with a pointer or yardstick while bent over a desk in front of the whole class." African American children attending segregated schools in the 1950s and 1960s, these writers attest, were routinely subjected to painful and sometimes severe physical punishments, often for small lapses or minor transgressions.

Corporal punishment was used in many white schools at that time, too, especially in the tradition-bound South, which was slow to heed the mounting calls from progressive educators for its abolishment.

Its widespread use in Roman Catholic schools of that era is legendary. Even today, it is still legal in twenty-two states, including all the states in the old Confederacy except Virginia. Yet from what I could infer from my discussions with both white and black teachers in Louisa in 1970, corporal punishment was far less common and much less severe in the county's white elementary schools than in its black ones. What might account for this disparity? Why was corporal punishment such an integral part of many black children's school experience in that era? And why was its use endorsed by so many African American parents, teachers, and administrators?

I didn't ask these questions in 1970. I was blind to the way my opposition to spanking children was deeply conditioned by my own class status, racial identity, religious affiliation, regional ethos, and family history. Quick to judge both the practice and its practitioners, I didn't recognize the powerful cultural forces that shaped Mr. Thompson's views about discipline. I didn't see, for instance, that for him and many other African American educators and parents, corporal punishment was a logical response to Jim Crow, a system that simultaneously undermined their authority and pressured them, through brutal acts and terrifying threats, to teach their children the necessity of absolute obedience. Seeking to protect black children from dangers far more threatening than a spanking—dangers arising from whites' abuse of power—they relied on physical punishments to bring home the dire consequences of defying authority. Inasmuch as their own authority was compromised by whites, who patronized and humiliated them in front of their children, many must have also felt the need to reestablish it in their homes, even if that meant resorting to force.

"There could be no protest, no argument, when an adult spoke," Deborah McDowell writes of her upbringing in the black community of Bessamer, Alabama; "You simply obeyed." When she openly disobeyed her great-grandmother on the night of a devastating fire, her punishment was swift and memorable: she was hit "upside my head" and given "licks on my arms, my legs, around my shoulders." Her great-grandmother's fury, a response to a crisis that must have made the adult woman feel keenly the child's vulnerability, surely erupted from the smoldering fear that, as a black woman in Jim Crow Alabama, she was ultimately powerless to protect her great-granddaughter. Beating a child must have enabled her—for a moment—to beat back that fear, allowing her to feel in charge. Yet if it temporarily empowered her, the punishment she inflicted emphatically reinforced the power relations of the very system that kept her down, for by insisting that her black grandchild unquestioningly obey people in authority, she implicitly taught her to be subservient to whites who, in the segregated South of the 1950s, occupied almost all the positions of authority outside the home and black community.

Debra Dickerson describes a more routine form of corporal punishment she and her siblings received at the hands of her mother, who was raised in the Deep South. Whenever they forgot to address their mother as "ma'am," she "called" them "to her for a smack." Dickerson depicts her mother here as a "stern taskmaster," one who was nevertheless loving and nurturing and who sought to instill a sense of responsibility in her children. But I wonder what else motivated those smacks. Memories, perhaps, of her embarrassment when whites withheld this title of respect from her own mother? A desire to attain in the confines of her home the respect denied her by the outside world? Resentment at the tenuousness of her own authority? Fear that her children were terribly vulnerable should they fail to follow the required rules of etiquette when speaking to whites? Or maybe she was a stern taskmaster because she believed the "undying truism" that Gerald Early recognizes as informing his own parenting: "I cannot be soft because it will make [my daughter] soft, and soft black children cannot survive in this world."

Early, who isn't an advocate of corporal punishment, admits that he doesn't know if this "undying truism" is in fact true. His point is that, whether true or not, he had fully internalized it. An assumption about the vulnerability of "soft" black children, one that can be traced all the way back to slavery, thus influenced the way he raised his daughters in the late twentieth century. His musings are illuminating, for they suggest that the disciplinary practices of black parents and educators that I have been describing here were deeply rooted in the past, and particularly in the collective memory of slavery and Jim Crow. Corporal punishment, much of it brutal, was of course widely used by white planters to enforce obedience, coerce labor, and punish defiance in their slaves. Without it, there was no feasible way of maintaining the institution of slavery. Even after the abolishment of slavery, its violent legacy survived. From the period of Reconstruction through the civil rights movement of the 1960s, white people in many parts of the country, and especially the South, threatened, beat, whipped, shot, hung, tortured, terrorized, and lynched blacks who dared to exercise their rights or assert their equality.

A disturbing comment by Marcus Sterling Hopkins, the federal Freedman's Bureau agent sent to Louisa County to supervise Reconstruction, suggests, too, that many of those who had been enslaved replicated the harsh forms of punishment they had known at the hands of their masters when disciplining black children. In a diary entry dated January 13, 1868, Hopkins writes of his efforts to find homes for newly freed slave children who had been separated from their families or orphaned. Noting how freedmen were eager to take in children who were old enough to work in the fields (and thus, like white slave owners, to reap the economic benefits of their labor), he notes with some consternation that "in such cases their parental and guardianship disciplines are very severe."

In oral histories collected in Virginia during the 1930s, former slaves tell how they were shackled, whipped, and beaten by their white masters for relatively minor offenses like "shirking" and "sassing," as well as for more serious acts of disobedience. In one of these stories, a female slave named Toots is subjected to such a cruel punishment for talking back to her master that she dies from her wounds. Her master then holds her brutal death up as a warning for the rest of the slaves:

> Ole Toots answre Marse Riles back one day. He tied her to de drum of de wheat thrasher. Den he let de fan beat her till she fell an' tol' her ole man if he want her, to come an' git her. He took her to his cabin, an' de po' thing died de nex' mornin.' He tol' de res' of us, "Dat's what you git effen you sass me." An' you sho' would. Git yo' thirty an' nine fo' lookin' hard. Thirty and nine? Dat was 'bout fo'ty licks an sometimes mo.

Resorting to an especially horrific punishment, the slave master Riles used physical force to reassert his authority in response to a slave's impertinence. He then pointed to the slave's mutilated body to underscore his point: "Dat's what you git effen you sass me."

Sassing was an unpardonable offense at Morton Elementary. Until I read about Master Riles and Ole Toots, I couldn't understand why Mr. Thompson reacted so angrily to children who "answered back" to him or to me. His insistence on punishing a young child for a few defiant words or a cocky attitude seemed irrational, the punishments he meted out for such behavior unnecessarily severe. Often, the offending child was merely trying to explain his side of the story or making an understandable effort to defend himself from what he felt was an unjustified accusation. Sometimes, the child was accurately correcting Mr. Thompson or me. "Let him speak," I wanted to shout at Mr. Thompson, whenever he lit into one of my students for talking back. "Listen to what he has to say." But I had grown up with a father who loved nothing more than to provoke me to challenge him, a man so assured of his own authority that he could play with it, share it, give it away. I carried with me no ancestral memories of bullwhips or threshing machines, no stories about family members struck dead for a single, rash act of defiance.

Mr. Thompson, in contrast, had grown up black in the South during the Jim Crow era, a time when even a small misstep by a black youth—an inadvertent violation of the rigid code of etiquette that governed all relations between blacks and whites, a smart-alecky remark made impulsively in the presence of a white adult, an admiring glance at a white girl—could result in harassment, violent recriminations, even death. A native of Louisa County, a descendent of slaves, a product of segregated schools, an African American educator who had to take orders from whites in positions of power over him, he viewed the world through a very different lens. Student behavior that seemed completely innocuous to me struck him as provocative, rebellious, disrespectful. He interpreted any hint of defiance as a threat to his authority, any assertion of will as a violation of the accepted code of behavior, endangering both the offending child and the social order.

One of his "undying truisms," I see now, was the lesson the planter Riles sought to instill in his slaves: the weak must submit to the powerful, who can and will defeat them if they resist. That truism informed the way he interacted with the white county officials who were his superiors, causing him to perform countless ritual acts of deference in their presence, all the while keeping his anger in check. It guided his philosophy of education, underscoring for him the urgency of teaching black children to obey authority. It also shaped his image of himself as Morton's principal. He was, after all, the school's chief authority figure, and he wielded his power with the zeal of a man who believed his position gave him the right to demand total submission from the children in his charge. In his effort to protect black children from a white world that disadvantaged and endangered them, he paradoxically embraced a model of power derived from that white world and its slaveholding past.

History helps to explain, and may even validate, Mr. Thompson's reliance on corporal punishment. The order it imposed was certainly preferable to the chaos in my classroom. But I witnessed daily its emotional cost. Ervin's large dark eyes, perpetually guarded, suspicious, hurt, accusatory. Henry's extreme repression, his anxious effort not to offend stiffening his body, freezing his emotions, stifling all spontaneity. Wendell's paranoid fear that he was being singled out for reprimand and his compulsive monitoring of others in his endless quest to prove that his classmates, not he, deserved to be paddled. Subjected to frequent physical punishments, many of my students automatically resorted to threats of violence to resolve their conflicts. I remember Clinton repeatedly vowing that his Mama would come to school the next day and beat up whatever friend had crossed, annoyed, or wronged him. Even the girls threatened each other with bodily harm. Here is a series of notes I confiscated from Cheryl and Jeanine:

> "I am going to knock you on the floor JH when we go the bathroom."
> "Oh really girl. If you do I is going to kill you. Yes or No."
> "Give me another pices. If you don't I am goin to beat you up."

Distrust, anxiety, fear, anger, the desire to retaliate, the impulse to bully: all were by-products of Mr. Thompson's disciplinary practices. So was resentment. Still seething over a severe reprimand she had endured at Mr. Thompson's hands two years earlier, Ramonia bitterly recounted one day how terrified she had been when the principal falsely accused her of intentionally tripping a girl named Glenda Jones as the class walked in line to the cafeteria. "Mr. Thompson came over to me and yanked me out of the line so hard my arm hurt," she told me. "He yelled at me, really loudly, right in my face, for tripping Glenda. And he shook me by the shoulders until I cried. But I didn't trip Glenda," she protested indignantly. "I didn't even touch her. Glenda Jones tripped over her own two feet." Sighing, she added,

"Everyone at home fusses at you. Then, you come to school and you get it all over again."

Gerald Early recalls a similar incident from his childhood, his anger surfacing with sudden force forty-some years later. When his daughter asks him, "'Did you like getting slapped around in school?'" he is surprised by the intensity of his response. "I was silent for several moments, as if I were trying very much to measure an answer that would have the proper sort of parental weight to it," he writes.

> But actually, at that moment, I was recalling with almost crushing immediacy one afternoon when my elementary school gym teacher slapped me viciously across the head because he thought I had been whispering in line. I wanted very much to cry but could not in sight of the other children. But I felt, at the moment, the wretched cruelty of this arbitrary justice (for I was not the person who was whispering) and the deep humiliation of this harsh authority. . . . "No," I said matter-of-factly, "I never liked getting slapped around and I never liked school. Not a single day of it. It felt just like prison. I couldn't wait to get out."

How many of my students felt that their school was just like prison? The extent to which they viewed it as an oppressive place came home to me one day when I watched a group of girls in my class immersed in "playing school." After declaring a portion of the blacktop playground their imaginary classroom and choosing Cecily to be the teacher, they threw themselves wholeheartedly into their role-playing. But their school had no pretend math lessons or reading groups, no play recess or spelling bee. Its students gave no recitations; its teachers, no praise. Instead, Cecily, mimicking the authoritarian teachers she saw all around her, cracked down hard on her "students." Brandishing a huge stick, she chased them furiously around the playground as they ran from her in mock fright. "I'm going to beat your butt until its red," I heard her yell, her voice hard-edged and threatening, "and then you'll behave." Were my students, too, counting the days when, like prisoners who had done their time, they could escape school? Would they forever associate school with the humiliation of being slapped around, the pain of having their butts beaten red?

Mr. Thompson's insistence on obedience, no questions asked, may have been a necessary lesson in navigating the culture of Jim Crow, but it disadvantaged my students in the classroom. If they insisted on the validity of their own perceptions, if they tried to explain their reasons for disagreeing with an adult's assessment, if they told a narrative that ran counter to the authorized one, if they challenged the rules, they were accused of "answering back" and threatened with a beating. In such a climate all kinds of qualities that contribute to learning—inquisitiveness, experimentation, risk taking, skepticism, active listening, independent thinking—get suppressed. Scared children aren't inclined to ask questions. Anxious children aren't able to focus. Alienated children aren't likely to join in on a class discussion. Anne Moody describes the chilling effect her elementary school teacher's routine beatings had on her school performance. Recalling the intimidating tactics that this man, a minister, used to discipline his students in the one-room black school she attended as a young child in rural Mississippi, she writes: "I was so scared of him I never did anything. I hardly ever opened my mouth. I don't even remember a word he said in class. I was too scared to listen to him. Instead, I sat there all day and looked out the window at the graveyard and counted the tombstones." Her withdrawal was a psychological defense against the harshness of her teacher's discipline, but it had a deadening effect on her, rendering her as silent as the corpses in the graveyard outside her classroom window.

This silencing is not at all the lesson privileged white children learn in their elite schools, where they are trained to become the country's future leaders and power brokers. In those schools, students are systematically taught how to question authority. They are encouraged "to inquire, to challenge, to be adventurous," "to take risks," "to think critically, creatively, and independently," "to develop a fuller sense of autonomy" and "a feeling of self-worth and self-confidence," "to come to respect . . . the strength of their own hearts," to be "independent thinkers," "to avoid standardized solutions to problems," "to live by [the] motto 'Dare to be true,'" all forms of answering back. Through these lessons, they are being socialized to take over America's boardrooms, run its government and businesses, invent its new technologies, and preside over its courtrooms, hospitals, research laboratories, and university classrooms. My students, in contrast, were being socialized to take orders. They were learning how to become compliant and docile workers.

The African American writers I cite here, it is true, escaped that fate. Men and women of prodigious talent, they all have remarkable stories to tell, ones that trace their deepening engagement with an African American intellectual tradition that raises the most profound questions about American society and embraces the transformative potential of education. Their stories typically involve as well high family expectations, dedicated black teachers and mentors, and a supportive black community. Most of these authors eventually attended predominantly white schools as pioneers in early efforts to achieve racial integration. Hunter-Gault was one of the first two African Americans to attend the University of Georgia, enrolling there in January 1961, where she was "greeted by mobs of white students, who within forty-eight hours would hurl epithets, burn crosses and Black effigies, and finally stage a riot outside [her] dormitory." Porter won a scholarship to Amherst College, leaving his isolated black community in rural Georgia in 1968 to attend a prestigious, predominantly white New England school, a place that initially seemed "like a foreign country" to him. Dickerson attended an integrated magnet school for gifted elementary students in the late 1960s, her bus shuttling her between her inner-city neighborhood and the privileged world of middle-class suburbia where she felt "like Cinderella at the ball." Recalling the challenges they faced leaving their families and communities and entering an alien and sometimes hostile white world, each reflects on the impact their early experiences with integration had on their lives.

It is impossible to say how the lives of these writers would have been different had the civil rights movement not successfully challenged Jim Crow and created new educational opportunities for them as young African Americans. Long before enrolling in integrated schools, they had already distinguished themselves as students. Some had become avid readers on their own, turning to books to compensate for inadequate schooling; others enjoyed the special attention and encouragement of talented black teachers who recognized their potential and pushed them to achieve. But their experiences attending integrated schools with middle- and upper-class children inevitably changed them. Many tell of the enormous gulf that opened up between them and their black communities when they returned from their integrated schools having assimilated prevailing middle-class, white attitudes towards authority. Porter, for instance, observes that

Amherst's ethos—with its emphasis on independent thinking and rigorous, intellectual questioning—was "antithetical" to that of his black community in rural Georgia, and he describes how his increasing willingness to question received ideas, examine the premises of his religion, and dispute beliefs held by members of his family and community created a painful distance between him and them.

Henry Louis Gates explicitly attributes to school integration the sharp generational divide he witnessed in the way members of his family viewed children's "rights and responsibilities and their relation to authority." According to him, older relatives who had "graduated from the colored high school" in his West Virginia hometown adamantly believed that black children should be taught to submit to authority, "both white and familial," and did not tolerate any form of answering back. But those in his own generation, who had grown up attending integrated schools, held strikingly different views of authority. They chafed against the traditional code of behavior that required them to defer to their elders and to whites, and they openly challenged their older relatives and whites in positions of authority over them. "I heard it times beyond counting: That boy's got too much mouth," he writes, describing how his uncles disapproved of his tendency to take a stand, speak his mind, argue with his parents, defend himself, or "answer back." They viewed his mother's willingness to tolerate his defiance "as a threat: it represented chaos, disrespect for tradition, order, containment," a view he believes was a product of their education in the town's segregated black schools, where they had learned the same undying truism that informed Mr. Thompson's disciplinary practices. His uncles, Gates writes, believed his youthful defiance "was reckless—insufficiently heedful of the fact that the white world could crush us all anytime it wanted to," and they feared for him. "Because I flouted the rules," he explains, "they thought I would come to a bad end, and they took pleasure in letting me know that. Deep down, I think they were frightened for me. And deeper down, I think I frightened them."

Gates attributes his uncles' fears to "integration anxiety," but he does not specify the reasons why his experience in an integrated school caused him to behave in ways that aroused those fears. He doesn't say, for instance, whether corporal punishment was any less common or less severe in the integrated school than the colored one, or whether his teachers there were more likely to encourage their students to raise questions or were more tolerant of answering back than teachers at the colored school. It is clear, however, that for an intellectually gifted student like him, integration was liberating. It allowed him to prove himself in a larger arena where he easily outperformed his white classmates and earned the admiration of his white teachers. In place of the lessons his uncles had learned at the colored school—the importance of tradition, order, containment; the practical need for deference and submission—he learned from his experience in an integrated school to question a tradition that marked him as inferior and to critique an order that relegated him to the lower rungs of society and tried to contain him. Fifteen years after the elementary school in Gates's hometown of Piedmont, West Virginia, was integrated, my students still attended a segregated school that, in its philosophy of education and its methods of discipline, closely resembled the "colored" school that Gates's uncles attended in the 1940s. Two years after the adolescent Gates, as valedictorian of his high school class, delivered a graduation speech that addressed controversial issues like Vietnam and civil rights and urged his classmates "to defy norms"—a speech he had "surreptitiously" written on his own "because this was not allowed," surprising his teachers with a different speech than the one he had rehearsed—my students were still learning that it was reckless to speak up because those in power could crush them at any time. For his bold defiance, Gates received a "big wink" from the white teacher in charge of the ceremony. For their small acts of defiance, my students knew Mr. Thompson's paddle awaited them.

## I've Got a Surprise for You

A fight erupted on the playground one morning. I rushed toward the circle of curious children who had quickly gathered to watch. Shouting and jeering, they had taken sides and were egging on the two quarreling boys. I wasn't at all surprised to discover Marcus, dead center, throwing punches. But I didn't recognize his antagonist, a tall, lanky sixth-grader, much bigger than Marcus. I could see the two of them scuffling on the ground, each fiercely pummeling the other as I made my way towards them. Someone must have alerted Mr. Thompson, for he appeared before I had managed to separate the combatants. Expertly breaking up the fight, he ordered the two boys to his office. I herded my students back to our classroom, relieved that the drama of the fight was over. But it wasn't. Matilda had already taken her seat when Reginald entered the classroom. As he passed her desk, he kicked it angrily. Bam, bam, bam. With every kick, the desk shook noticeably. Matilda's whole body shuttered from the vibrations. She was on the verge of tears.

"You know what you've done, girl," Reginald muttered as he took his seat behind her. "It's all your fault John beat up on Marcus."

I couldn't imagine why Reginald was blaming Matilda for the playground brawl. One of the most popular girls in the class, she ordinarily stayed above the fray, and she never got in trouble. Scolding Reginald for his outrageous behavior, I instructed him to leave Matilda alone, and I tried to get the class to focus on their spelling lesson. But Mr. Thompson soon came barging into the room. He had talked to Marcus and the sixth-grader, and he was furious. Not at the older boy who had started the fight. Not at Marcus who had readily accepted the challenge. But at Matilda.

"What on earth made you think you could get John Pointdexter to do your dirty work for you?" he demanded of her, his tone fluctuating between outrage and ridicule. "And why would John be the least bit interested in helping you out? Do you think you're that pretty? I want you to tell me why John would pick a fight for a little girl like you. Surely, you don't expect me to believe he was willing to fight Marcus just because you asked him to." His voice heavy with sarcasm, Mr. Thompson made his suspicions clear.

Matilda crumbled in the face of his withering interrogation. She began to cry, and I could see that her whole body was trembling. But Mr. Thompson continued to rebuke her in front of her classmates. After he stormed out of the room, Matilda became inconsolable. She sobbed violently. Her hands, held out from her sides, shook wildly and repetitively, as if they were fantastic windup toys over which she had no control. Then she began to hyperventilate, desperately gasping, in short, shallow breaths, for air. As I tried frantically to soothe her, some of the boys began to taunt her. "She's faking!" they cried in derision. "She's faking! She's faking!" But Matilda was not faking.

It took me days to piece together Matilda's story. How Marcus had been harassing and frightening her. How her fear had driven her to enlist the help of the older boy, who rode her bus and was big enough not to be cowed by Marcus's bullying tactics. How when John told the younger boy to keep away from Matilda, he had set off the volatile Marcus, who responded to John's warning by threatening Matilda, vowing "to cut her stomach open" to get back at her. How she had told John about the terrifying threat, and he had challenged Marcus to a fight on the playground with everyone watching. How her carefully concocted plan had backfired, intensifying Marcus's hostility, turning Reginald and some of Marcus's other pals against her, and causing Mr. Thompson to hold her responsible for the playground fight, a fight she had never meant to incite.

Matilda's story seemed to me to be very clearly a story about male bullying. Why was Mr. Thompson so quick to interpret it as a story about female transgression? He appeared to have no sympathy for the little girl who was afraid, though he had to know that Marcus was a very real danger to the other students in my classroom. Even worse, he could only see Matilda's plea for protection as a form of seduction — a deliberate act of provocation on her part — despite the fact that she was only ten and pre-pubescent. Instead of putting a stop to Marcus's bullying, he blamed Matilda for trying to protect herself. Even though, by turning to a boy for help, she was hardly challenging the gender hierarchy, he seemed threatened by her sense of agency, her willingness to take action on her own. At the time, I vaguely understood that Mr. Thompson's impulse to blame Matilda — and to sexualize, ridicule, and control her — reflected the traditional, patriarchal beliefs of Louisa's black community, of southern society, and, indeed, of mainstream American culture in 1970. The feminist movement of the late twentieth century was still in its infancy, and I was just learning to use words like "patriarchal." But I'd been taught by my fiercely independent mother and my playfully nonconformist grandmother to believe that women were men's equals, and I chafed at Mr. Thompson's male-centered view of the world.

Our clashing views about women's status complicated many of the interactions between us. I found myself, more than once, responding to Mr. Thompson's assumptions about gender roles by forging alliances with the girls in my class. In those instances, the categories of white and black seemed far less relevant than the categories of male and female. I remember, for instance, sympathizing with the girls in my class when they complained that they couldn't use the school's jungle gym, which was the only piece of equipment on the playground. The jungle gym was off limits to them because they were required to wear dresses to school, and there could be no climbing or hanging upside down or skinning the cat in a dress. While the boys owned the jungle gym and the baseball field, the girls were confined to a bare square of asphalt, good for jumping rope and hopscotch, but not much else. I let them in on a strategy from my own tomboy days: why not wear shorts under their dresses? The next day, six or seven of the girls excitedly told me their mothers had permitted them to take me up on my suggestion. At recess, they raced to the jungle gym and immediately began to climb, dangle from, and turn somersaults on the iron bars. Their exuberance lasted maybe ten minutes. Then a gruff voice interrupted their joyful play. From the upstairs window of his office, a furious Mr. Thompson shouted down at me. "Get those girls off the monkey bars right now, and don't let them get near them ever again."

Once, three of the boys in my class cunningly manipulated Mr. Thompson's assumptions about women, at my expense. I had spotted them fighting at the far end of the baseball field, Clinton and Lonnie ganging up on Derrick, Derrick ferociously punching back, the three of them dropping to the ground, fists flying. I'm sure there would have been black eyes and bloody noses had I not quickly intervened. After calming them down and reprimanding them, I sent all three of them to Mr. Thompson with a note describing the fight. But minutes before the final bell sent students scurrying for their buses, they returned from the principal's office, all smiles. I knew from the look on their faces that they had miraculously been spared Mr. Thompson's paddle. They had escaped punishment, I later learned, by agreeing on their way to the office to present a united front, telling the same tall tale to the unsuspecting principal: there had been no fight. "We were just playing hard," they'd told him, "but Mrs. Hallahan, she couldn't see we were just rough housing. She thought we were hurting each other, but we weren't. We were just having fun. We're all good friends, and that wasn't any fight she saw." Mr. Thompson believed the boys' story. Quick to assume that I couldn't recognize when boys were just being boys, he took their word over mine and decided not to punish them.

The next day, however, he roared into my classroom, as angry as I'd ever seen him, and hauled the three boys off to be paddled. By then he had realized he'd been snookered. An apologetic Mr. Thompson told me later how he had discovered the boy's duplicity. Shortly after they had convinced him they had not been fighting, he had met with Mr. Drumheller, the University of Virginia professor who was serving that year as a consultant to the school district. Mr. Drumheller had been on the school playground that afternoon and had informed him of an especially vicious fight at the far end of the baseball field. "Those boys were really going at each other," he told Mr. Thompson. "If their teacher hadn't stopped them, some one could have gotten seriously hurt."

For all our differences, I liked Mr. Thompson. He was an amiable and good-natured man with a robust sense of humor. He was also an able administrator: hardworking, responsible, attentive, a man who took his job seriously and did it with pride. He tried his best to help me, and I depended on him. But I didn't understand him. And he didn't understand me.

"I've got a surprise for you," he announced one morning, pleased as punch with his secret. "But you have to wait until this afternoon. As soon as school is out, I'll come by your room and explain." Then, his eyes afire with anticipation, he added knowingly, "I'll have someone with me, someone you're going to be very interested in meeting." I felt like a child being teased with the promise of a very special birthday surprise. Excited, but intuitively sensing the obligation to be pleased. And frustrated that everyone else seemed to be in the know but me.

The surprise was indeed a big one: a teacher's aide for my class. Her name was Mrs. Coomes. Mr. Thompson had worked with Dr. Martin, the white superintendent, to hire her, getting the school board's approval and interviewing a number of applicants before selecting her. I had been left completely in the dark throughout the entire process. No one had ever informed me that I was to get an aide, and no one had consulted me about the person who would be hired to help me. Had they done so, I would have asked for — begged for — an aide from the African American community who could help me forge connections with the parents of my students. Someone like Ramonia's mother, a teacher's aide in Mrs. Perkins' second-grade classroom, or like the genial Mrs. Perkins herself, a woman who affectionately bantered with my students in the hallway, always appealing to their sense of family pride and reminding them that she would be talking to their mothers at church the next Sunday.

The last person I would ever have chosen to be my aide was Mrs. Coomes. A white woman in her early sixties, Mrs. Coomes was not a native of Louisa County and had no connections to the black community. She was a plain-looking woman, thin and wiry, with short gray hair and deep-set, hazel-colored eyes, not noteworthy except for their intensity. Outspoken and opinionated, she let me know daily just what she thought of hippies, Vietnam war protesters, black radicals, civil rights organizers, and Communists, all of whom, she was convinced, were part of a vast conspiracy to bring down America. I didn't need to ask whether she believed in white supremacy. She had grown up dirt poor in the mountains of western Virginia, and she loved to tell me about her hardscrabble childhood. Her stories—gothic, grotesque, darkly funny—fascinated and unsettled me. Once, she told me about the time she escaped the fury of her abusive mother by climbing a big oak tree. She took refuge in its highest branches where, safely beyond the reach of the abhorred hickory switch, she huddled all that November day, shivering and alone. While her mother cursed and raged at her from below, she defiantly stayed put, answering her mother's angry shouting with taunts of her own. There was something chilling about the way she told this story, an odd lack of emotion in the way she recalled her mother's drunken violence and her own distress. Mrs. Coomes appeared to feel no pity, no compassion for the treed child.

Married three times, she had raised ten children, an accomplishment that, in her mind, earned her the requisite credentials as an expert in child rearing. "I've been bringing up children all my life," she liked to tell me, "first my younger brothers and sisters, and then my own children, all ten of them. I've had a whole lot more experience with little ones than you've had," she would boast, "and I know a thing or two that you don't." And then she would recite her litany of "truths" about children. "All kids are liars," she cautioned me whenever I took a child for his word, aghast at what she saw as my naivete. "You can't trust a word they say. Not a single word. If you don't watch out, I'm telling you, they'll try to pull something over on you every time. Children aren't angels. No siree. They've got the devil in them, they do." Beating children was her preferred method of discipline. "You have to beat the demons out of them," she liked to say. She was flabbergasted at my reluctance to paddle my students. In her mind, a good thrashing was the solution to almost any problem a child presented. "I always whipped my sons if they started a fight," she proudly told me, "and I whipped them if they didn't take up for themselves."

Openly advocating a double standard, Mrs. Coomes adamantly believed that girls should be treated differently than boys because of their sexual vulnerability and the predatory nature of men. "When my girls were teenagers," she told me, "I kept an eye on them all the time. I didn't permit them to leave the house, ever, except to go to school and church. They used to beg to attend dances, church socials, their high school prom, but I wouldn't hear of it. I made it my business not to allow them to go anywhere near where there were boys, because I knew the boys would take advantage of them." She was eager, however, for her sons to seek out the very experiences she denied her daughters, explaining that she wanted them "to get exposed to all kinds of girls."

Mrs. Coomes liked to boast that she had brought up all her children "to live decent lives." But even as she bragged to me about her parenting skills, she chronicled her children's woes (two had been blue babies, one suffered from chronic anemia, one was retarded, and a third one spastic) and filled me in on the details of what sounded like deeply unhappy lives. One son had failed two grades in school; another had caused her all kinds of trouble when he was growing up, getting into fights and playing hooky, and was now in prison; a third son was an alcoholic, struggling, without much success, to stay sober. One of her daughters had been a chronic runaway when she was a teenager; another had repeatedly snuck off to have sex with an older man in the woods; yet another was currently seeing a psychiatrist about her husband who, she explained to me without elaborating, was "queer but makes good money."

In some ways, it was helpful to have Mrs. Coomes in the classroom. Because I had so many students, I could always find something for her to do, and I was grateful for the energetic way she responded to my requests. During reading period I could focus my attention on one reading group at a time, while she made sure the other students were working quietly at their desks. If a student didn't understand a math problem or a reading assignment, I could ask her to work individually with him while I continued teaching the rest of the class. I also tried to invent ways to use Mrs. Coomes to help me maintain order. I even used her to try to counter the culture of punishment by rewarding good behavior, though my experiment was overly ambitious and only semi-successful. But our fundamental assumptions about children and discipline were so antithetical that her presence introduced a whole new set of tensions to an already tense classroom.

When, during science class, Reginald asked how astronauts orbiting space managed to go to the bathroom, Mrs. Coomes was deeply offended. She was equally shocked by my willingness to take Reginald's query seriously. I thought his question was a sign of a curious and intellectually engaged child, but she thought it was disgusting and firmly believed Reginald should be spanked for asking it. I had to fend off her clear disapproval before I could even attempt to deal with Reginald's question. She was also critical of the way I handled an argument that broke out among some of the girls during recess one spring afternoon. Instead of squelching it and reprimanding them, I took their disagreement seriously and tried to mediate their differences. The girls openly vented their anger, spewing out fighting words and registering their complaints, but in the end they agreed to make up and end their bickering. I felt I'd dealt with this crisis thoughtfully and effectively, but Mrs. Coomes was outraged that I'd let their argument continue. "It was shameful, what those girls were doing out there on the playground," she told me later that afternoon, "airing their grievances in public like that. There's no excuse for such behavior. It was embarrassing to watch. And shame on you for not stopping them. Believe me, it doesn't do any good to talk to children about why they're quarreling. You just end up fueling the flames. Those girls didn't need any more talking; all they needed was a good healthy beating." Not one to keep her judgments to herself, she made sure my students knew she disapproved of the way I was handling things, further confusing them.

Mrs. Coomes had no tolerance for weakness, vulnerability, or difference. She was especially set off by Samuel, the troubled white boy in my class whose father had abandoned him after his mother's death. She found his high-pitched giggles offensive, and we argued vehemently when I refused to let her spank him for the annoying way he laughed.

I tried to tell her about his emotional problems, but she was unmoved. "I'd like to wring his little neck when he giggles like that," she told me. "There's no excuse for him. Of course he can control himself. My husband deserted me when my son was a baby, but that's no reason for him to be disturbed." She was similarly unsympathetic to Marcus, insisting that his fits of rage were deliberately staged, and to Derrick, scoffing at the tears he shed when he tried unsuccessfully to read.

But she also took a dislike to some of the class leaders. I couldn't believe it when, at the end of one school day, she declared that Ramonia had "the vilest temperament in the class." Ramonia! What could she be thinking? This was the girl who had reached out to me in my frustration, writing me a note about her "ashamement" and asking for my forgiveness; the girl who had stoically endured a toothache rather than upset her mother who could not pay for a dentist; the girl who was so worried about the state of my soul that she had invited me to attend her church. Yet something about this bright, confident, and affectionate child set Mrs. Coomes off, eliciting a reaction in her that was intense and visceral. I only began to comprehend her reason for disliking Ramonia a couple of weeks later when, during a lively discussion, Ramonia openly took issue with some of her classmates. They were all imagining how much better their lives would be if only they were as rich or as talented or as famous as the people they saw on TV. Only Ramonia disagreed, declaring emphatically, "I want to be just who I am." Smiling at her wonderful sense of her own self-worth, I was surprised at that moment to see Mrs. Coomes glare angrily at the little girl, her disapproval palpable. Only then did I realize that the very qualities I admired in Ramonia—her self-assurance, her independence, her courage, her strong belief in herself—rankled Mrs. Coomes. She found these traits "vile" in a little black girl, apparently because they made her "uppity."

I was never told why Mr. Thompson and Dr. Martin chose Mrs. Coomes as my aide. They probably believed her age and experience would provide a corrective to my youth and inexperience. They must have known as well that she was a proponent of corporal punishment and was willing to carry out the spankings they felt my students needed. But I believe they also chose her because she was white. Both men, I think, automatically assumed that, because I was white, I would prefer to have a white aide. Certainly, Mr. Thompson tended to see Mrs. Coomes and me as related in our whiteness; in his mind, we were both, first and foremost, "white people." Yet I felt far less kinship with Mrs. Coomes than any of the black teachers, parents, and children I worked with at Morton. Even though I recognized how her view of the world was shaped by her impoverished Appalachian childhood and working-class experiences, experiences far different than my own, I recoiled from her rigidity, her fierceness, her repression, her racism, her values, her judgments, and, especially, her lack of empathy and self-reflection. Except when my students assumed I had a special kinship with the white boy Samuel, this is the only time in my life I have ever experienced what African American writers refer to as "involuntary relatedness," and it infuriated me. I couldn't understand why Mr. Thompson would assume I had anything at all in common with Mrs. Coomes. And yet white people make similar assumptions about blacks all the time, seeing race as a category that trumps all other categories (class, wealth, education, nationality, regional identity, religion, political affiliation, family, gender, age, temperament) and drawing no distinctions among a Jamaican immigrant taxi driver in New York City, a high school math teacher in California, a small business owner in Dallas, a graduate student in Boston, a gang member in Chicago, a factory worker in Detroit, a Creole socialite in New Orleans, a crack addict in Atlanta, a farmer in Alabama, an Ivy League–trained lawyer in Washington, D.C., because they see only black. But when Mr. Thompson automatically assumed I would like a woman who was so different from me that she might as well have been from Mars simply because we were both white, I wanted to call foul.

There was another reason why my principal and superintendent wanted me to have a white aide. The elementary schools were to be integrated the next year. Because I was one of only a handful of whites teaching in the county's black elementary schools that year, both men viewed my classroom as a test case for integration. Instead of focusing on my ineptness and inexperience, they saw only that black children were giving a white teacher a hard time, a situation that could not be tolerated, for it seemed to confirm the fears of many in the white community that the presence of African American children in the formerly white schools would be disruptive. By hiring a white aide strict enough to straighten out my class, they sought to allay those fears, proving that black students could be made to obey white teachers.

They were determined to prepare my students for the difficult transition to an integrated school, where they would be expected to behave according to a code of rules written by whites. It never occurred to either man that, in the face of impending integration, a white teacher like me might have much more to learn from an African American than a white aide. Nor did they ever imagine that the example of a white and a black working closely together in the classroom might provide a more meaningful preparation for integration than two whites imposing their wills on a class of black children.

## They Ran Away for What We Said We Don't Know

The day before spring break—a long Easter weekend—was one of those spectacular March days that distinguish a southern spring from anything the North is capable of producing. The sky could not have been a more intense blue, the sun could not have radiated a more comforting warmth, the breeze could not have blown more mildly and gently. And every tree, it seemed, chose that day to burst into joyous bloom. I had already planned to celebrate the upcoming holiday with special activities and treats, and the intoxicating spring weather heightened the festive mood of the class. I remember the grins as the students shared the jelly beans I'd given them, the laughter as they joined in the silly math games I'd organized, the happy concentration as they drew vases of flowers, inspired by the copies of impressionist paintings I'd hung at the front of the room. By afternoon recess, they were all euphoric. Drenched in sunshine and goodwill, they felt no lingering hostilities, knew no divisions or conflicts.

But as April advanced, peaceful days like this one became increasingly rare. I was having more and more trouble controlling my class. Some of the boys began acting out on an almost daily basis. Trips to the principal's office were becoming routine for many of them. As the noise level rose to unacceptable heights, many children were finding it hard to concentrate on their work. Some reported feeling anxious. Looking now at the many handwritten notes my students gave me, I can chart a steady decline in my effectiveness as I failed to find a workable method of discipline and allowed the class to spin out of control. Early in the semester, the notes were hopeful and full of affection. "I love you Mis Hallahan do you love me? Yes or no," wrote one anonymous student. "Dear Mrs. Hallahan," Kevin confided, "I love you. Do you love me. Please say yes." In some of these early notes, the children eagerly looked to me for help or support with their school projects:

> Dear Mrs. Hallahan,
> How are you? I like you very much. I think you are a nice and
> pretty teacher. Matilda and I are going to make a collest of rocks.
>    We have a sandstone—a snow rock—a spong rock—and a
> shale.
> We like to make collest of enything. We want you to help us in our
> collest. Will you Please. I must close for now.
>    Sincerely yours,
>    Ramonia
>    Tirish
>    Jackson

And they were quick to express gratitude for the smallest favor. "Dear Mrs. Hallan," Sharon wrote after I gave her a piece of paper to draw on, "may I have the other blue sheets if you don't need them or want them, please?" After signing her name—"truely yours, Sharon"—she added a postscript: "And I really like the sheet you gave me. This might be a little to write but I do love you."

By the middle of the semester, however, the children's notes to me began to acknowledge the problems I was having controlling the class. "I like these little children," Cecily observed in a long missive, "but they to bad. They doesn't do what the teacher tell them to do but only they want the teacher to do what they do." A troubling ambivalence crept into their expressions of affection and admiration. "We have a nice teacher," Cheryl began warmly, adding, "she is kind and sometime mean sometime we make her mean and sometime she make us mean." In an extended note, Matilda oscillated between complaint and praise: "I do not like this mean class. They are to noisie aren't they? . . . I think you will make a good teacher. We will learn more work if we didn't have so much talking. You are very Pretty Teacher." And Sharon felt compelled to write me to apologize for the behavior of the other students, pledging to do her best to help out and desperately hoping the others will shape up:

> Dear Mrs. Hallahan,
> How are you? Fine I hope. I guess I know how you feel. I'm just writing to tell you that I'm really sorry that the class is making so much noise. But I'm really writing to tell you that I'll do the best I can. I really hope that they will get better.
>> Your friend always
>> Sharon M. Crawford
>> P. S. I hope they will get better.

By mid-April, however, even one of my staunchest allies has had enough:

> Dear Mrs. Halldan,
> I'm tird of being in this room. You told me that you was going to do something about this. But you told me that the first of the week. You have not don anything about it.
>> Ramonia Jackson may move out of this room
>> Sign

---

By early May, I was desperate. Mrs. Coomes and I couldn't agree on anything. Rather than relying on her to help me restore order, I found myself trying to protect my students from her harsh discipline, her prejudices, her stinging criticisms. Mr. Thompson was understandably becoming impatient with me. And parents were beginning to complain. I didn't consider quitting, though, until the day I met with Mr. Thompson and Dr. Martin to discuss the problems I was having. Mr. Thompson laid out his concerns — how the disorder in my classroom interfered with learning, jeopardized safety, fostered bad behavior, and undermined his authority. His concerns, I knew, were all legitimate. Dr. Martin's response took me completely by surprise. Instead of focusing on my failures or addressing my inadequacies, he placed the blame fully on my children and their parents. Turning to Mr. Thompson, he proceeded to lecture him. "These children should have learned how to behave before they were ever sent to school," he declared. "Since they clearly haven't, the only logical solution I can see is to send them back home until they can learn to conduct themselves properly. Whenever they give Mrs. Hallahan trouble," he ordered Mr. Thompson, "I want you to expel them from school. I don't care if you have to expel half the class. These children need to learn they can't act this way in school."

I knew in my gut that Dr. Martin was siding with me solely because I was white. His defense of me had no basis in fact; everything Mr. Thompson was telling him was true. But Dr. Martin's assessment was grounded in racist assumptions so old, so deep, and so unexamined that no evidence Mr. Thompson could lay out before him could possibly carry any weight. For a fleeting moment, I was tempted to accept Dr. Martin's support. His solicitousness was gratifying; his kindness to me flattering. Feeling besieged, I initially appreciated his impulse to protect me, his judgment that I was not to blame. But I was to blame. My classroom was spiraling into chaos, my students were in distress, their parents were voicing their concerns, and my principal was pleading for an intervention. If I accepted Dr. Martin's backing, I would implicitly be acquiescing to the racist assumptions behind it. Indeed, I would be the direct beneficiary of them. I could avoid an official reprimand, keep my job, retain my self-image and my social standing, but at a terrible cost. I would have to live with the knowledge that I mattered more than a roomful of African American children simply because I was white and they were black. I began to think that my students might be better off if I resigned.

I agonized for days before turning in my resignation. I had never failed at anything before, and I hated to think of myself as a quitter. I tried to tell myself that I could hold the class together for the few remaining weeks of the semester. And I worried that turning the class over to yet another teacher so late in the year might be even more disruptive for my students than my sticking it out. Then I learned from Mr. Thompson that Mrs. Stockton, the class's original teacher, was willing to return now that her baby was two months old. She would be able to quickly restore order to my classroom. And my students knew her well, so her return should not be too disruptive. In January, I had looked askance at Mrs. Stockton's teaching methods, sure I could do a better job. The irony was not lost on me that now I viewed her as a kind of savior. I submitted my resignation at the end of the first week in May. Dr. Martin replied immediately. In a warm and supportive letter, he once again took my side, advising me not to feel disheartened by my experience at Morton and encouraging me to pursue a career in teaching. The tone of his letter is kind, gracious, caring. Yet in it, he subtly reiterates his belief that the two of us, as white people, are different from, and superior to, the black children at Morton: "I fully understand how you feel about the type of discipline necessary to control the children at Z. C. Morton," he wrote me, turning my failure as a disciplinarian into a problem caused by African American children. "I, too, object to corporal punishment and have never used it during my years of school work." This from the man who had no compunctions about sending the abusive Mr. Snead to teach at Z. C. Morton.

When I told my students that I would no longer be their teacher, many of them were upset. Timothy — the boy who lived alone in the log cabin with his grandfather — refused at first to believe me. "Are you really not going to be here tomorrow?" he asked. "Not at all? Will you come visit us? Will you come visit us tomorrow?" At the end of the day, as I was saying my good-byes and giving farewell hugs, Matilda told me sadly, "I'll go alone to bed tonight and when I'm all by myself in my room I'll cry and cry." I don't know how they adapted to the return of Mrs. Stockton, or how they understood my leaving them, although I do have one note, pressed into my hand when I returned to the school a few weeks later for its annual teacher-student baseball game, that suggests they found the transition confusing. It was the last note I received from any of my students. Here is what it said:

Dear Mrs. Hallahan
We want you to come back Cheryl, Gloria, Annie Mae, Sharon. When you left they don't talk then Mr. Thompson came in the room. He said who is going to teach us. We said we don't know then Mrs. Perkins came in and said where did you and Mrs. Coomes go to. We said they ran away for what we said we don't know.
P.S. write Back
From Cheryl Purcell

# It Was a Long Time Ago

*It was a long time ago.*
*I have almost forgotten my dream.*
*But it was there then,*
*In front of me,*
*Bright like a sun—*
*My dream.*
  *—from "As I Grew Older" by Langston Hughes*

## Sanco Pansy's Cottage and the Louisa County Public Library, 2001

left Louisa that June, and I didn't return for thirty-one years. In the intervening time, I went to graduate school and became a professor of English. I divorced and remarried (twice), acquired stepchildren, had a daughter, and raised a family. After studying and teaching at a number of universities, I joined the faculty of the University of Iowa and settled in Iowa City. I did not stay in touch with any of my students in Louisa. But whenever I moved, I carried with me a simple cardboard box, the letters LOUISA printed boldly across the top in black magic marker. Sealed inside were the notes, drawings, and mementos my students had given me, samples of their schoolwork and projects, photographs I had taken of them, all my lesson plans, and a journal I had kept that spring. In each new house I occupied—the rustic log cabin in North Carolina; the nineteenth-century farmhouse on a hill in upstate New York; the efficiency apartment near the Museum of Science and Industry in Hyde Park, Chicago; the redwood contemporary in Oklahoma; and the cozy 1920s cottage and the roomy, sunlit house in the woods in Iowa—I stored the box in some out-of-the-way place and forgot it. In all that time I opened it only once, when an African

American colleague at the University of Oklahoma asked me to give a guest lecture about my experience teaching in a segregated school to her psychology class. Occasionally, during a class discussion or at a party, I would tell a story about my experience at Morton Elementary School, but otherwise I boxed and shelved my memories, too.

The Louisa box might have remained sealed and forgotten on the shelf in my Iowa City basement had I not learned, shortly before my fiftieth birthday, that a rare malignant tumor was growing in the salivary gland at the base of my tongue. Up until the moment my otolaryngologist, looking up from the scope she had threaded so delicately through my nose and down my throat, gave me the bad news, I thought I knew exactly what the next chapter of my life would entail. The script was already written: I had just begun an academic book on Renaissance comedy; I was expected to become the next departmental chair; I had courses to teach and graduate and honors students' theses to direct; and I had committed myself to deliver papers, give lectures, read manuscripts, evaluate tenure files, and serve on a range of university committees. But after a twelve-hour surgical procedure in which a tumor the size of a Ping-Pong ball was removed from my tongue, a few days of being unable to speak at all, two weeks recovering in the hospital, six weeks of radiation therapy that burnt the skin of my neck and face and made my mouth painfully sore, and three months of subsisting only on liquids delivered through a stomach tube, I no longer had any idea how my future would unfold. I didn't even know if I had a future.

The story I had to tell about Louisa suddenly seemed more important, more compelling, and more urgent to me than any of my scholarly projects or professional commitments. I'd always assumed I would tell it someday. Now, perhaps in response to the sense of powerlessness I had felt by being, even if temporarily, without a voice, the frustration of being hungry in the midst of abundant food, and the indignity of being perceived by strangers as incompetent or strange, I knew that day had arrived. My motivation was not just personal. As the twentieth century was drawing to a close, many of the issues I had grappled with in 1970 were resurfacing in new forms. A major Harvard University study announced that the nation's public schools were becoming increasingly re-segregated. The federal courts rescinded a number of high-profile, well-established school desegre-

gation plans that had been put in place in the early 1970s. Scholars
began sounding the alarm about an achievement gap between white
and black students. Many were raising provocative questions about
the impact of integration on black achievement. Some even wondered
aloud whether integration had turned out to be a good thing for black
students after all. With all these issues in mind, I retrieved the forgotten box, opened it up, and began to study its contents. And I decided
to write this book.

As I planned my first trip back to Louisa, eager to begin research,
I checked the Internet for places to stay in Louisa County. I was surprised to discover that the Rebel Motel, a modest 1950s-era roadside
motel just east of the town of Louisa, was still in business. It was already a little tawdry in 1970, and I couldn't imagine staying there. But
for all the years that had elapsed, this local motel apparently still had
no competition. Then I discovered that some of the manor homes on
former plantations in Louisa and its adjacent counties had recently
been converted into luxurious country inns. Their polished promotional materials are clearly aimed at a far different clientele than that
of the seedy Rebel Motel. And yet, like the Rebel Motel, these inns
seek to evoke nostalgia for an illustrious, lost past. Many of these
inns offer lodgings in eighteenth- and nineteenth-century structures
where slaves once worked or lived. One inn in Louisa County, for
instance, rents out "Sanco Pansy's Cottage." Featuring a "redwood
bath with double jacuzzi tub" and renting for $495 a night, it is named
after a slave who once worked on this plantation, a man who, according to the inn's Web site, "followed his master throughout the
War between the States and is buried on the property." Invoking the
romantic myth of the Old South and sentimentalizing the relation
between master and slave, inns like this one render invisible the labor that made—and still makes—the life of leisure and privilege on
these plantations possible.

That myth—and what it stands for—still has a powerful hold
on the (white) American imagination, so much so that businesses far
from the geographical South appropriate and commercially exploit it.
Just outside the northwestern Pennsylvania town where I grew up, for
instance, in a county that sent soldiers to fight for the Union army,
an inn named "Tara" invites its customers to recapture "the glori-
ous days of the Old South." There, fourteen miles from the town of

Mercer, where ardent and outspoken abolitionists sheltered runaway slaves on a station of the Underground Railroad, hiding them in a secret compartment and teaching them to read and write, guests can stay in rooms called "Plantation Suite," "Gen. Robert E. Lee's Room," and "Confederate Getaway." There, twenty miles from the shores of Sandy Lake, where escaped slaves from Virginia lived unharmed in a settlement known as Liberia from 1825 until the Fugitive Slave Law of 1850 forced them to flee to Canada, locals flock to eat in restaurants named "Stonewall's Tavern" and "Old South Armory."

Whether in Virginia or less likely places like Pennsylvania, these inns artfully erase the reality of slavery in order to market fantasies about the Old South. Affluent professionals seeking a weekend escape from the pressures of the nation's capital don't, of course, want to think about the "cruelty" of "white slave patrols" who administered "whip lashings" to Louisa County slaves "for leaving the plantation at night" in dependencies like the one they are renting. And families on vacations to celebrate weddings, anniversaries, and birthdays don't want to be reminded of "those lashings of the *heart*" that Henry Box Brown describes as the cruelest consequence of slavery, namely the intense emotional suffering of parents, children, spouses, and siblings forcibly separated from loved ones sold to strange slave masters on faraway plantations. But reading about these inns, I couldn't help wondering how my former students, the descendants of Louisa slaves, felt about tourists being encouraged to visit plantation inns near their homes in order to recapture "a quieter, more sensitive time" and to "contemplate the untimely demise of the Old South." The romantic appeal of the Old South had no hold over me. I wasn't traveling to Virginia to indulge in "a groaning board of Southern favorites prepared from the season's bounty"; I wanted to know if there were still hungry children living just down the road.

I eventually found a place to stay in neighboring Orange County at a more modest bed-and-breakfast whose proprietors were able to convey the beauty and history of their eighteenth-century plantation house without unduly idealizing antebellum life. I flew to Washington, D.C., with my teenaged daughter Susannah, rented a car, and drove South, recognizing along the way familiar towns and landmarks, yet feeling disoriented by the suburban developments, commercial strips, and heavy traffic in places that I remembered as sleepy little towns.

I was relieved when we finally turned onto a less-traveled secondary road leading to our bed-and-breakfast and pleased to find it at the end of a long driveway, sitting gracefully at the crest of a hill, with sweeping views of the countryside.

Eager to see the place where I had lived thirty-years earlier, I persuaded Susannah to take an exploratory drive with me before dinner. My first impression as we crossed the county line into Louisa on a backcountry road was that very little had changed in my thirty-year absence. We passed large swaths of pine forests and smaller acreage planted in oats, wheat, and hay. From time to time, we saw a lone driveway disappearing into a thick woods or a gravel road leading to a tiny settlement of modest, single-story homes and house trailers. Occasionally, a small, unimposing church appeared, standing, deserted, in a clearing, waiting to be filled with worshipers on Sunday morning. As we approached the town of Louisa, we began to see some larger Victorian homes, with gables and wide porches. I recognized the long, white building of the J. S. Purcell Lumber Company, fronting the railroad tracks that parallel the main street through town; the stately red brick courthouse with its white pillars and impressive dome; the tall stone and bronze monument dedicated to the Confederate soldiers of Louisa County; the quaint shops lining the picturesque town square.

But as we drove through the town, I quickly realized how much had changed. There was a newer brick medical center, a nursing home, some government-sponsored housing. And on the eastern edge of the original town, where the Rebel Motel had once stood alone, a sprawling complex of fast food restaurants, grocery stores, chain stores, and asphalt parking lots had invaded former farm fields. Traffic lights had been installed and turning lanes built to control the busy commercial strip. Beyond this strip, there were office buildings, an industrial park, and a renovated airport.

The biggest surprise for me, however, came when I drove west on Route 22 toward the town of Mineral and discovered, on my right, an impressive academic campus housing the county's consolidated high school and middle school, a school administrative building, and a public library. Only the high school—originally the county's all-white high school—had stood on this site in 1970, and the part of it that I recognized had been dwarfed by newer additions. All the other buildings—including a sprawling middle school and a substantial public library—had been built after my departure. Parking the car, I walked with Susannah into the library, an attractive brick building that was almost brand new. I marveled at its spacious rooms, well-stocked shelves, and up-to-date computer stations. As I watched an assortment of children, some African American, some white, doing what children do in libraries—curling up in a comfortable chair to read, spreading out a creative project on a table, listening to a story being read aloud, searching for information on a computer, checking out a stack of books—I was overwhelmed by the memory of the cramped bookmobile, with its pitiful selection of frayed books, that pulled up to Morton Elementary once a week. Feeling a little bit like Rip Van Winkle, I tried to impress upon Susannah how utterly different things had been thirty-one years earlier when the schools were segregated and there were hardly any books available for black children and no public library.

I wondered if the painful process of desegregation that I had witnessed in 1970 had wrought this extraordinary transformation. Perhaps the elimination of the dual school system had freed up money to invest in books and libraries and classrooms, just as the integrationists had predicted. Maybe integration had even broken down the color line, bringing African Americans and whites together through their shared commitment to public education. But my speculations, though not entirely wrong, were highly simplistic. There was, I learned, another reason why a county that had historically resisted investing in public education or providing quality schools for black children had financed these impressive public school and library building projects. In the very year that Louisa County had implemented court-ordered desegregation of the schools—the year I had lived there—the Virginia Power Company had completed its North Anna Nuclear Power Plant in eastern Louisa County, flooding the North Anna River to create Lake Anna and opening it to recreational use. With this nuclear plant and the development spurred by the reservoir came a massive infusion of tax revenues—eleven million dollars in the year 2000 from Virginia Power alone (in a county of only 25,627 residents). This windfall enabled county officials to increase support for public education without raising individual property taxes at all. In fact, the county boasts that its property taxes today are the lowest in the entire state of Virginia.

I thought about the irony of this, for I had adamantly opposed this nuclear power plant. I had objected to the flooding of sensitive wetlands, the destruction of historic buildings, and the displacement of the poor from their homes. And, like many others, I was concerned about the safety of nuclear energy as well as its long-term environmental consequences. The men who had championed this nuclear power project were, to the best of my knowledge, the same men who had fought school desegregation and adamantly opposed raising property tax increases to improve the county schools, even when that meant consigning the county's African American children to shamefully inadequate schools. Now I stood admiring the integrated public library and public school buildings built from the taxes generated by their nuclear power plant.

Over the next couple of days, Susannah and I set out to locate the most promising sites for our research. The County Historical Museum, housed in a little brick building that had formerly been the county jail, was chock full of interesting artifacts and staffed by friendly volunteers. But we were disappointed to discover that its exhibits told only the stories of Louisa's white settlers, planters, and Revolutionary and Confederate soldiers. There was virtually no evidence that African Americans had, from the very first days, been an integral part of the county's history. I bought a book on Louisa County history there, but it, too, was largely silent about the history of the county's black residents, mentioning African Americans only once, in a two-page illustrated discussion of the county's Negro schools. A sizable room in the public library devoted to local history included a wider range of useful materials. Most helpful, though, were the archives of the local newspaper, the *Central Virginian*. Its staff allowed us to work all day in a little room next to the main office, bringing us the large bound volumes of archived newspapers we requested and indulging our desire to hole up there for hours at a time.

I hoped on that trip to find some of my former students, many of whom, I guessed, were still living in the area. I wanted to talk to them about their memories of Morton Elementary, their subsequent experiences in the newly integrated schools, and their present lives. But once I was actually in Louisa, I was surprised at how self-conscious I became, how acutely aware I was of being an outsider, a white person with no ties to the black community. I had no idea how I would be received if I actually did manage to locate some of my former students. Would they even remember me? Might they harbor ill feelings towards me? Might they resent my sudden reappearance or regard my questions as intrusive? And why should they agree to talk to me at all, a middle-aged white woman from Iowa, showing up suddenly with a tape recorder, asking a barrage of questions and claiming to be writing a book about something that happened thirty years ago?

An hour with the local phone book convinced me that finding them was going to be much harder than I had anticipated. If any of my female students were still living in the county, they had, by marrying and taking their husbands' names, disappeared without a trace. But it wasn't much easier to find the names of my male students in the phone book. I didn't know whether most of them had left the area or had unlisted numbers or used only cell phones; perhaps they had no phone at all or lived with relatives. And, though I was sure most of the parents of my students still lived in the area, I couldn't remember any of their first names. Worse still, because the family names of my students and other African Americans in the county had typically derived from a relatively few white planters who had owned their ancestors, virtually everyone I was looking for had a common surname shared by many, many others (black and white) living in the area. I knew I needed to make contact with someone in the black community who could help me, but all my initial attempts — writing an African American member of the school board who had grown up in Louisa, stopping by some of the black churches, searching the phone books — proved unsuccessful.

During that first trip back I did, however, learn a little bit about how my students had fared in the newly integrated schools. In June 1978 the local newspaper ran a front-page story about that year's graduating class at Louisa High School, along with a photograph of the graduates. And there they were, the members of my 1970 fourth-grade class, in caps and gowns. Or at least some of them. I counted sixteen from my class of thirty-eight who were among the one-hundred-and-sixty-six students receiving diplomas from the county high school that year. Six more were among the seventy-eight nongraduating members of the senior class. Sixteen others were missing altogether from the long list. Though a few of the missing might have moved away and graduated elsewhere, it was far more likely that they had simply dropped out of school. All sixteen, I noted, were among the poorest and most disadvantaged children in my class, and as ten-year-olds, all had struggled academically. I live in a midwestern university town where, for decades, more than 90 percent of the students who attended public schools graduated from high school. And thus, despite all I knew about the inadequacy of their early schooling, I was still stunned to learn that only 40 percent of my students had earned a high school degree.

But I was also thrilled to discover, through newspaper stories and the 1978 high school yearbook, just how accomplished some of my students had become. In an integrated high school with a majority white student body, they had established themselves as leaders and talented musicians, actors, artists, debaters, and athletes. Feeling all the pride of a fiercely devoted mother, I took stock of their achievements: two were senior class officers and three others served on the student council (one as its vice president); three were selected for regional choir, two had won district awards in drama, and two were band members; nine had lettered in football, basketball, wrestling, cross country, and/or track, and one had been the manager of the basketball team. Matilda had been elected vice president of her class and vice president of the student council, and she had garnered awards in both music and drama. And then there was James, who had excelled at everything, it seemed, winning district awards in debate and drama, serving as photographer of the yearbook and president of the science club, running cross country, participating in Boys State and the Student Cooperative Association and the Literary Club, and acting in a regional theater production of Steinbeck's *Of Mice and Men*. Named to the honor roll, he was off to Old Dominion University.

James, however, was the only one of my students who appeared to be headed to a four-year college or university, though I later learned that Ramonia also went to college and perhaps others did too, at a later date. According to the newspaper article, James was one of only thirty-five students, black or white, in the entire senior class bound for a four-year college. The article describes the plans of the other members of the graduating class without giving their names. Eighteen planned to attend two-year colleges, five more were going to technical schools, fourteen were joining the armed forces, two had secured positions in business, and two more in the department of highways.

The rest were taking jobs as secretaries, sales clerks, cooks, waitresses, auto mechanics, beauticians, medical aides, surveyors, truck drivers, service station attendants, and upholsterers. The county's public schools, it appeared, had not encouraged them to set their sights on higher education or offered the kind of curriculum that prepared very many of them for college.

I collected everything I could find about my former students, but I wasn't able to trace any of them until, on a later trip back, I stumbled across a list of all the staff members who had worked at Morton Elementary School when I had taught there in 1970. As I scanned it, I zeroed in on one name, "Lillian Jackson, teacher's aide." She almost surely was Ramonia's mother. I consulted the local phone book and found a current listing for a woman with that name. Could this be the same Mrs. Jackson who had been so friendly and helpful to me thirty-some years earlier? If she were, I had a hunch she would be willing to talk to me, and I decided to try to contact her. After asking for directions at the local post office, I drove to her house in the country. Greeting me at the door, she was understandably wary and a little flustered when I identified myself and asked her if she was Ramonia's mother. But Mrs. Jackson remembered me and listened politely as I explained my project. Soon she was telling me about Ramonia and filling me in on what she knew about her classmates. She helpfully gave me Ramonia's address, Sharon's married name, and the first names of some of my students' parents. I now had some valuable clues, enough to lead me to some of the students I most wanted to find.

## When I Am Big Enough I Want You to Come See Me

"One day when I am big enough I want you to come see me." Matilda was ten when she wrote me this note on March 24, 1970. Thirty-four years later, in September 2004, I went to see Matilda. Sitting at a little table in the Starbucks where she had suggested we meet, I watched for her out the large storefront window. The coffee shop was part of a new suburban shopping complex in Pantops, just east of Charlottesville. Its parking lot and sidewalks were bustling with people on their way home from work, most of them headed to Giant

Foods to grab something for dinner. I scanned their faces, wondering whether I would recognize Matilda, a person I hadn't seen for more than three decades. Although I was prepared to meet a forty-four-year-old woman, I was looking for the pretty ten-year-old girl I'd preserved in my memory.

I had arrived in Charlottesville two days earlier, hoping to interview a number of my former students during my week's stay. But my plans were quickly unraveling. Although I had written to Reginald before my trip, I hadn't been able to connect with him either before or after my arrival in Virginia. No one answered the phone at his home, though I made repeated calls. I had succeeded in reaching Sharon by phone a few months earlier—just hearing her warm, assured voice had elated me—and she had graciously agreed to see me when I next visited. But when I tried to contact her to set up an interview, I got only her answering machine, no matter what time of the day I called. She never returned my messages. I learned later that she had been ill and was nearly blind. And Ramonia, who had indicated she was interested in talking to me, was suddenly skittish when I tried to arrange a meeting. She confided in a letter that she didn't believe she had anything helpful to tell me, though she was pleased that I remembered her so fondly and was curious to know why. We corresponded by e-mail after I arrived in Virginia, but though she continued to keep open the possibility of a meeting, she couldn't seem to bring herself to commit to an actual time and place. Later she wrote me a detailed letter, telling me that she had received her B.A. from Virginia Commonwealth University, a postgraduate certificate in information systems, and an M.S. degree in logistic management from the Florida Institute of Technology.

Matilda, however, had not just been willing to talk; she had immediately entered into the spirit of the project. "It has been such a long time," she wrote me when I first contacted her, "and the strange thing is I didn't even know your first name! All I could remember is Mrs. Hallahan and I remember you wearing a cute creme colored dress with brown tights and brown clogs. Your hair was long and pulled back. Funny how some things just seem to stick out in your mind—things that you think are not important in your memories." I recognized in her response the instincts of a fellow memoirist. If the others saw my request to talk as intrusive or intimidating, Matilda seemed to approach it as an opportunity, a chance to unearth buried memories and examine her past.

I recognized her as soon as I saw her making her way towards Starbucks. The same easy confidence, the same pretty round face, the same spontaneous smile. When I met her at the door, we hugged like old friends. Matilda laughed when I showed her the note she had written me so many years ago, a black fourth-grader's hopeful, if pragmatic, invitation to her white teacher. But she also made it clear that she felt, by seeking her out after so many years, I had in fact honored her childhood request. She welcomed my questions and answered them freely, her voice—low, slightly husky—radiating warmth.

Matilda—or Tillie, as she is now called—explained that, after graduating from high school, she had fought with her parents, who objected to her plans to enroll at a music school—she played the clarinet—and instead wanted her to take business and secretarial classes at the local community college. "I wanted to go to that music school like you wouldn't believe," she confided, the memory of her adolescent aspiration still very much alive. Denied her dream, she had rebelled, announcing that if she couldn't go to music school, she wouldn't go to any school at all. And so she had taken a job at the new nuclear power plant directly out of high school. For the past twenty-five years, she has worked at the local jail in Charlottesville, where she currently holds the senior position in human resources and reports directly to the superintendent. Her college-educated husband, who taught in the public schools for eight years, is the deputy superintendent of the same jail. They have two school-aged daughters. "I was really excited to have the chance to talk to you," she told me. "But my husband wasn't convinced I should meet with you. He wanted to know why I was so sure I could trust you. We both work at the jail, you know, and he kept reminding me that there are all kinds of strange people out there." She laughed. "I just told him, if my time has come, so be it."

I wanted to know what she remembered about her years at Z. C. Morton Elementary School, and I was especially interested in learning how, as a child, she had viewed being segregated from the county's white schoolchildren. She pointed out that young children tend to accept the status quo without questioning it. "As a child," she told me, "you don't even think about" the fact that you're required to attend a segregated school. "You just do it." As an adult, she admitted, she had virtually forgotten that Morton was a Negro school. In fact, she told me that when my research assistant had read her the names of her former fourth-grade classmates over the phone, hoping to find out what she knew about their whereabouts, she recalled thinking to herself, "how odd; every one of them is black." Shrugging her shoulders, she explained, "I've *never* thought about the fact that all of us children at Morton were black. Never thought about it." After more than thirty years of integration, she could hardly believe she'd attended a segregated school.

When prompted, however, Matilda did remember that her fifth-grade year at the newly integrated Louisa Elementary School had been trying. Her white teacher, she believed, had been unnecessarily severe, and she sensed at the time that this teacher was harder on the black students than the whites. "She was so mean. I remember her hitting me with a ruler, and I didn't think I deserved that at all. And the other kids she hit were black, too." She recalled, too, that she was acutely aware of how different things seemed at the newly integrated school. I asked her whether the white children had accepted her. She had no memory of any overt acts of hostility, but one girl's comment about the white children's attitudes towards black children had stuck with her. She had befriended a white student named Debbie Burch, who had recently moved from Texas and was thus new to the school, too. Debbie's father was in the military, and she had traveled widely. Once, Debbie said to her—and here, Matilda did a pitch perfect imitation of a Texas drawl, Debbie's words indelibly fixed in her memory—"In Texas we do things differently than you'all do here." When Matilda asked her what she meant, Debbie elaborated. "White people there are a whole lot friendlier to blacks than they are here." Coming as it did from an outsider, this single, offhand observation had given Matilda a startling new insight into racial relations in her own hometown. She also remembered thinking to herself, "Debbie is a white friend. She's a good friend, and she's white." And then, after only a few months, Debbie moved away.

If the initial transition to an integrated school was difficult, Matilda quickly adapted. She credited this to her parents, who taught her that change was part of life and encouraged her to learn how to try new things. Matilda stayed close to her best friends at Morton—Cecily, Sharon, Ramonia, and a girl named Darla who had not been in my class — but by the time she was in high school, she had many white friends, too. "Especially the guys," she laughed, noting playfully that she "was well endowed" and hinting that the white boys had found her attractive. An integrationist at heart, she acknowledged that it was easy for her to "fit in": "I just made it work." She expressed no nostalgia for Morton at all. "I feel very fortunate to have been part of integration. The fact that we ended up getting books, a library, and experience interacting with whites really helped prepare us for the larger world."

I wondered how typical Matilda's experience had been. She had, I recalled, been a very self-assured and sociable child and a natural classroom leader. I could easily imagine her crossing the color line to befriend white children and could envision them being drawn to her. Brought up in a family she described as "very spiritual," she had, she told me, always been taught "to see people as people," an ethical principle that must have served her well during the period of school desegregation, when racial fears were rampant. In addition, Matilda was light skinned, with features that conformed to white ideals of beauty, attributes that surely, if unfairly, worked to her advantage in the adolescent culture of a newly integrated high school. Then, too, she may well have been predisposed to embrace integration because of the experiences of her own family. "My grandmother's father," she told me, "had Indian and white blood, and he passed for a while as a white man, moving back to the area only when he was dying. I remember his pale skin and beautiful, curly black hair," adding "my grandmother looked white." Surely, I speculated, some of my other students — those perhaps who were less gifted, or more bashful, or darker skinned, or more isolated — found the transition to the integrated school more traumatic than Matilda.

Matilda herself had personal knowledge that school desegregation was traumatic for some African American students. Her older sister had suffered terribly when she was transferred from the black high school to the newly integrated white high school in her final high school year, even though she shared with Matilda the same spiritual values, parental guidance, leadership potential, light skin, and great-grandfather who passed for white. Matilda attributed their radically different responses to school integration to the difference in their ages. While she was only ten, her sister was seventeen when her school was integrated. "By the time you're seventeen," Matilda observed, "you think your way of doing things is the right way. By then, the whites had their own way of doing things at their high school, and the blacks had theirs, and no one wanted to change. But when you're a ten-year-old kid, you're much more open to new ways of doing things and it's a lot easier to blend in." Laughingly, Matilda then confided to me, "When my older sister found out you were going to interview me, she objected, insisting that *she* was the one you should talk to, because she 'caught hell' when the high schools were integrated."

I jumped at the chance to talk to Mary, who was eight years older than Matilda—and just four years younger than me. She agreed to meet me a few days later, at the same Starbucks where I had talked to her younger sister. More reserved than Matilda, with a composed and serious demeanor, Mary seemed a little uncomfortable talking to me at first and somewhat guarded. The two of us, after all, had no shared memories, no emotional bonds from a common past, and there wasn't the easy rapport between us that I had felt with Matilda. Nevertheless, she had a story to tell, and she wanted me to hear it.

In contrast to Matilda, who spent only four years in a segregated school, Mary spent only one year in an integrated school. She was a senior in the fall of 1969 when the county desegregated its two high schools, sending all the black students to the formerly all-white Louisa County High School. Before that, she had attended a small Negro elementary school—Ferncliff—in rural Louisa County for seven years, and the consolidated Negro High School—A. G. Richardson High—from grade 8 through grade 11. After her high school graduation, she enrolled in an all-black business school in Richmond, and she has worked at Albemarle County's Social Services for most of her adult life. There, she helped initiate diversity training and supported efforts to recruit and hire more minority social workers. Although she has some white friends, most whites, she confided, don't want to talk about racial issues, a reluctance that sometimes frustrates her.

Mary's memories of the Negro high school are almost entirely positive, and she looks back at her segregated school with nostalgia. All of the teachers at that school were black, and she recalls that they gave their students lots of attention, nurturing, encouraging, and supporting them in their studies. At Richardson she was active in extracurricular activities, fully involved in the school's social life, and a serious student. But all that changed when she and her classmates were sent to the formerly white Louisa High School at the beginning of their senior year. There, she felt as if she had been dropped into an alien culture without any guide or instruction. All the white kids knew the language and understood the customs, while she and her black classmates from Richardson were left to flounder, unwelcome outsiders unable to crack the white school's secret codes. She wistfully observed, too, that there was a cultural divide between her classmates from Richardson and the few, select black students who had been attending the white high schools for a couple of years under the county's "freedom of choice" program. Those students were as fluent in the language and customs of Louisa High School as the white students, and as comfortable there, a fact that unsettled and riled her. Perhaps their successful integration felt to her like a betrayal; perhaps it served as a rebuke to her, invalidating her own sense of alienation.

All of Mary's teachers that year were white. To her, they seemed aloof and cold. She felt they were uninterested in her welfare and indifferent to her academic efforts. None of them gave her the close, personal attention she was accustomed to at Richardson. Because of a scheduling glitch, she was not admitted into the shorthand class she had registered for until a week or so into the semester. But her teacher made no effort to help her catch up. She felt she was on her own and found herself struggling to understand the work she had missed. She resented what she saw as an entirely new and unfair set of expectations, suddenly imposed on her in her very last year of high school. At Richardson she had been told she had completed all the required math courses, but at Louisa High she discovered she needed another math course to graduate and was forced to enroll in business math, a subject she detested. She couldn't understand her English teacher's methodology and hated his class. Her World History teacher, she allowed, was nice to her, even excusing her from completing some of the assignments. She recalls having to work very hard, all the time, just to get by.

Socially, Mary and her friends from Richardson stuck together and did not mix with the white students. She did not participate in any extracurricular activities that year. Deeply alienated from the newly integrated high school, she felt as if she had been "robbed" of her senior year. At a time when she should have been at the top of the pecking order and a class leader, she found herself displaced by whites and forced to accept their way of doing things. In a year when she had expected to participate in the time-honored traditions of Richardson High School, she discovered, to her horror, that those traditions had been cavalierly discarded, superceded by the traditions of the white school to which she had been exiled. Rather than breaking down the color line, the year Mary spent at the integrated high school had, for her, only fortified it. She never felt she belonged or was welcome at the former white school, and her experience there intensified her attachment to the black community and her estrangement from whites. Her deep sense of loss has not dissipated over the years. Like most of her black classmates, she doesn't attend high school reunions. She got rid of her class ring. She has never considered Louisa High School "her" high school. And she remains bitter about the way she was treated that year, viewing Louisa's white elite today as perpetuating the same sense of superiority she encountered thirty-four years ago. Whites in the county, she told me, are still grabbing land, holding onto power, and resisting change.

That painful year at Louisa High School made Mary skeptical about whether whites can teach black students as fairly and effectively as African American teachers. Although she has no children of her own, many of her black friends, she told me, are deeply concerned that white teachers and school administrators are too quick to stereotype their children, and especially their sons, unjustly assuming they will cause problems, disciplining them too harshly, and even assigning them to special education classes for children with behavioral problems. Mary's year at Louisa High also gave her an interesting perspective on my own experience at Morton. When I told her I was the first white teacher my students had ever had, her response was quick and pointed. "They probably resented you," she concluded. This possibility had never occurred to me, and I didn't want to believe what was to her so self-evident. Breaking out of my interview mode, I assured her, somewhat defensively, that I was certain my students hadn't resented me. I wanted her to see how they had reached out to me and confided in me and in all kinds of ways tried to forge connections with me. Days later, however, as I drove alone through a remote and beautiful part of Louisa's countryside, Mary's words hit me with their full force. "They probably resented you." Of course, I thought, remembering Wendell's defiant assertion: "No white woman is going to tell me what to do," Derrick's conviction that I kept him from seeing Miss Broderick because he was black, Ervin's accusation that I cared only about my "brother," the white boy Samuel. Why hadn't I been able to see this?

I asked Mary how she thought her eleven years of segregated schooling had shaped her. Because she had experienced school desegregation as a traumatic loss and remembered Richardson High with such fondness, I expected her to counter the argument that racially segregated schools are inherently harmful to black children. Inviting her to reflect on that argument, I noted that, in the *Brown v. Board of Education* decision, the court had asserted that "segregation of white and colored children in public schools has a detrimental effect upon colored children. . . . It generates a feeling of inferiority as to their status in the community that may affect their hearts and minds in a way unlikely ever to be undone." When I read her these words, she did not take issue with them as I had anticipated. Instead, she teared up. Visibly moved, she explained how profoundly racial segregation of the county schools had affected her. "Growing up," she told me, her hurt and anger barely contained, "I always felt that I had to perform much, much better than white people, just to prove myself." She paused, and then added sadly, "And, you know, I've never really stopped feeling that way."

Only eight years apart, Mary and Matilda are both technically "baby boomers." But they find themselves on opposite sides of a generational divide, a divide created when the public schools were desegregated. Mary, who attended segregated schools from 1958 to 1969 and an integrated one in 1969–1970, proudly identifies with the community, traditions, and values of the Negro schools even as she feels strongly that de jure segregation had a lasting, negative impact on her. Her younger sister Matilda, who attended a segregated school from 1966 to 1970 and integrated schools from 1970 to 1978, however, has almost no recollection that her elementary school was ever segregated. Educated primarily in integrated schools, where she thrived, she feels no nostalgia for the old Negro schools and does not seem the least bit burdened, as Mary is, by the stigma of having once been legally required to attend racially segregated schools.

Because of segregation, Mary's school experience was closer to her mother's than her younger sister's. Even though the five-room Ferncliff Elementary School was almost new when she enrolled there in 1958, and therefore in better condition than virtually all the other Negro elementary schools at the time, its PTA complained to the Louisa County School Board that very year that it had "inadequate heat" and "no indoor toilets," no cafeteria, and no auditorium. The one-room school at nearby Bell's Crossing that her mother Josephine had attended from 1940 to 1947 was even more primitive. It had no running water or electricity, no indoor toilets, and just a wood stove for heating, Mrs. Timberlake told me in a phone interview. There was only one teacher for all seven grades.

In those years, Matilda and Mary's mother explained, the county did not provide buses for African American children, even though it funded buses for white children, and she had to walk three miles each way to school every day. She recalled how, on her walk to school, she and the other black children had to pass the white elementary school, and the white children used to come out of the building and harass them, calling them names and humiliating them. Since the county's only black high school was too far away for most of its students to reach on foot, their parents had to hire a private bus to get them to the high school. By the time her daughter Mary began school, the county was providing buses for its African American students. However, as late as 1960, I knew from my research, black parents were pleading with the school board to replace the "unsafe buses" that were being used to transport their children. And in 1961 they complained about the use of "a 1946 bus that leaks and breaks down regularly" to take black children to school.

The Negro high school that Mary attended from eighth through eleventh grade, A. G. Richardson High School, was built shortly after her mother had graduated from the school it replaced, Louisa Training School. Richardson's physical plant, though far more modest than the county's white high school, was a marked improvement over Louisa Training, which had comprised a number of separate, aging frame buildings. Mrs. Timberlake recalled getting wet and cold while changing classes in bad weather and eating at a cramped cafeteria next to the coal bin. What was most insulting to her, however, was the fact that the county mandated that she and her other African American classmates use different textbooks and follow a different curriculum than their white peers at Louisa High School. This policy guaranteed that, even though they graduated from the only public high school available to them, Louisa's African American students did not have a certified degree because they hadn't been allowed to follow the state's standard curriculum, the one used at Louisa High. In addition, while the county's white students were required to complete twelve years of schooling to earn their degrees, schooling for black students ended after eleventh grade, again putting them at a disadvantage. By the time Mary was in high school, a twelfth grade had been added, but the Negro school still did not offer a number of courses—Latin I and II, Advanced Math, Journalism and Speech, Art, Shorthand I and II, Horticulture—that were available at the white high school. Instead, it offered basic and remedial courses not in the curriculum at the white high school—General Mechanics, General Music, Record Keeping, Remedial Reading.

Matilda, however, spent only a year at Ferncliff Elementary, and then three more years at the segregated but much larger Morton Elementary before completing her education in integrated schools. Unlike her mother and sister, she seems to have few memories of the stark inequalities that plagued the dual school system when she entered school, and it appears she harbors little of the resentment towards the unfairness of the old system that understandably still rankles Mary and her mother. She does not appear to struggle with any "feeling of inferiority as to [her] status in the community" or to feel that opportunities were denied her because of her race. When I explained the title of my book to her, however, she identified with it instantly. "Dream Not of Other Worlds," she repeated. "I guess that's what my parents told me when they refused to allow me to attend music school. They just couldn't imagine that someone like me, who had spent her whole life in Louisa County, could find a place for herself as a professional in the music world."

When I asked her about her own daughters' experiences at their integrated elementary and middle schools in Fluvanna County, a rural county adjacent to Louisa, she reported that both children are well-adjusted and thriving. Her elder daughter plays soccer and is a cheerleader; her younger daughter participates in soccer, band, and choir. Matilda did voice some frustration that each is the only African American on her soccer team. When I asked whether her children's schools teach black history and literature, she told me that her younger daughter is always doing reports on black authors, and she rattled off the subjects of recent ones: Harriet Tubman, Madame C. J. Walker, Nellie Lee Love.

But she did tell me that her older daughter initially had problems in school, problems that began when, as a first grader, she enrolled in a small, rural elementary school—in the same building where Matilda had participated in one of the early Head Start programs—after her family moved from Charlottesville to rural Fluvanna County. Until then, her daughter had thrived in an integrated pre-school and an integrated Christian school in Charlottesville. "There aren't many black people who live near the lake, where our house is located, and this school was predominantly white. I felt the teachers there, who were all white, were prejudiced," Matilda explained, almost apologetically. "Every day, it seemed, they would send home a letter, saying there was a problem with my daughter." One time, a child kicked Matilda's daughter in the shins and used a racial epithet against her; the offending child was not punished. Another time, when her daughter's finger was accidently crushed in a bathroom door and she screamed in pain, her teachers yelled at her. When her daughter began having trouble with her schoolwork, Matilda urged the teachers to have her daughter tested, but they refused. "I don't know if it was because she was black, or because they didn't want to deal with the problem," she told me, her indignation at the teachers' inattention something I, as a mother, completely understood. I listened in admiration as she described how she had effectively intervened. "I took things into my own hands and went to the university and had her tested myself. Once I took them the documents and showed them that she had been diagnosed with ADD [attention deficit disorder], they finally began to address the problem." Still, she couldn't help wondering if her daughter had been "somewhat traumatized by being one of the only blacks in the school and by the way the white teachers and children treated her." Things improved markedly when that particular school was closed and her daughter was sent to a larger, consolidated school, one that had a more enlightened pedagogy and many more African American students.

Toward the end of my interview with Matilda, I asked her what she knew about her classmates at Morton. She told me that Derrick —the boy who had pounded his fist on the wall and protested that he had problems, too—was dead. So was quiet, petite Vernice, a teenaged victim of carbon monoxide poisoning that occurred when she and her boyfriend parked on a lover's lane. Matilda didn't remember Samuel, the white foster child, or Victor, the boy who missed his bus. She didn't know what had happened to William, the hungry boy who had wolfed down his lunch before school started, or Emmeline, the fastidious girl who was so appalled at the condition of her white neighbor's house. And she had no idea what became of Marcus, the troubled foster child from Alexandria who had terrorized the class. But she knew that Cecily, the feisty little girl who had given me the stolen lilacs, was — true to her ambition and drive — living in California. Matilda confirmed that Sharon, the thoughtful child who had stood up to the white bully at the gumball machine, was married and living in Louisa County. She also told me that Ramonia's father had made it home from Vietnam, but that he and Ramonia's younger sister had both died recently. Reginald, the boy who was scolded for saying he saw the moon in the daytime, was married and living with his family in Louisa County. And his good friend James — the talented boy who always had his head buried in a book and had made the instructive collage about Martin Luther King and was the only child in my class to go on to college — became a highly successful commercial photographer in Atlanta. His pictures, Matilda told me proudly, had appeared in major venues like the *National Geographic*, a fact I later confirmed when I discovered James's professional Web site. Gazing on the powerful photographs posted there, taking note of their astounding range and distinctive style, I tried to imagine how the ten-year-old country boy I had known had become a sophisticated urban photographer whose work took him to some of the world's most exotic and interesting places. But then I recalled that James had always been a dreamer.

Matilda and I talked energetically for more than an hour and a half. We had met late in the afternoon, after she had finished a full day's work and done some errands, and she must have been exhausted. It was dark by the time we were wrapping up our discussion.

"Your husband is going to think I've kidnapped you," I joked.

"It's really interesting how you made me take a look at my past," she told me, refusing to accept my apologies for keeping her so long. "Most white people around here aren't comfortable talking about issues of race with African Americans, so I've found our talk very useful, very helpful."

By the end of our conversation, I had abandoned any pretense that I was still conducting a formal interview. I found myself telling her more and more about what I had discovered in my research, filling her in on bits of local history she hadn't known, telling anecdotes about her and her classmates. We worked together to try to reconstruct memories of particular classroom incidents, she offering glimpses from the child's perspective, me from the adult's. She began peppering me with questions: "What did you do after you left us?" "What possessed you to write this book?" "Will you contact me when the book comes out?" As we parted, she assured me that my project had "certainly made a difference to me." After I had returned to Iowa City, I received the following e-mail from her in response to a thank-you note I had written her:

> It was really good connecting with you last week. It was very heart-warming to see that I had written a letter to you asking you to come see me when I was older and you did! . . . My sister enjoyed talking to you and so did my mom. You have just enlightened us so much on things that we saw but took for granted because "that is the way it is" and you saw that some of it was totally wrong. God Bless you for what you are trying to do by educating people on "how it really was."

## Mr. Thompson's Story

Matilda vividly recalled her terror during the incident when Marcus threatened to "cut out my stomach," but she couldn't remember what had set Marcus off or how Mr. Thompson had handled the crisis. "I remember something happened outside, but I can't recall why Marcus was so angry at me. I was really nervous after he threatened me, and I just flipped out. I remember my hands — I couldn't control them — and my body felt like pins and needles. They took me out of the room and I curled up in a ball and they gave me nerve medication, which I had to take for a week or so. My mother was very upset at the way the whole thing was handled." I apologized for failing to protect her from Marcus, pointing out that if I had been a more effective disciplinarian, I could have kept him from bullying her. Then I told her what I remembered about the incident, filling her in on what I understood had led to the playground threat and telling her how angry Mr. Thompson had been at her. Later in the interview, she returned to this traumatic event. "Now that we've been talking," she told me, "I'm remembering more and more about the incident with Marcus. I can actually see Mr. Thompson standing over me. He was so big and menacing." She seemed to be recovering a long-buried memory, and with it accessing the fear she had felt as a vulnerable ten-year-old child. I worried, however, that by telling her my version of the story, I had planted the image of an angry Mr. Thompson in her mind.

The very next day I learned that Mr. Thompson was retired and still living in Louisa County. I wondered if he would be willing to talk with me. I left a message on his answering machine, asking him to call me, and within seconds, my cell phone rang. It was Mr. Thompson. He was eager to talk. I arranged to meet him on Monday morning at the public library. Mr. Thompson pulled into the parking lot shortly after I did, and got out of his car. He'd aged, of course, but he was every bit as tall and imposing as I remembered him, so I was amused when, looking me over, he said, with some surprise, "You're not as short as I remembered." Perhaps my age, or my PhD, lent some gravitas to my 5-foot 4-inch frame, obscuring a little the twelve-inch difference in our heights. We then discovered that the library was not open on Monday mornings. Dismayed, I asked him if he knew of a suitable place where we could talk. At first he deferred to me, telling me he'd go anywhere I suggested. "You're the boss," he said. But when I pointed out that he knew the area much better than I, his demeanor changed completely.

"How about going to my church?" he suggested brightly. "It's not too far away, and there's a nice, quiet meeting room we can use there. The church is closed today, but I have a set of keys."

"Perfect," I said. Since his church was in the direction I would be headed after our interview, I followed him in my rental car, thinking as he led me deep into the countryside, how implausible this scenario—a black man and a white woman meeting alone at an isolated, African American church in rural Virginia to talk about racial issues—would have been thirty-four years earlier.

Mr. Thompson led me into a large room and flipped on the fluorescent lights. He joked about having to use a cane; I explained that I'd had oral surgery and radiation that made my speech sound a little strange. We sat down at a long cafeteria table, two grey-haired people who hadn't seen each other since he had been my supervisor when we were both relatively young. I set up my tape recorder. When I asked him about his early life, he was quick to respond, details and stories about his boyhood spilling out. Not only was he a Louisa County native, he was, he told me proudly, living today on the very same property where he had been born. When he was growing up, he recalled, all the adults took responsibility for raising him and the other children in their small, black community. "I had to answer to all of them," he laughed. But, he confided, mocking himself ever so slightly, "I didn't get into very much trouble. I was one of those goody, goody boys." He'd attended a two-room Negro elementary school in the town of Mineral from grades 1 through 7, and then he'd gone to the old Louisa Training School for grades 8 and 9. "It was called a training school," he explained sarcastically, "because we blacks were to be trained, not educated."

Like Matilda's mother, who was a few years older than he, he remembers having to walk to school because there was no bus for black children. "The school buses for the white kids used to pass right by us as we trudged along with our books," he recalled. He completed grades 10 and 11 at the brand new A. G. Richardson High School, which still didn't offer a twelfth year of schooling while he was there. At that time, the county's black and white high schools, he noted, used different grading systems. "You could pass with a lower grade if you were black," he told me, indicating just how condescending and insulting he had found this to be when he was young. He remembers feeling, too, that "we blacks had to do twice as much as the white students to get any recognition as students."

When he graduated from high school he had, he felt, only a few options. "Either I could become a barber or a tailor, or I could go to college and become a teacher." He chose to go into education and enrolled at Virginia Union, a black college in Richmond, commuting at first by train (his father worked for the railroad, which qualified him for a free pass) and then rooming in the house of an elderly black woman in Richmond during the week. In the summers he worked in Atlantic City to earn his tuition. Mr. Thompson told me that he had initially planned to be a high school history teacher, but the language requirement stymied him. He had had only the most rudimentary French at Richardson and couldn't keep up in his college French class. So he decided to go into elementary education instead. Shortly after graduating from college, in the fall of 1959, he began teaching seventh grade at the Negro elementary school housed in the old Louisa Training School. The next year he moved to the brand new school that replaced it (the building where I would teach ten years later) and was soon named a teaching principal, eventually becoming a full-time principal.

Mr. Thompson was animated and talkative as he reminisced about his early years in Louisa. Though he was well aware of the injustices of segregation, he also expressed nostalgia for a time when African American teachers were elevated to a special status in the black community and treated with such deference and respect that "if your parents heard you were punished at school, they'd punish you again as soon as you got home." I pressed him about the challenges he must have faced as a black administrator at a time when virtually all the power was in the hands of whites. But he was uncomfortable with my efforts to get him to analyze the racial politics of that period and resisted the narrative I wanted to impose. He viewed himself as someone who "got along" with his white supervisors, even though he assured me "I wasn't the type of person to bow and scrape." Although he admitted he "had some problems" with one white administrator, he liked others and felt he could work with them. I asked him if he and the teachers at Morton had any say in choosing the textbooks they used. He explained that they were, in fact, sent copies of textbooks that were being considered for adoption and invited to make recommendations, but that the books were chosen by majority vote, so "the other side" always got its preference.

In response to my question of whether he had any say in who was hired at Morton, he assured me that he was routinely consulted. When I pointed out to him that I was hired without ever meeting him, let alone being interviewed by him, he became a little defensive. Revealing some ambivalence towards Dr. Martin, the white superintendent at the time of my hiring, he nevertheless defended him, telling me that Martin "got better at consulting with me as time went on." I refrained from reminding him that Dr. Martin had suffered a stroke and resigned ten months after hiring me. But then he recalled an anecdote that countered his own position. He had a vivid memory, he told me, of attending a summer wedding while he was Morton's principal. "I was reading the wedding program before the ceremony began and was stunned to discover that the bride had taken a position at Morton Elementary. I was completely in the dark about that, and I was furious that nobody had informed me about this hire."

I was eager to hear about his experience when the schools were desegregated. But he remembered almost nothing about the battle over desegregation, explaining that he had not been active in that struggle. When the elementary schools were finally integrated in the fall of 1970, Morton became a school for grades 5 through 7, and he stayed on as its principal. He remembers encountering some racial hostility from white parents and students. During a conference with a white parent whose son had repeatedly defied Mr. Thompson's request that he take off his hat while in the school building, the father refused to believe that his son had misbehaved.

"My boy doesn't lie," the man asserted, stone-faced, after Mr. Thompson explained the problems his son was causing.

"Well," Mr. Thompson told him, ending the conference, "that must make me the liar and therefore there is nothing more to say."

Another time a white girl was sent to him for using the word "nigger." "I confronted her," he recalled. "I told her, I didn't know what a nigger was and could she please describe one to me. And then I said to her, 'The next time you see a nigger, I want you to come and tell me, so I can find out what one is.' She got very upset and cried, and I don't think she ever used that word again."

Mr. Thompson was quick to point out, however, that there were prejudices on both sides. He told me about the time a white teacher reported to him after the school year that some black students had been harassing a white student throughout the school year. "I was very upset that he hadn't told me earlier, so I could have disciplined those boys." He also recalled that black parents had vehemently opposed the appointment of a white male teacher who had been sent to Morton. Since this incident had probably occurred before desegregation, I wondered if the white man in question might have been Mr. Snead, the other fourth-grade teacher and the only white male teacher at Morton when I was there, the one that, Mrs. Stockton had told me, had in a previous job broken the arm of a child. But to my dismay, Mr. Thompson had no memory of any such abuse or of the militaristic tactics of the white man whom I had watched march his terrorized students around the playground. Nor could he verify my version of why Mrs. Stockton's class had so many more boys than Mr. Snead's. If he and I were recalling the same man, he had turned the man's story into one about black parents' prejudices against white teachers, while I had used it to illustrate the indifference of white educators to the welfare of African American students.

I was surprised, too, when Mr. Thompson denied that any black administrators or teachers had been demoted because of the desegregation of the schools. I remembered my husband telling me how the former black principal of A. G. Richardson had clearly seen his new assignment—I can't remember now whether he was made the principal or the assistant principal of the newly integrated junior high where Bill worked—as a demotion, one that assured the newly integrated high school would be run by a white principal. And I knew that throughout the South, many black administrators and teachers suffered similar fates when the public schools were finally integrated. Mr. Thompson acknowledged that Richardson's principal had indeed been assigned to a lower-status job. But he pointed out that he himself hadn't been demoted. "I continued as Morton's principal after the school was integrated," he told me proudly. I asked him how long he had served as principal. "After a couple of years," he explained, "I was appointed to be the eighth-grade Assistant Principal. Later, I was moved to the school board office where I became a Visiting Teacher, visiting the homes of truants and problem kids." He paused, and then, wincing, said quietly, "I guess you could call that a demotion."

Mr. Thompson looms large in my memory of Morton Elementary. But as I sat and talked with him that day, I realized that he had only the vaguest memories of me and my classroom. A funny story about one of my students. My miniskirts. The fact that I had trouble controlling my class. The thirty-eight Morton students whose faces and stories are seared in my memory are just a few of the thousands of Louisa students he has worked with over his forty-odd years in the county's schools, and he can recall only a few of them. The others are a blur to him, easily confused with their sisters, cousins, nephews, even their own children, or not recollected at all. For him, the tumultuous semester I spent in Louisa is indistinguishable from many others of that period—one of nearly seventy he has spent in Louisa County—and therefore impossible for him to recall in any detail. I was glad to see him again, glad to sit with him at the table in the social hall of his church and be reminded of how good-natured, gregarious, and unjudgmental he can be, how nonmenacing. But, I came to see, he was deeply enmeshed in the ongoing life of a county I had made the object of analysis. He had learned not to ask the very questions I most wanted to raise. And who was I to criticize him for making his peace with his community and living happily on the property where he was born?

## Thomas Jefferson Elementary School, 2004

I drove out to the old Z. C. Morton Elementary School on a warm, late September day in 2004. It was still in use, but it had been joined with the adjacent building where Bill once taught, originally the Negro high school, and the combined buildings had been extensively renovated. It had also been renamed. No longer bearing the name of the African American educator, Zelda Carter Morton, it was now known as Thomas Jefferson Elementary School. I had first discovered this name change on the school's Web site, which gives no clue that the school was ever a segregated, Negro elementary school or had ever been called Z. C. Morton. Underneath a banner displaying a portrait of Jefferson, the official "School History" tells how it came into existence in 1987 when the county merged Louisa Elementary School, "built in 1907," and Mineral Elementary School, "built in 1910"—both originally white schools—with Louisa County Intermediate School. The Web site omits any mention of the fact that the Intermediate School buildings had originally housed a Negro elementary school and a Negro high school. It gives no dates for when the actual buildings of the present-day school were built and tells no story about them. Instead, it erases from the collective memory the very existence of these Negro schools. Of my school.

When I asked him about this name change, Mr. Thompson told me that the school board had formed a committee to rename all three elementary schools. It had at the time assured the public that none of the schools would be named after an individual, thus mitigating the concerns of many that the new names might be racially divisive. But to the deep dismay of the African American community, when the names were announced, two were in fact named in honor of individuals, both famous white Virginians, both slave owners. The third was named Trevalians, after the place in Louisa County where Confederate soldiers had forced a Yankee retreat.

I had driven past Thomas Jefferson Elementary School on my earlier summer research trips, but this was the first time I had visited Louisa during the academic year, when the school was in session. On this visit, I parked my rented car at the front of the school and walked in the main entrance. Signing in, I was given a visitor's pass and directed to the front office. Mr. Thompson's office had been in a cramped and dingy space on the second floor of the building, but the current office occupied a number of spacious rooms in a central area on the first floor. I waited at a long counter, behind which a number of secretaries and other staff members worked efficiently at well-appointed desks. I explained to the receptionist who I was and asked if the principal might be free to talk to me. She invited me to take a seat in a small waiting area while she conferred with the principal. I sunk into a comfortable chair and looked around. An impressive bust of Thomas Jefferson presided over the busy office. On the wall just to my left hung three handsome, framed posters, one a portrait of James Madison, the second of James Monroe, the third of John Marshall. All major figures in American history, all Virginia natives — and all white. I checked the other walls, but there were no images of any African Americans in the main office.

The principal emerged from the adjacent office and greeted me courteously, if somewhat guardedly. Jo Ann Wagner was a pleasant-looking white woman, probably in her early forties, with a brisk, professional manner. She hesitated, for just a split second, after hearing my request. I could tell she was sizing me up. Then she made up her mind. Yes, she said, she would be happy to talk to me. I followed her into her large, comfortable office. Mrs. Wagner was smart, energetic, and upbeat. She told me that she had been working at the school since 1987, the year it was turned back into an elementary school and named Thomas Jefferson. She has served as its principal since 1999. I could tell right away that she was an able administrator, the kind of person who believed wholeheartedly in what she was doing and was fully committed to accomplishing the tasks at hand. In striking contrast to the white superintendent in 1970 who had made it clear to me he did not believe my poor black students had the capacity to learn,

Mrs. Wagner had high expectations of all the students at her school. She was especially proud that, even though it was a Title I School and thus at least 40 percent of its students lived below the poverty line, Thomas Jefferson had recently been fully accredited, an accreditation based in part on its students' scores on achievement tests. In the preceding year, I later learned, about 60 percent of the school's current black fourth graders and 75 percent of its disadvantaged students had passed the state's Standards of Achievement tests in language arts, though the results on another statewide achievement test were somewhat lower and revealed a significant achievement gap between African American and white students.

With the combined space of the old black elementary and high schools, Thomas Jefferson Elementary is much larger than the original Z. C. Morton, which when it opened in 1960 had only 12 class rooms and 14 teachers to serve its 503 African American students, a ratio of nearly 40 students per teacher. The school's current enrollment, Mrs. Wagner told me, was around 700 students, approximately 35 percent of whom are African American. Instead of a tiny 14-member staff, however, the school now has a faculty of 57, including 34 teachers in grades kindergarten through fifth grade, 11 Special Education teachers, 4 Title I Reading teachers, 2 additional reading specialists, a Gifted and Talented teacher, a teacher in charge of two preschool classes for disadvantaged children, an art teacher, a music teacher, a P. E. instructor, and a librarian. It also has 2 social workers, a psychologist, a speech therapist, a nurse, a guidance counselor, and a resource officer. Additionally, Mrs. Wagner shares administrative duties with two assistant principals. When I asked her about the extraordinary improvements at the school since I taught there in 1970, she explained that, in addition to the large infusion of tax money from the nuclear power plant, the schools had been extremely fortunate to have had committed and forward-thinking leaders "who went after that money." She did not mention integration.

I asked if there were any racial tensions at the school. My question seemed to take her by complete surprise. She looked at me as if I had just asked if any of her teachers had ever taken their students on a field trip to the moon. "Absolutely not," she assured me, adding, with complete conviction, "Children are color blind. They don't recognize color at all. They don't see racial differences; they see everyone as 'just people.'" As I listened to her earnest assurance that children are oblivious to their own or others' racial identity, I thought about how conscious my fourth-graders had been of being "colored," how attentive they had been to my racial affiliation with the white boy, Samuel, how much the girls had made of my long, straight hair. Was it possible that such racial awareness had completely disappeared in the thirty-odd years since I had taught at this school? Could it be that school integration had truly produced a generation of children who were color-blind? Before I could pursue this issue further, Mrs. Wagner continued her thoughts on this subject. "Sometimes, of course, kids will use words" — she left to my imagination what those words might be — "but," she explained confidently, "there isn't really any racist motive behind those words. They're just using them to get at the other kid." I puzzled over her interpretation, wondering why it was so important to her to believe that a slur hurled in anger was drained of its racist content. When I pushed her a little about her conviction that children were innocent of racial differences and prejudices, she allowed that "some children learn prejudice from their parents." But she wasn't inclined to reflect on when that learning took place or how it might affect the interactions of white and black students at her school. I sensed her discomfort with my line of inquiry. Either because of her role as school spokesman or because my direct questions about race breached some unspoken rule of southern etiquette, she was reluctant to talk openly about race relations at Thomas Jefferson.

I changed the subject from race to poverty. I wanted to know whether the problems of poor children that I had witnessed — hunger, toothaches, lack of medical care, financial anxieties, insecurity, burdensome responsibilities at home — still plagued some of the children in her school, undermining their ability to concentrate on their school work. And I wondered whether she still encountered some parents who struggled to help their children with their school work because they, themselves, were not fully literate. I was especially interested in learning whether the integrated Thomas Jefferson School — so much better funded than Morton — had been able to address effectively the problems that poverty had caused so many of my students. A little defensive at first when I broached the subject of poverty, Mrs. Wagner assured me that virtually all the parents of her students were literate, and many had college educations and good jobs. She viewed the families who sent their children to Thomas Jefferson school as middle class and bristled at my mention of illiteracy. I wasn't sure how to reconcile the picture she painted with the fact that as a Title I school, at least 40 percent of its students lived below the poverty line. Or the fact that, in 2000, the county's own comprehensive plan advocated an expansion of "adult literacy programs to reach the approximately 23 percent of Louisa County citizens with reading impairment."

Mrs. Wagner did, however, acknowledge that many of the poorer children arrived at school without the vocabulary and knowledge of their middle-class peers, and she described an impressive range of programs the school had instituted to help these children catch up. Beginning with preschool classes for disadvantaged children who are behind in normal development, the school also provides poor children who are struggling academically with close, individual attention from well-trained Title I teachers, as well as small group instruction in math and reading, tutoring, and extended learning after school. None of these programs was available to my students in 1970.

I was curious to know more about the school's eleven special education classes. Mrs. Wagner informed me that 14 percent of the students at Thomas Jefferson were in special education, and this figure struck me as high. At the same time, I knew that Marcus and Samuel and Derrick and Louis and Donna desperately needed the specialized knowledge and extra attention such classes provide. According to Mrs. Wagner, the school offers a range of special education classes that serve children with learning disabilities, children with behavioral problems, and children with various levels of retardation ("the educable mentally retarded," "the trainable mentally retarded," and "the severely mentally retarded"). Aware of the national concern that too many African American children are placed in special education, some without proper evaluation and others — especially boys — because they are stereotyped as potential troublemakers, I asked her what percentage of students in the school's special education classes were black. My question flustered her. She said she had no idea what the breakdown was, that she doesn't keep figures on the racial makeup of these classes. When I pressed her, she said vaguely that the racial breakdown was probably "about even." I asked her if that meant the special ed classes were approximately 50 percent black and 50 percent white (and thus had a disproportionate number of black students), and she said "yes." But, of course, without any access to the records of these children and without any expertise of my own, I could draw no conclusions about these figures.

Finally, I asked Mrs. Wagner if it might be possible for me to visit a fourth-grade class. She thought for a moment and then very graciously agreed, as long as the teacher she had in mind — Mrs. Lombard — was willing. "Mrs. Lombard is an experienced teacher," she told me. "She's been working at the school since 1972 — shortly after it was integrated and was made an intermediate school serving grades 5 through 7. I'm pretty sure Mr. Thompson was still the principal when she came here." Excusing herself, she hurried off to see if Mrs. Lombard would agree to my visit, temporarily leaving me alone in her office. I glanced around the room, admiring the way Mrs. Wagner had transformed a large, institutional room into a cozy space, one that must have felt warm and inviting to the children who were sent to speak to her. I laughed at the playful collection of pink flamingoes, admired the photograph of her children on the desk, and studied the pretty white angel ornament dangling from a peg. And then I began to survey the pictures on the walls, all of them carefully chosen, it was clear, to appeal to children: a Raggedy Ann doll on a chair with a teddy bear and blocks; three country boys with straw hats; a young boy, Amish perhaps, sitting at a table with a teddy bear; two girls playing on a see saw; a girl in a long dress and bonnet, standing in front of a nineteenth-century schoolhouse, being greeted by her teacher and classmates. As my eyes moved from picture to picture, I began to wonder whether an African American child or parent would feel as comfortable as I did sitting in Mrs. Wagner's office. Every human figure in every picture, I noted sadly, was white. And I wondered: is this what it means to be color-blind?

I returned to Thomas Jefferson Elementary School the next morning and was directed to Mrs. Lombard's fourth-grade class. It was housed in the very wing where I once taught, in a room just one door down from my former classroom. Walking through that door, I felt a little like Alice, walking through the looking glass. I instantly recognized the room, its rectangular dimensions, the low shelves beneath its long row of windows, the view of the field behind the school. For a dizzying moment, I had the physical sensation of standing at the front of it, thirty-four years earlier, looking out over long rows of desks, my students staring back at me. But at the same time, nothing at all was as I remembered it. The shelves that had once been nearly empty were crammed with books, including a dictionary for each child in the room. Every inch of wall space was covered with educational materials—not the trite or condescending things that so often decorate the walls of elementary classrooms, but interesting stuff, including maps, historical posters, artwork, and a quilt. Whole sections were devoted to science, history, geography, and reading. The regimented rows of desks I remembered were gone, replaced by two long tables, arranged in a "V" formation in the center of the room. Children intent on their work sat around the tables, some of them quietly collaborating with each other. In the back corner a circle of chairs was arranged for small group work. Beside it was a bin full of more books. Counting twenty-one students in the room (a twenty-second one arrived with a pass towards the end of my visit), I tried in vain to recall how thirty-eight children had ever crammed into a room this size.

Most disorienting of all to me, though, was the fact that virtually every child in the room was white. Thirty-seven of my students had been African American, but only four of Mrs. Lombard's were, and all four of them were girls. I hadn't anticipated that the class I would be observing would be nearly all white or that it would have no African American boys at all, and I was sorely disappointed. I wondered why only 18 percent of Mrs. Lombard's students were African American when the school overall was 35 percent African American. Perhaps a few black students were absent on this day. Maybe the demographics of this year's fourth-grade class were skewed or the other fourth-grade classrooms had a much higher proportion of black students. But I couldn't help wondering whether I might find the African American boys missing from this classroom in one of the school's special education classes for children deemed to have behavioral problems. I later learned that all the students were present that day. And I was told that because students are grouped by reading levels before being assigned to classrooms, the racial makeup of each class varies.

I had, as planned, arrived just in time for reading class. Mrs. Lombard invited one of the three reading groups to join her in the circle at the back of the room. She gestured for me to pull up a chair just outside the circle so that I could observe the group, and she reached into the bin beside her and retrieved a copy of the group's book for me. It was not one of the deadening, homogenized stories like the ones I had been required to teach, but a wonderful work of fiction by an award-winning African American writer.

I knew immediately that I was watching a master teacher at work. Effortlessly commanding her students' attention, Mrs. Lombard raised a series of interesting questions that instantly sparked discussion. Hands waved. Girls squealed to be recognized. Boys shouted out answers. She listened thoughtfully as each student responded, following up on one child's answer, pushing another to go farther, engaging the rest of the group in evaluating yet another's interpretation. And she worked at drawing out the quieter students, telling them she wanted to hear what they had to say. Even as she raised open-ended questions about the characters, themes, and plot of the book, she continuously coached her students on reading strategies. She made it clear to her students that she loved this book, that she thought it had something powerful and important to say, and that its language was something to savor and remember.

Mrs. Lombard had an easy rapport with her students. For the duration of each half-hour discussion, as she engaged them in analysis and interpretation, she also kept up a running patter with them about their various foibles, affectionately teasing one child for his restlessness, gently chiding another for her daydreaming, using endearing terms and colorful southern slang to describe, and reflect back to them, their errant behavior. She had a knack for letting her students know she was aware of their small lapses without embarrassing them, and she understood how to keep them in line without making any threats or administering any punishment. While she devoted her attention to the small group before her, the other students worked quietly together on written assignments at the main tables. On the few occasions when they became a little too loud, Mrs. Lombard raised her voice ever so slightly and reminded her "peanut gallery" to whisper. Mr. Thompson's paddle seemed like a very bad dream.

When I arrived, the four African American girls were sitting together at the far table. When Mrs. Lombard convened the first reading group, one of them, a petite and pretty girl named Keisha, got up from the table to join the circle of students gathering in the corner. I watched her as her group began to discuss its assigned book, *The Well*, a work of fiction by the African American writer Mildred D. Taylor.

This was the most advanced reading group, and Keisha followed the discussion attentively. Except for a boy who admitted that he hadn't read the assigned pages, however, she was the quietest child in the group. Perhaps she was simply shy and reticent by nature, but I noticed how carefully she observed the other children in her group and wondered whether she felt self-conscious about being the only African American child in it. How did she feel, I wondered, sitting among her white classmates, listening to them talk about a southern black family's terrifying confrontation with a bigoted white sheriff?

Mrs. Lombard referred to an earlier discussion in which the group had grappled with why the book used the forbidden "n-word," reminding them of how the author was, with this racial epithet, trying to convey the mean-spirited and racist nature of the villain who used it. And then she asked why the two protagonists—innocent boys—would have been in danger of being killed "back then"? "Because they're black!" a number of the children shouted confidently. Keisha lowered her eyes. Sitting silently beside a blonde-haired girl to whom she seemed attached, Keisha smiled in admiration when Mrs. Lombard praised her friend, then reached out and touched her blonde hair. Keisha was the only child who didn't raise a hand when the teacher asked, "How many of you have ever been sunburned?" When her session was over, she did not join the other children in her reading group at the near table, but instead walked to the far table where the other three African American girls were sitting.

All three of these girls, along with three white boys, were in the third reading group, which was discussing a book by Jane Wagner called *J. T.* This book, too, was about an African American child, a city boy who adopts a badly hurt, one-eyed alley cat. The class was using an edition that included illustrations from a movie based on the book that was made by the black photographer and filmmaker Gordon Parks Jr. I was surprised when all three girls expressed some dissatisfaction with this appealing book. They wanted to know why they couldn't read *The Well* instead. I wondered whether they had been eavesdropping on the first group's discussion of that book and were intrigued by its story about a southern black family. Maybe Keisha, so quiet among her white peers, had told them all about it when they were alone together. Perhaps the three girls sensed, rightly, that *The Well* was a more mature and challenging book than the one they had been assigned, and they longed to be considered worthy of it. Mrs. Lombard did not dismiss their request out of hand. "I'm seriously thinking of letting you read this book this year," she confided in them, "because I think you can handle it."

All of them then wholeheartedly entered into the discussion of *J. T.* Unlike Keisha, who had seemed intimidated in her all-white group, they were completely relaxed and uninhibited in theirs, easily holding their own with the other (white) children in their group. Once, Jade complained to Mrs. Lombard that she never called on her. Mrs. Lombard immediately directed her next question to her, playfully addressing her as "Miss Never-Called-Upon." Later, when Jade was practically bouncing out of her chair in her effort to be recognized, Mrs. Lombard put her arm around her and patiently explained, "I know you have something to say, but I want to call on Ashley first, because, even though she's not as dramatic as you, I can tell she really wants to say something too." When the students were discussing the word "wise" and Jade declared that "a wise person is someone who uses good judgment," Mrs. Lombard made a point of praising her comment.

As the reading period drew to a close and the children prepared to go to lunch, I thanked Mrs. Lombard for allowing me to visit and left her classroom. In the hallway, students from another class had already lined up outside their classroom and begun moving in single file toward the cafeteria. Suddenly, just in front of me, on my right, a classroom door burst open. A teacher, a young white woman, emerged with an African American boy of about eight or nine in tow. Before I could comprehend what was happening, she had expertly wrestled him to the floor, using what appeared to be a deft, well-practiced maneuver. The boy squealed loudly as he struggled with her, futilely trying to escape her sure hold. Unflustered by his kicks and shouts, she hovered a few inches above him, continuing to physically restrain him. Trying not to stare, I walked as quickly as I could around these two entwined figures on the floor. Ahead of me, I could hear a teacher admonishing her cafeteria-bound students—"don't look," "don't look"—and urging them to "walk on." Rattled, I followed them through a set of swinging doors. On the other side, the teacher stopped the line and turned around to address her wide-eyed students. "Remember," she told them earnestly, "how we've talked before about how some of the classrooms on our wing are for children with special needs. That little boy is one of those children. I want you to understand that his teacher would not have been treating him that way if it weren't absolutely necessary." The children, sobered, nodded their heads as they processed this information and marched on to lunch.

I handed in my visitor's badge, signed out, and walked into the too-bright sunlight. But I couldn't get the scene in the hallway out of my head. It was clear from the startled responses of the other children that what I had witnessed was unusual, an unsettling incident that required explanation. Remembering my own inept responses to Marcus during his frightening and threatening outbursts, I was certainly not going to second-guess a special education teacher trained to act decisively when a student behaves in a way that endangers himself or others. And, I kept reminding myself, the teacher in the hall had not been beating the angry boy, as Mr. Thompson had beaten Marcus; she had been employing physical techniques to restrain and quiet him. Still, the image of the raging black boy crumpled helplessly on the floor, his white teacher towering over him, lingered.

I had just spent an hour and a half with a gifted teacher, in a school building that had undergone a miraculous transformation since I had taught in it thirty-four years earlier. I had sat in Mrs. Lombard's well-ordered classroom, marveling at the small class size, the abundance of books and materials, the imaginative selection of award-winning fiction, the expert pedagogy, the absence of any corporal punishment, the well-behaved and highly engaged students. If, in 1970, I could have waved a magic wand over my Morton classroom, this was exactly the classroom I would have wished for. Except for one crucial element: in my ideal classroom, my fantasy classroom, Reginald and James, Sharon, Ramonia, and Matilda, William, Cecily, Victor, Emmeline, Annie Mae, and Chester—and not just four little black girls—would have been there, soaking up what Mrs. Lombard had to teach them. They would have been sitting among the white children, talking and laughing with them, and not isolated at one end of the table. And, during the discussion of the story about the nineteenth-century African American family, they would have been confidently sharing their insights and experiences with their teacher and classmates.

As I walked to my car, the elation I'd experienced observing Mrs. Lombard and the distress I'd felt witnessing the hallway incident gave way to a profound sadness. Even though I was gratified to see what a huge difference integration—and the county's significant financial investments—had made in the quality of Louisa's schools, I couldn't help lamenting the costs of this progress. I regretted the dispersal of the tightly knit black community that had formed around and given life to Z. C. Morton Elementary School. There wasn't much evidence that anyone at Thomas Jefferson stood in the hallways as Mrs. Perkins had done so magisterially, laughing her hearty laugh and reminding wayward students about the talk she'd have with their mamas when she saw them at church next Sunday. And I was chagrined, as a white person, to see how reflexively the county's white elite had re-conceived the former Negro school in its own image. Chagrined, and saddened, for I was quite sure that Mrs. Wagner had not intentionally decorated her office walls only with pictures of people who looked just like herself or consciously removed the black thread of the school's history from its Web site, unraveling a tapestry more colorful and intricate than she cared to admit. I guessed, too, that the committee members who had chosen to name the school after an eminent Virginian had never even thought about the fact that the man they were honoring had been a slave owner who had fathered children with his slave mistress or ever once considered naming the school after an eminent black Virginian. Fretting over Keisha's timidity and the absence of any African American boys in Mrs. Lombard's class, I wondered how many Sharons and Matildas might be withholding their penetrating insights in Thomas Jefferson's integrated classrooms, how many Reginalds and Chesters might be exiled from the regular classroom because of their restless inquisitiveness.

Before getting into my car, I looked back at the plain brick building where I had as a very young woman learned so much about discrimination, poverty, power, inequality, racial identity, and the longings of ten-year-old children. But Z. C. Morton Elementary School was no longer there. Turning away, I slid into the seat of my car, started the engine, and drove out onto Route 33, leaving Thomas Jefferson Elementary School, with all its impressive accomplishments and all its unsolved problems, behind.

# Afterword

*To fling my arms wide*
*In some place of the sun,*
*To whirl and to dance*
*Till the white day is done.*
*Then rest at cool evening*
*Beneath a tall tree*
*While night comes on gently,*
      *Dark like me—*
*That is my dream!*
*—from "Dream Variations" by Langston Hughes*

A year after I quit my job at Z. C. Morton Elementary School, I took a summer work-study job at the Wright School, an integrated state elementary school for emotionally disturbed children in Durham, North Carolina. There, I assisted an experienced teacher with a master's degree, working closely with the young children in our classroom and supervising them and the school's other students during afternoon recreation sessions. After my experience in Louisa, I was astonished to find myself in a public school where everything worked: the classrooms were filled with books, creative materials, and educational games; the teachers were exceptionally well-trained and committed; a low faculty-student ratio allowed them to devote a significant amount of attention to each child; students followed a curriculum specifically designed for their individual needs and abilities; they had to complete their lessons with 100 percent accuracy, eliminating failure as an option; everyone from the director of the school to the teaching aides had high expectations of all the students, many of whom advanced three academic years in their brief, four-month residential stays; and discipline problems were handled firmly but humanely, with misbehaving students encouraged to reflect on their behavior and to take responsibility for their actions. All these children had emotional or behavioral problems serious enough to warrant their removal from their regular schools and were, in a sense, outcasts, in danger of being exiled from all they knew. Except they had landed at a school determined to save them from that fate. Wright School was only a couple hundred miles south of Louisa, but I felt as if I'd entered another galaxy.

That summer I had the opportunity to observe African American and white children who had previously attended segregated southern schools interact with each other for the first time. My experience gave me hope in the promise of school integration. Every sunny afternoon another young teaching assistant and I took groups of children to a nearby public swimming pool that had only recently been integrated. As soon as classes were over, we would load the kids onto the school's squat, peculiarly shaped bus — affectionately known as the Blue Goose — and head off to the pool, Tom driving, me in the back with the children. Almostly daily on the bus, I took part in one of their favorite rituals, holding out my arm for its color to be compared to the different colors of the many, much smaller arms, thrust into the aisle for inspection. I watched in fascination as the children, dressed only in their bathing suits, examined each other curiously, intently, but with not a hint of mistrust or hostility. They playfully patted heads to see whose hair was silky or kinky or wavy or frizzy; carefully studied the unusual paleness of one child's skin, the dark chocolate hue of another; and, with childlike wonder, examined their physical similarities and differences. They were not color-blind, but neither were they trapped inside their culture's rigid racial prejudices. Jostling along together in the Blue Goose on those hot afternoons, they acted as if they belonged to one happy, boisterous clan, though, in fact, they came from upper-, middle-, working-class, and poor families, both white and African American, from across the state.

Many of us back then naively believed that once the courts had completely dismantled Jim Crow and eliminated de jure segregation of the public schools, the promise of a fully integrated society, so palpable at Wright School in the summer of 1971, would be realized. We imagined countless scenes similar to the one I witnessed on the Blue Goose naturally occurring in schools and playgrounds across the country. And we were confident that, once African American children were allowed to go to school with white children, the disadvantages they had historically suffered would evaporate, and they would thrive. Products ourselves of a segregated society, only a few of us who were white had ever had any close contact with an African American community, as I had in Louisa. Most of us hadn't yet learned to be attentive to cultural differences or to imagine how those differences might play out in the classroom. Nor did our idealized vision take into account the role socioeconomic status plays in a child's education.

Filled with optimism, we failed to anticipate the negative impact school integration would have on some black children or to comprehend the lasting power of destructive racial stereotypes. We never imagined that the centuries-old prejudice that viewed African Americans as intellectually inferior—what the African American journalist Brent Staples has called "the presumption of stupidity"—would persist despite decades of integrated schooling. We thus did not foresee that some teachers and school adminstrators would continue to expect less of their African American students, holding them to lower standards, assigning them to basic classes for noncollege-bound students, dumping them into special education classes, and otherwise segregating them from white students on academic tracks in the same schools. Nor could we have predicted that, far into the future, this enduring prejudice would have the power to negatively affect even very high achieving black students, substantially lowering their test scores when they most felt the need to disprove it.

We would have been shocked in 1970 to learn that fifty years after the *Brown* decision was handed down, some prominent educators would seriously question whether integrated schools were better than (or even as good as) segregated schools for African American children. Or that decades after Brown was finally enforced, conflicting cultural assumptions would persist, causing even dedicated and well-meaning white teachers to misunderstand their black students, confuse them by using pedagogical strategies alien to them, and have trouble disciplining them, just as I had my Louisa students in 1970. And it never occurred to us that, once given the educational opportunities denied their ancestors, many African American young people—especially, but not exclusively, those growing up poor in blighted areas of the country—would equate doing well in school with "being white" and walk away from those opportunities rather than put their racial identity at risk or betray what they understood to be their culture.

Even more unimaginable to us back then was the possibility that the nation's schools would eventually become re-segregated. Yet that is now happening. A series of recent court decisions has permitted school districts to end court-ordered desegregation plans that were put in place in the late 1960s and the 1970s, even though 67 percent of black students in the United States today now attend schools in which fewer than half the students are white, a higher percentage than in 1972. The school district in Clarendon County, South Carolina, whose lawsuit was part of the original *Brown* case, is now 98 percent black, the local whites having fled to private and parochial schools like Clarendon Hall, which currently enrolls only 3 percent "students of color." White flight to the suburbs and private schools has made de facto segregation the norm in many American cities, giving the northern states of Illinois, Michigan, New York, and New Jersey the dubious distinction of having the nation's highest levels of segregation in their public schools. One state even appears to be reintroducing de jure segregation: in April 2006 the Nebraska legislature passed a controversial plan to *segregate* Omaha's public schools, dividing the city's school system into three districts, one predominately black, one predominately white, one predominately Hispanic. And in a surprising move, the U.S. Supreme Court has agreed to consider in its 2006–2007 session the legality of any student enrollment plan that takes into consideration the criterion of race, thus raising the possibility that all plans to achieve racial balance in the nation's public schools will be declared illegal.

Thirty-five years after my hopeful rides on the Blue Goose, the integration of America's public schools, always a divisive issue, seems more complicated and less utopian than it appeared to many of us during the civil rights era. With policy makers on both the right and left raising troubling questions about its desirablity, utility, and practicality, the country's commitment to school integration appears to be waning. Yet as the nation's population becomes increasingly diverse and the public schools become multiracial, the challenge of educating children from different racial, ethnic, and economic backgrounds has never been more urgent or the need to forge an integrated society more essential. Educators, politicians, journalists, and sociologists, as well as concerned parents, are currently engaged in a national debate, often contentious, about how to meet this challenge. Many conservatives, including some influential African Americans, blame the public schools for failing to educate poor and minority children and advocate redirecting public funds to private and parochial schools in the form of tuition vouchers. The Bush administration has pushed through legislation known as No Child Left Behind which seeks, among other things, to assure that minority, poor, and disabled children receive the same attention and are held to the same high standards as other students. Liberals point to the success of affirmative action programs and press for extending them, even as opponents of these programs seek to have them overturned in the courts. Meanwhile, many educators have developed "multicutural" pedagogies that specifically attend to racial, ethnic, and cultural differences in the classroom and celebrate diversity.

By telling the story of a single, segregated "Negro" school in one rural Virginia county, I hope to keep alive a past that is in danger of slipping away, a past that I believe has much to teach us about the challenges facing our public schools today. But the past I recall in this book is not simply fading from memory; it is being rewritten and even erased. The desire of white people to forget, or radically revise, the embarrassing history of Jim Crow schools is understandable. But burying this history, or whitewashing it, has unintended consequences. It conceals the harm done to black children in the name of white supremacy, allowing old wounds to fester and past wrongs to go unacknowledged. It fosters the misconception that, as one local historian wrote about Louisa County, "school desegregation was carried out with dispatch," and thus impedes white Americans' ability to understand the experiences or address the grievances of African Americans who were denied access to schools and universities as recently as the early 1970s. It also obscures the fact that the suspicions many black youths exhibit toward school, and toward the intellectual traditions of Western culture taught in school, are grounded in a history of exclusion and exploitation not of their own making. In doing so, it prevents these young people from understanding how that history has shaped them while impeding white educators' ability to reach them. And it denies African American children access to an intellectual tradition of their own, one in which blacks risked their lives for the right to be educated; courageously fought to establish Negro schools in the face of white hostility; and brilliantly mined Western culture, using its treasures subversively to liberate and empower their people.

Another reason the history of black education in the Jim Crow South should not be forgotten is its potential to shed light on our own thinking about educational policies and pedagogies. The proposal to use public money for tuition vouchers to parochial and private schools, for instance, is not a new idea. I've shown how segregationists in Virginia sought to use a similar voucher system to prevent school integration during the period of Massive Resistance, even though it threatened to impoverish the public schools. Although vouchers are not now being proposed as a way to preserve segregation, its proponents express the same deep distrust of state education and the same hostility toward public institutions as the segregationists of an earlier era, and they are as unsympathetic to the belief that a well-funded public school system is vital to a democracy as the nineteenth-century southern politicians who, unlike their northern and midwestern peers, adamantly opposed universal education and the establishment of "free" schools. Will the implementation of tuition vouchers, it seems fair to ask in light of this past, leave only the poorest and most disadvantaged students in public schools that are drained of the funds necessary to educate them?

The No Child Left Behind Act directly addresses the historically low expectations that have undermined the education of black children like the students I taught in Louisa. But its potential is severely limited by the tax policies of the very adminstration that champions it, policies that favor the wealthy and, by design, starve government programs that benefit the poor. These policies, I would point out, closely replicate those implemented by southern Democrats in the former Confederate states shortly after the Civil War and kept rigidly in place throughout the first half of the twentieth century. As I have shown in my local history of Louisa County, these tax policies were used then to empower a small elite class of wealthy landowners, to the detriment of public schools, public libraries, and the education of African American, working-class, and poor white children. That history raises serious questions about how the idealistic goals of No Child Left Behind can possibly be realized at a time when federal aid to educational and social programs that support poor children, such as Head Start, the free lunch program, Pell grants, and Medicaid, is being slashed.

Although affirmative action programs explicitly seek to redress the wrongs done to African Americans in the past, their efficacy is undercut when whites—implicitly resorting to the the centuries-old "presumption of stupidity" that burdens black children—express doubts about the credentials of blacks who have benefited from these programs. To some degree, then, affirmative action inadvertently perpetuates racial prejudices, stigmatizing people who have received preferential treatment, no matter how brilliant they are or how successful they have become. Even the ideal of cultural diversity is sometimes invoked in potentially harmful ways that are reminiscent of an earlier era. It has recently become the mantra of academic administrators who seem far more interested in engaging in public relations campaigns than in educating black students. What message are these administrators giving African American students when they boast that their presence on campus is important because it helps sheltered white students prepare to live in a multicultural world among all kinds of people utterly unlike themselves? How different is this, really, from all the other ways in the past that blacks have been viewed primarily in terms of how they could be of service to privileged white people? And why aren't these administrators proclaiming instead the importance of having African American students on campus because of their intellectual promise, academic achievements, and creative talents?

If, as these examples suggest, a shameful past still haunts the corridors of America's schools and universities, the changes ushered in by the *Brown* decision and subsequent civil rights legislation have nevertheless transformed public education and the society it serves in the years since I taught in Louisa County. Black children can no longer be legally denied access to a public school because of their race; much of the South has become successfully integrated; and Jim Crow is dead. African Americans who were the pioneers of school integration now teach in formerly all-white universities, work in formerly all-white law firms, write for formerly all-white newspapers, and hold management positions in formerly all-white companies. Their children enjoy educational opportunities that would have been unimaginable to them in their own childhoods. Although the country has not yet succeeded in fully integrating its schools or its society, the promise I sensed on the

Blue Goose in the summer of 1971 has been at least partially realized. Lest we lose sight of that promise, allow me to tell one final story about my summer at the Wright School and an unlikely friendship between two ten-year-old boys — one white, the other black.

Jonathan arrived at Wright School a week before Maurice. He was from an affluent white family and had grown up, indulged and over-protected, in a small town in eastern North Carolina. On his first trip to the public pool, he held back when the other children jumped exuberantly into the water.

"This pool is dirty," he announced. I could hear the alarm in his voice, the barely contained terror.

"No it's not," I assured him. "It's inspected routinely by the state health agency. The city wouldn't be allowed to operate it if it weren't clean," I said, though I knew he wasn't concerned about the amount of chlorine in the water.

"But it is dirty," Jonathan protested, now near tears. "It's very dirty." And then, as if perhaps I were being inattentive or dense or negligent, he gravely informed me, "There are a whole lot of black people swimming in this pool."

I led Jonathan to a nearby bench to talk. Sitting with him in the hot North Carolina sun, I explained that the color of one's skin had nothing to do with cleanliness. I reminded him that everyone, black and white, had to take a shower before entering the pool, so nobody in the pool should be dirty. I pointed out that the Wright School had a number of African American students and teachers, and that the rest of us happily shared the classrooms, bathrooms, water fountains, and cafeteria with them. But nothing I said shook his conviction that the pool was dirty, and dangerously so. He declared emphatically that he would never, ever swim in a pool with black people.

"You don't have to swim if you don't want to," I shrugged, trying hard neither to validate nor to escalate his fears. And I left him sitting all alone on the bench. Turning my attention to the other children, I laughed with them as they gleefully turned somersaults, played tag, and dived for pennies in the cool water. A few minutes later, I noticed Jonathan approaching the pool. He hesitated for a long time at the edge, anxious and uncertain. And then he jumped in. I silently celebrated the plunge he had taken.

Maurice arrived the next week. Only a few months younger than Jonathan, he was smaller, much skinnier, and black. Maurice had been orphaned when he was only a toddler, and he had recently been removed from the home of an elderly black man who, though unrelated to him, had been caring for him since his mother's death. Social workers had determined that the man was too old, too ill, and too poor to adequately parent Maurice, who was declared a ward of the state and separated from the only caretaker he could remember. His second-grade teacher, a white woman who evidently had no sympathy for his situation, declared him unmanageable, reporting in disgust that "Maurice crouches under the desk, eats pencils, and behaves just like an animal." Her report hardly prepared us for the little boy who showed up at the Wright School that July. As soon as we met him, all of us on the staff were immediately smitten. Plucky, curious, and affectionate, Maurice had a big heart, and he opened it to anyone willing to pay the slighest bit of attention to him.

Before taking him to the pool that first week, I asked him, as I asked every new student, whether he knew how to swim. "Oh, yes, ma'am," he assured me. "I love to swim. I can't wait to get in that pool." I could see my colleague Tom, out of the corner of my eye, shooting me a dubious look.

"Well," I went on, "before you go into the deep end of the pool, you have to show Tom and me that you can swim all the way across the pool and back. Do you understand?"

"Yes, ma'am. That won't be any problem."

When we arrived at the pool that afternoon, Maurice ran to the edge of the water with all the other children and hurled himself enthusiastically into the water. But while the others quickly resurfaced, Maurice sank with sickening speed to the bottom of the pool. I could see his small body thrashing wildly, ineptly, as he panicked, gulped in water, and flailed helplessly. Tom instantly jumped in and hauled him out, but the damage had been done. Maurice was terrified of swimming. I held him on my lap, his thin body shivering in the ninety-five-degree heat, and tried as best I could to comfort him. But none of my assurances or promises to keep him safe could persuade him to get back in the pool. And then, miraculously, Jonathan, of all children, walked over to where we were sitting with a look of concern on his face. Taking Maurice by the hand, he led him gently to the ladder at the shallow end of the pool and began to coax him into the water. I could hear him tell Maurice that he had to let go of his fear because being afraid would only make it that much harder to learn to swim. And I watched in amazement as the white boy who had only the week before been terrified to swim in a pool with black people reached out to the black boy and helped him face down his own demons. Jonathan spent the entire afternoon walking patiently with Maurice around the shallow end of the pool, even though the other boys periodically shouted to him to join them in the deeper water. And by the end of the afternoon, Maurice got brave enough to bob his head under water and even make his first attempt to float. Whenever I hear someone doubt the value of school integration, I think of the bond formed that day between Jonathan and Maurice. "That," if I may appropriate the words of Langston Hughes, "is my dream."

# Notes on Sources

## A Part of Me

Pictures from the art exhibit at Apple Grove Elementary School appear in the *Central Virginian*, May 21, 1970, and May 28, 1970.

## Concerning This Little Frightened Child

In 1970 only a very small percentage of Louisa families was affluent: approximately 6 percent had annual incomes above $15,000 (equivalent to about $68,400 today); a minuscule .004 percent (four out of one hundred thousand) made more than $50,000 (about $228,200 in today's dollars). More than 40 percent of African American households were officially classified as living below the poverty line. More than half of the homes owned or rented by families living below the poverty line lacked some or all plumbing. All statistics are from *1970 Census of Population*, Bureau of the Census, U.S. Department of Commerce, vol. 1, part 48, pp. 114–550.

The statistics I cite on the number of slaves, the tax revenue produced by slaves, and the percentage of whites who were slave owners in antebellum Louisa County are based on the 1860 census and taken from Crandall A. Shifflett's *Patronage and Poverty in the Tobacco South: Louisa County, Virginia, 1860–1900* (Knoxville: University of Tennessee Press, 1982), pp. 8, 11, and 118n11. My discussion of the lives of African Americans in Louisa County after the Civil War is based on this book, and I am deeply indebted to Shifflett's careful historical research and probing economic analysis. I quote directly from *Patronage and Poverty*, pp. 102 and 25.

Ramonia Jackson Stith recently informed me that her mother found a foreign-born dentist in neighboring Orange County who was willing to treat African American patients.

Gerald Early's story is taken from *Daughters: On Family and Fatherhood* (Reading, MA: Addison-Wesley, 1994), pp. 6–11.

My discussion of the Twin Oaks commune draws on an article, "Paradise Not Quite Lost," that appeared in the *New York Times Magazine* on August 3, 1997, pp. 24–29, and from Kathleen Kinkade's *A Walden Two Experiment: The First Five Years of Twin Oaks Community* (New York: Morrow, 1973), as well as from my 1970 visit. I quote from p. 24 of the *New York Times Magazine* and from p. 74 of Kinkade's book. Kinkade writes that "our commitment to this Community is made quite deliberately, knowing that there are other choices open to us."

## Reach Up Your Hand, Dark Boy, and Take a Star

Citations to the local newspaper, the *Daily Virginian*, are to the following issues: December 21, 1967; January 23, 1958; March 27, 1958; May 5, 1960; and August 24, 1961.

My discussion of John Mercer Langston draws on the first volume of William and Aimee Lee Cheek's biography, *John Mercer Langston and the Fight for Black Freedom, 1829–65* (Urbana: University of Illinois Press, 1989), especially pp. 7–48. I quote from pp. 2 and 17 of this biography. Langston himself tells the story of his return to Louisa in 1867 in his autobiography, *From the Virginia Plantation to the National Capitol* (1894; New York: Johnson Reprint Corp., 1968), pp. 267–273. Langston quotes General Gordon, p. 270.

I am indebted to Paul Everett Behrens's study, "A Survey of Negro Education in Louisa County" (master's thesis, University of Virginia, 1949), which gives a detailed and exhaustive description of Louisa's Negro schools in the late 1940s, includes photographs of many of these schools, and compares the resources and physical plants of the white and Negro schools.

In relating the history of Louisa's Negro schools and the efforts of African American parents to provide schools for their children, I have drawn on Behrens's M.A. thesis, pp. 12–18; Alberta Guy Despot's "Negro Education," in Pearly Mills Harris, *A Brief History of Education in Louisa County* (Orange, VA: The Orange Review, 1963) pp. 55–57; and Eugenie Trainum Bumpass's "Education," in *Louisa County, VA 1742–1972*, compiled by Eugenie Trainum Bumpass

(Louisa County, VA: Louisa County 250th Anniversary Committee, 1992), pp. 93.

My statistics on the level of education attained by Louisa's blacks are drawn from the *1970 Census of Population*, Bureau of the Census, U.S. Department of Commerce, vol. 1, part 48, pp. 114–550.

The passage about one black family's response to the *Challenger* disaster is quoted from Kristin Hunter Lattany's "Off-Timing: Stepping to the Different Drummer," in *Lure and Loathing: Essays on Race, Identity, and the Ambivalence of Assimilation*, edited by Gerald Early (New York: Penguin, 1993), pp. 173–174.

The history textbook I was required to use in 1970 was titled *Virginia's History* (New York: Charles Scribner's Sons, 1956). It was written by Raymond C. Dingledine Jr., Lena Barksdeile, and Marion Belt Nesbitt and illustrated by Lois Maloy. I cite pp. 256–257, 281, 269, and 275–280. In its discussion of slavery, the book explains that

> Northern and Southern people did not think alike about slavery. The Northern people did not need much help to work their small farms. The planters in Virginia and in the South needed many men to work for them. They had slaves to do the work. . . . The planters did not know how they could free their slaves and keep their plantations going. Some people in the North said that the Southern people had to free their slaves no matter what happened to their plantations. The South said that the North had no right to tell them what to do. (pp. 256–257)

A copy of this textbook is in Special Collections at the University of Virginia Library in Charlottesville.

For the story of Henry Box Brown's life and escape, see Charles Stearns's *Narrative of Henry Box Bown* (Boston: Abner Forbes, 1849); *Narrative of the Life of Henry Box Brown, Written by Himself* (Manchester, U.K.: Lee and Glynn, 1851); and Jeffrey Ruggles, *The Unboxing of Henry Brown* (Richmond: Library of Virginia, 2003).

I quote from the "The Diary of Marcus Sterling Hopkins," January 13, 1868; February 2, 1868; September 20, 1868; November 4, 1868; March 24, 1868; April 8, 1868; May 20, 1868; January 7, 1868. Hopkins was the Freedmen's Bureau agent sent to Louisa County to supervise the education of the newly freed slaves. His diary is in Special Collections at the University of Virginia Library in Charlottesville.

## Larger Than Truth Can Be

My discussion of the history of the *Brown* decision draws on a number of sources, most notably Richard Kluger's *Simple Justice: The History of Brown v. Board of Education and Black America's Struggle for Equality* (New York: Knopf, 1976). In his analysis of the oral arguments and judicial decision in the *Brown* case (pp. 667–747), he quotes from both the November 1954 briefs and the April 1955 oral arguments, including the passages I cite, which are at pp. 723–724. In his discussion of earlier judicial opinions that permitted racial segregation, Kluger includes the following quote from *Plessy v. Ferguson* (1896): "'The most common instance of this [state-sanctioned separation of the races] is connected with the establishment of separate schools for white and colored children, which has been held to be a valid exercise of the legislative power even by courts of States where the political rights of the colored race have been longest and most earnestly enforced,'" p. 75.

Excerpts from the oral arguments of Archibald Robinson and Lindsay Almond are cited from *Argument: The Oral Argument before the Supreme Court in Brown v. Board of Education of Topeka, 1952–1955*, edited by Leon Friedman, with an introduction by Kenneth Clark and Yale Kamisar (New York: Chelsea House, 1983), pp. 423, 428, 433, 434, and 435. Robinson explicitly answers the accusation that southern whites are responsible for the low level of academic achievement among blacks, saying "I know that it may be said, well, that is your fault, you denied them opportunity, you denied them equality. It is the result of environment. We think that is irrelevant in this case," p. 428.

The laws forbidding the education of slaves and free blacks that I cite here are printed in June Purcell Guild's *Black Laws of Virginia* (New York: Negro Universities Press, 1936), pp. 117 and 167.

For a discussion of the origins and history of Jim Crow, see William H. Chafe, Raymond Gavins, and Robert Korstad, eds., *Remembering Jim Crow: African Americans Tell about Life in the Segregated South* (New York: New Press, 2001); John Egerton, *Speak Now against the Day* (New York: Knopf, 1994); Peter Irons, *Jim Crow's Children: The Broken Promise of the Brown Decision* (New York: Viking, 2002); Kluger, *Simple Justice*;

Jerrold M. Packard, *American Nightmare: The History of Jim Crow* (New York: St. Martin's Griffin, 2002); C. Vann Woodward, *The Strange Career of Jim Crow*, 3rd ed. (New York: Oxford University Press, 1974).

Throughout this chapter I quote from African American oral histories drawn from *The Negro in Virginia*, compiled by federal workers in the Writers' Program of the Works Progress Administration (New York: Random House, 1940; repr., New York: Arno Press and the New York Times, 1969), pp. 269, 60–61, and *Remembering Jim Crow*, edited by William H. Chafe, Raymond Bavins, and Robert Korstad, pp. 179–180, 183, and 186–188. These first-person accounts by African Americans corroborate Kluger's assertion that "a major share of the financial load [of educating blacks after the Civil War] was carried by Northern-based philanthropies that brought some light to the darkness but served as well both to relieve the states of their obvious responsibilities and to inculcate a severely restricted life outlook among the colored children. Had they lifted the eyes of the blacks too far above the cotton fields, the Northern schoolmarms would soon have been sent packing," *Simple Justice*, p. 633. I also cite first-person accounts of violence against freedman schools and teachers. The first is from a letter written on July 22, 1867, in Forsyth, Georgia, and signed by "George H. Clower, William Wilkes, etc. Freedmen"; the other is from the *New Era* (February 17, 1870). Both are quoted in *The Trouble They Seen: Black People Tell the Story of Reconstruction*, edited by Dorothy Sterling (Garden City, NY: Doubleday, 1976), pp. 297–298.

For a discussion of Margaret Douglass's efforts to teach free blacks, see Philip S. Foner and Josephine F. Pacheco, *Three Who Dared: Prudence Crandall, Margaret Douglass, Myrtilla Miner — Champions of Antebellum Black Education* (Westport, CT: Greenwood Press, 1984). Arrested for starting a school for free blacks in Norfolk, Virginia, Douglass was advised that "'it is a violation of the law to teach any person of color to read or write, slave or free, and an act punishable by imprisonment in the penitentiary,'" pp. 60–61. She and her daughter were charged because they "'did . . . unlawfully assemble with diverse negroes, for the purpose of instructing them to read and to write, and did instruct them to read and to write, contrary to the act of the General Assembly, . . . and against the peace and dignity of the commonwealth of Virginia,'" p. 63. Her actions were described in court as "'manifestly mischievous,'" and she was accused of having spoken of her "'regard for the colored race'" with "'indiscreet freedom,'" p. 70.

My source for the records of the Louisa planters David Watson and Thomas S. Watson is the "Watson Family Papers, 1760–1890, Louisa County," in Special Collections of the University of Virginia Library in Charlottesville. I quote from "David Watson's Account Book, 1813–1830"; "David Watson's Cash Book, 1821–29"; and Thomas S. Watson's Account Books of 1858–1859, 1865–1866, 1869–1879, and 1880–1882. Crandall Shifflett cites the Virginia commissioner of agriculture in *Patronage and Poverty in the Tobacco South*, p. 55. He discusses white planters' views of the freed slaves, pp. 33–34, and the efforts of freedmen to keep their families intact by contracting out their children to white farmers, pp. 31–32.

Kluger quotes the chairman of the faculty at the University of Virginia in *Simple Justice*, p. 85; Carter Glass is quoted in *The Negro in Virginia*, p. 239. My discussion of the disenfranchisement of Virginia's African American citizens is drawn from Kluger, *Simple Justice*, p. 458; James W. Ely Jr., *The Crisis of Conservative Virginia: The Byrd Organization and the Politics of Massive Resistance* (Knoxville: University of Tennesee Press, 1976), p. 22; and Robbins Gates, *The Making of Massive Resistance: Virginia's Politics of Public School Desegregation, 1954–1956* (Chapel Hill: University of North Carolina Press, 1962), p. 143. Kluger writes: "To assure that those who needed schooling the most—the poor-whites and the new black freedmen—would not get it, the re-enthroned Virginia aristocracy busied itself with a series of measures that effectively disenfranchised the lower orders. . . . Democracy in Virginia was dealt a nearly mortal blow" by the 1901–1902 State Convention, p. 457. He also writes that "Virginia's government was more thoroughly controlled by a reigning oligarchy than that of any other state in the South. . . . Democrats appointed by the unshakably Democratic legislature ran the election machinery in every one of Virginia's 100 counties," and they "supported taxes favorable to corporations and other business interests, strong curbs on organized labor, and tight restrictions on expansion of public-nuisance services such as education, health, and welfare," p. 458. Gates cites an interview with the black civil rights lawyer Oliver Hill: "Hill claimed that many of those Negroes who paid the poll tax did not register and vote. 'Pressure from the boss' and the courthouse politicians 'made it too much trouble.' The registrars in the Southside counties were often white women. If a Negro objected to being told to come back some other time, he was accused of being sassy to white ladies and was threatened with the loss of job," p. 143.

The reminiscences of John Lewis are taken from Howell Raines, *My Soul is Rested: Movement Days in the Deep South Remembered* (New York: Putnam, 1977), p. 71, and John Lewis, *Walking with the Wind: A Memoir of the Movement*, with Michael D'Orso (New York: Simon and Schuster, 1998), p. 46.

Kluger discusses the history of public education in Virginia in *Simple Justice*, p. 456.

The article "Louisa County Struggle for Free Schools, 1868–1878," appears in the *Central Virginian*, March 28, 1957. The quotation from the diary entry is also cited in Pattie Cooke, *Louisa County History: A Co-operative Effort* (Louisa, VA: 1993), p. 62, who takes it from the *Louisa County Historical Society Magazine*, no. 1, p. 18, which prints Haley's diary. Pattie Cooke summarizes the history of public schools in Louisa County in *Louisa County History*, p. 62. The suggestion that the desegregation of the county's schools happened quickly and painlessly appears in *Louisa County, VA 1742–1992*, compiled by Eugenia Trainum Bumpass, p. 92.

My discussion of Virginia's Massive Resistance derives from a number of sources, including Numan V. Bartley, *The Rise of Massive Resistance: Race and Politics in the South during the 1950's* (Baton Rouge: Louisiana State University Press, 1969); Ely, *The Crisis of Conservative Virginia*; Gates, *The Making of Massive Resistance*; Matthew D. Lassiter and Andrew B. Lewis, *The Moderates' Dilemma: Massive Resistance to School Desegregation in Virginia* (Charlottesville: University Press of Virginia, 1998); and Benjamin Muse, *Virginia's Massive Resistance* (Bloomington: Indiana University Press, 1961). I cite Gates, quoting Albertis S. Harrison Jr. and Robert Y. Button, two black belt senators, p. 189; Ely, pp. 64, 61, 51, 68, 74–75, 130–131, and 135; and Muse, p. 128. Ely uses the term "passive resistance" in chapter 8.

Asked to explain the operation of the public school system in Virginia, Lindsay Almond told the court that "the school boards of Virginia are appointed by a school trustee electoral board which board in turn is named by the circuit judges of the various circuits comprising the counties of Virginia" (Friedman, *Argument*, p. 431). Even juries were selected by appointment. An article in the local Louisa paper describes how the county court annually appoints from two to nine citizens to choose the list of "jurymen" (*Central Virginian*, January 11, 1968).

The article about the activity of the segregationist group appears in the *Central Virginian*, October 20, 1958. In my discussion of the struggle to desegregate Louisa's public schools and of white resistance to integration, I cite the following issues of the *Central Virginian*: May 20, 1954; June 7, 1962; May 12, 1960; May 5, 1960; February 22, 1968; February 8, 1968; March 14, 1968; April 25, 1968; May 9, 1968; February 22, 1968; April 25, 1968; June 27, 1968; July 25, 1968; August 1, 1968; May 1, 1969; May 8, 1969; May 15, 1969; May 29, 1969; May 29, 1969; June 12, 1969; October 2, 1969.

The passage recalling the effect of desegregation on different generations of African Americans is from Henry Louis Gates Jr., *Colored People* (New York: Random House, 1995), p. 184.

# Where Is the Jim Crow Section on This Merry-Go-Round?

Timothy B. Tyson tells the story of his reaction to seeing the black child drink from a water fountain in *Blood Done Sign My Name* (New York: Crown, 2004), p. 41. The quotation about white supremacy appears in Tyson's book on pp. 111–112. For compelling anecdotes that tell how black children experienced white supremacy, see Marita Golden, *Don't Play in the Sun* (New York: Doubleday, 2004), p. 5; Toi Derricotte, *Black Notebooks: An Interior Journey* (New York: Norton, 1997), pp. 17 and 164; and Anne Moody, *Coming of Age in Mississippi* (New York: Dell, 1968), p. 39.

The legal descriptions of Louisa's freed blacks are all taken from *Free Blacks of Louisa County, VA*, transcribed by Janice Luck Abercrombie (Athens, GA: Iberian Publishing, 1993). John Boswell's will appears on p. 128. The story of John Poindexter is told in Jabez Quintus Massie's "John Poindexter, Jr. Joins the Baptists," in *Louisa County, Virginia 1742–1882*, pp. 61–62. The excerpt from the letter of Thomas Watson's daughter is quoted from Shifflett's *Patronage and Poverty in the Tobacco South*, p. 56. Except for this quote, I have relied on my own reading and analysis of the Watson Family Papers. All citations of Thomas Watson are from Thomas S. Watson's Account Books in the Watson Family Papers, Special Collections, University of Virginia Library in Charlottesville. I quote from Watson's Account Books of 1858–1859; 1861–1862; 1865–1866; 1869–1870; and from Watson's Ledger Book of 1882–1883. The Baptist Church issued a statement declaring the Negro to be subordinate to whites at its 1891 convention, held in Virginia. I quote this statement from Carrie Allen Mc-Cray's *Freedom's Child: The Remarkable Life of a Confederate General's Black Daughter* (Chapel Hill, NC: Algonquin, 1998), p. 76. All citations of Marcus Sterling Hopkins are drawn from "The Diary of Marcus Sterling Hopkins," in Special Collections of the University of Virginia Library. Dates of the passages quoted are, in order of their appearance: September 20, 1868; November 4, 1868; January 13, 1868; January 27, 1868; April 14, 1868; January 31, 1868; Februrary 10, 1868; March 28, 1868.

Hill's editorial appeared in the *Central Virginian* on April 23, 1970. Timothy Tyson discusses the response of most middle-class whites (and some middle-class blacks) to the civil rights movement in *Blood Done Sign My Name*, p. 318.

In a roundtable discussion, published in *"Brown* and Its Impact on Schools and American Life: A Dialogue," *Focus on Law Studies* 19, no. 2 (Spring 2004): 1–16, scholars from various disciplines present evidence demonstrating that America's public schools are becoming re-segregated. Michael Klarman reports that 98 percent of public school students in Clarendon County, South Carolina—one of the original *Brown* cases—are black, while 98 percent of the private school students in that county are white (p. 1). John Paul Ryan, serving as the moderator of this discussion, cites a report by the Harvard Project on School Desegregation which warns that "southern schools are again becoming increasingly segregated" (p. 8). And Gerald Rosenberg points out that 91 percent of public school students in Chicago are black, even though 40 percent of that city's population is white (p. 8).

An article in the *Central Virginian* explaining the Virginia tradition of celebrating Lee's instead of Lincoln's birthday appeared on February 8, 1968.

For a discussion of the negative effect of early-twentieth-century schooling on black children, see Carter G. Woodson, *The Mis-Education of the Negro* (Chicago: African-American Images, 2000), pp. xviii–xix.

## The Too-Rough Fingers of the World

For a useful discussion of the cultural differences in styles of discipline, see Lisa D. Delpit's *Other People's Children: Cultural Conflict in the Classroom* (New York: New Press, 1995). Delpit argues that middle-class white parents tend to pose their requests to children as questions, even when they expect those requests to be obeyed. African American parents, however, tend to be more assertive and to give commands. She suggests that many black children misunderstand their white teachers because their requests are made indirectly. And she believes that many black children do not automatically grant authority to an adult; instead, it must be earned. I believe her analysis sheds light on my inability to control effectively the children in my class.

I cite anecdotes and passages from the following memoirs: Charlayne Hunter-Gault, *In My Place* (New York: Farrar Straus Giroux, 1992), pp. 54 and 4; Gerald Early, *Daughters*, pp. 32–33, 58, and 33–34. Horace A. Porter, *The Making of a Black Scholar: From Georgia to the Ivy League* (Iowa City: University of Iowa Press, 2003), pp. 24 and 45; Debra Dickerson, *An American Story* (New York: Random House, 2001), pp. 19, 10, and 38; Deborah E. McDowell, *Leaving Pipe Shop: Memories of Kin* (New York: Norton, 1996), pp. 130 and 121; Anne Moody, *Coming of Age in Mississippi*, p. 21; Henry Louis Gates Jr., *Colored People*, pp. 184–185 and 191.

My quotation about the freedmen's school is from "The Diary of Marcus Sterling Hopkins," January 13, 1868. It refers to Hopkins's work establishing and supervising schools for freed slaves in Louisa County. This diary is in Special Collections, University of Virginia Library.

The story about the slave's punishment for sassing his master appears in *The Negro in Virginia*, compiled by the Virginia Writers' Project, p. 155.

I have taken descriptions of the educational goals of elite schools from the Web sites of the following independent schools: National

Cathedral School for Girls; St. Albans; Sidwell Friends; and Milton Academy.

## It Was a Long Time Ago

Descriptions of the country inns in Louisa and surrounding counties are taken from the Web sites of the following inns: Willow Grove Plantation Country Inn; the Clifton House Inn (which quotes from an article in the Condé Nast *Traveler*); and Prospect Hill Inn. Descriptions of Tara, the inn in Clark, Pennsylvania, are from its Web site.

In *Patronage and Poverty in the Tobacco South*, Crandall Shifflett summarizes the reminiscences of Charlie Robinson, a former slave of Thomas S. Watson Jr., which appeared in a local newspaper series, "Old Homes of Louisa." Robinson talks about the slave patrols and describes the whippings he received as a slave, p. 136, n. 39.

The quotation from Henry Box Brown, the Louisa-born slave who escaped to Philadelphia in a box, is taken from Charles Stearns, *Narrative of Henry Box Brown*, p. 15.

The account of my conversation with Matilda Timberlake Beauford comes from my taped and transcribed interview with her. My accounts of my interviews with Mary Timberlake and Josephine Timberlake rely on my transcription of the notes I took during these interviews. The account of my interview with my former principal, whose name I have changed, comes from my notes and my taped and transcribed interview with him. The account of my interview with the principal of Thomas Jefferson Elementary School relies on my transcription of notes I took during our discussion.

My summary of Louisa County's current economy is based on statistics that appear in the draft of "The County of Louisa, VA. Comprehensive Plan," October 26, 2000. According to the Louisa County Economic Development Web site, "Louisa County has the lowest machinery and property tax in the state."

The comment about the Ferncliff School is from the March 27, 1958, issue of the *Central Virginian*. The complaints about the buses are from that paper's May 5, 1960, and May 25, 1961, issues.

In 2005, 85 percent of white fifth-graders at Thomas Jefferson Elementary School, but only 68 percent of black fifth graders, met or exceeded Virginia's Standards of Learning in reading and language arts. Ninety-one percent of the school's white fifth-graders, but only 67 percent of its black fifth-graders, met or exceeded the state's standards in math. (These statistics are given on a Web site called greatschools.net.)

## Afterword

The Wright School for Reeducation, founded in 1963, is still in operation. It is funded by the North Carolina Department of Health and Human Services. Its original teachers were trained at Peabody College through a grant from the National Institute of Mental Health.

I cite an editorial by Brent Staples titled "The Presumption of Stupidity: Affirmative Action, Occupational Apartheid" that appeared in the *New York Times* on March 5, 1995.

In his groundbreaking research, the Stanford psychologist Claude Steele has shown how racial and gender stereotypes, when activated in the minds of his research subjects, substantially lower the test scores of highly capable students. His studies suggest that even very high achieving black students are negatively affected by the persistence of this prejudice. He writes of his findings in a book he co-authored with Theresa Perry and Asa G. Hilliard III, titled *Young, Gifted, and Black: Promoting High Achievement among African-American Students* (Boston: Beacon Press, 2003).

For a useful discussion of the way cultural differences between white teachers and minority students can negatively affect learning, see Lisa D. Delpit's *Other People's Children.*

For a discussion of the way school integration has failed black students, see Roy L. Brooks, *Integration or Separation? A Strategy for Racial Equality* (Cambridge, MA: Harvard University Press, 1996).

For recent discussions about the re-segregation of America's public schools, see, for instance, *School Resegregation: Must the South Turn Back?* edited by John Charles Boger and Gary Ordfield (Chapel Hill: University of North Carolina Press, 2005), and *Dismantling Segregation: The Quiet Revolution*, edited by Susan E. Eaton and Gary Ordfield (New York: New Press, 1996). Peter Applebome reports on the findings of a study conducted by Ordfield, co-director of the Civil Rights Project at the Harvard Graduate School of Education, in his essay "Schools See Reemergence of 'Separate but Equal,'" *New York Times*, April 8, 1997. Applebome notes that 63.6 percent of black students attended schools where fewer than half the students were white in 1970, as compared to 67.1 percent in 1996. Recent court decisions ending court-ordered desegregation plans include *Board of Education of Oklahoma City v. Dowell* in 1991 and *Freeman v. Pitts* in 1992. The Clarendon County lawsuit was known as *Briggs v. Elliott.* The Nebraska legislation was supported by the single black legislator, Ernie Chambers, who argued that it would give minorities more control over their children's education. This plan is being opposed by the NAACP.

According to Richard Kluger, the Democratic Party of Virginia "supported taxes favorable to corporations and other business interests, strong curbs on organized labor, and tight restrictions on expansion of public-nuisance services such as education, health, and welfare." This policy, Kluger adds, "kept most of [Virginia's] people ignorant and servile," *Simple Justice,* p. 458. For evidence of the impact of tax policies on the public schools today, see Brent Staples's editorial, "The 'Mississippification' of California Schools," which appeared in the *New York Times* on June 23, 2000. He quotes Peter Schrag, a columnist for the *Sacramento Bee,* who describes how Proposition 13, which froze property taxes in California, resulted in the "Mississippification" of California's once-excellent public schools. And he cites statistics showing that today, low-income children in Mississippi are more likely to have a fully certified teacher than low-income children in California, while California's fourth-graders had lower reading test scores than fourth-graders in Mississippi. In fact, California's scores on these reading tests, sponsored by the National Assessment of Educational Progress, were the lowest of all the states.

Many educators have raised additional concerns about the No Child Left Behind Act, including its heavy reliance on high-stakes standardized testing, its narrow focus on reading and math skills, its imposition of financial penalties on the very poor urban and rural schools most in need of additional funding, and its failure to take into consideration the socioeconomic factors that hamper the academic performance of poor children. Others complain that it diverts attention, energy, and money away from learning for its own sake—from the pleasure of learning—and unwittingly encourages the manipulation of scores, the lowering of standards, and even outright cheating. And some lament the fact that it ignores important areas of the curriculum like history, science, music, and art.

# Acknowledgments

I am very grateful to my colleagues in the English Department at the University of Iowa for their support while I was writing this book. Their enthusiastic response to an early draft of the first chapter, which I presented at a faculty colloquium, persuaded me to pursue this project at a time when I was tempted to abandon it and return to the more familiar and safer terrain of early modern drama. That they never questioned what a Renaissance scholar was doing writing a memoir about a segregated school in the Jim Crow South is a testament, I think, to our department's open and creative spirit. Patricia Foster, David Hamilton, Robin Hemley, Sarah Levine, and Susan Lohafer, all members of the department's nonfiction writing program, gave me much-appreciated encouragement, as did Ed Folsom, Miriam Gilbert, Kevin Kopelson, Kathy Lavezzo, Teresa Mangum, Susie Phillips, Garrett Stewart, Doug Trevor, Jon Wilcox, and Doris Witt. Harry Stecopoulos read drafts of two chapters and supplied me with invaluable bibliographic references, lending me copies of books he wanted me to read, helping me navigate recent criticism in the exciting area of African American Studies, and greatly enriching my understanding of race and class in America. Kathleen Diffley directed me to a number of useful works about Henry Box Brown and the antebellum South. Judith Pascoe made a particularly helpful suggestion about how I might traverse the gap between my narrative of a segregated classroom in 1970 and my return to that story in the twenty-first century. Horace Porter, Linda Bolton, and Peggy Smith (a faculty member in Iowa's College of Law) very generously talked with me about their experiences growing up black in the post–World War II South, each providing me with a distinctive and valuable new perspective on my experience in Louisa County. And when I was afraid that health problems would prevent me from completing this book, my chair at the time, Brooks Landon, immediately responded by arranging a semester's research assignment.

Two colleagues, Mary Lou Emery and Dee Morris, deserve special thanks. Mary Lou believed in this project when it was nothing more than an amorphous idea and, unlike its author, she never wavered in her conviction that it would find an audience. She read multiple drafts of every chapter, carefully attending to tone, voice, language, and narrative and wrote extensive comments that always managed to zero in on exactly what needed to be rewritten, rethought, or thrown out. I am especially grateful for her ability to tell me, gently but firmly, when a section was misconceived, an argument fallacious, an anecdote sentimental, all the while championing the larger project. Dee read a draft of the entire manuscript while she was on leave in Wales and had far more important and pressing work to do. Her detailed and insightful response helped me stand back from what I had written and get a better perspective on its larger design. By identifying the different strands of my narrative and showing me what worked and what needed further attention, she made the task of revision much easier and even, dare I say, pleasurable. All her suggestions made their way into this book. I will not even try to express my appreciation for the many extraordinary acts of friendship Mary Lou and Dee have shown me over the years.

Two good friends from my graduate school days at Duke University also made valuable contributions. Diane Mowrey joined me in Charlottesville on one of my summer research trips and helped out in all kinds of ways, cheerfully reading maps, consulting phone books, touring a museum, and chatting with strangers during our exploratory forays into Louisa County, all the while asking me probing questions about my project. Susan Ward read early drafts of the first three chapters, which greatly benefited from her finely honed editorial skills. She raised a series of provocative questions about my personal experience in Louisa that helped me reflect on that experience, and she also made a number of illuminating observations about class, poverty, race, and "race etiquette" that gave me valuable insights into southern culture. I especially appreciated her willingness to reflect on her own experience growing up white in a small North Carolina town in the 1950s and 1960s and to recall her own bewilderment and confusion as she tried to make sense of the rules and customs governing race relations at that time.

I am deeply grateful to my former student, Matilda Timberlake Beauford, for sharing with me her memories of our Morton Elementary classroom and to her sister, Mary Timberlake, and her mother, Josephine Timberlake, for agreeing to talk to me about their experiences in the county's segregated (and, for Mary, newly integrated) schools. I hope they understand what an important contribution they made to this book by reflecting so openly and honestly about the impact segregation and integration had on their lives. I also wish to thank my former principal, referred to in this book as "Mr. Thompson," for sitting down with me in the fall of 2004 and telling me about his experiences as an administrator, teacher, and student in the Louisa County school system. Thanks, too, to Jo Ann Wagner who very graciously agreed to talk to me about Thomas Jefferson Elementary School when she was the principal there, and to Mary Lombard, who kindly allowed me to observe her fourth-grade classroom and then dazzled me with her artful teaching. Many others in Virginia helped me when I was doing research on this book, including my former student, Ramonia Tirish Jackson Stith, and her mother, Lillian Jackson; the staff of the *Central Virginian*; the librarians and staff in Special Collections at the University of Virginia Library; the volunteers at the Louisa County Historical Museum; my research assistant, Emily Waterfield; and Reginald D. Butler and Scot A. French, the director and associate director of the Carter G. Woodson Institute for African-American and African Studies and its Center for Local Knowledge. I wish to thank the University of Virginia and the University of Virginia Library for permission to quote from the following unpublished manuscripts: Papers of the Watson Family of Louisa County, Virginia, Diary of Marcus Sterling Hopkins (1868, MSS 4656), and "A Survey of Negro Education in Louisa County," Paul Everett Behrens, Masters 5550, Special Collections.

Two chapters of this book were written at the University of Iowa's Center for Advanced Studies while I held a semester's developmental assignment from the university in the spring of 2003. I am grateful to its director, Jay Semel, not only for providing a quiet and collegial place to work, but also for his personal interest in my project. One of my research trips to Virginia was funded by a Spellman Rockefeller grant from the University of Iowa. Mimi van Ausdale ably served as my graduate assistant one summer.

It has been my great good fortune to work with the wonderful people at the University of Iowa Press, including its director, Holly Carver. From the moment the press's acquisitions editor, Joseph Parsons, contacted me out of the blue on a bleak winter day and asked to take a look at my manuscript, I have known that my book was in the able hands of professionals who truly care about the books they publish. I can't thank Joe enough for his early interest in my project, his enthusiastic and active support of it, and his strong commitment to publishing and promoting it. I am also very grateful to Carl Klaus, who encouraged the press to consider my manuscript after reading a brief excerpt from it and later sent me astute and very helpful suggestions for revision.

I also want to thank various members of my family for the many different ways they have contributed to this project. Although he was a physician by profession, my father, Gilbert Herman Diehl, was a teacher at heart, and the joy he took in intellectual inquiry, lively debate, and exuberant play has deeply influenced both my teaching and my writing. What I remember most about my father, who died more than twenty years ago, was his ability to reach out to, take delight in, and empathize with all kinds of people, regardless of their social position, race, ethnicity, nationality, or religious beliefs. I am especially grateful to him for encouraging me, at a very young age, to imagine and appreciate others' differences. My mother, Nancy Simons Diehl, died shortly before this book was completed, but before she died, she talked to me at great length about Alberta Sherwood, the remarkable woman who was our family's housekeeper when I was young. Her thirty-five-year correspondence with Alberta, and the mutual respect these two women had for each other, taught me that valuable friendships can be forged across racial and class boundaries. My sisters, Deborah Young and Eve Sliwinski, eagerly shared with me their experiences teaching in the public schools and their memories of our Pennsylvania childhood. Each of them read portions of the manuscript and made useful suggestions. My stepdaughter, Jamian Wetlaufer, encouraged me to pursue this project, as did Jennifer Lewis Smith and Daniel Lewis, my stepchildren from an earlier marriage. Both Jami, an intrepid genealogist, and Dan, a specialist in Amercan Studies, referred me to useful books on the nineteenth-century South.

My daughter, Susannah Lewis, was actively involved with my project from its inception. As a high school student, she worked as my assistant one summer, accompanying me on my first trip back to Louisa, where she proved to be a tenacious researcher as well as a delightful traveling companion. We spent many intense days working together in the archives of the local newspaper, and she helped me piece together the story of how Louisa's schools were desegregated. Susannah also read drafts of every chapter, and her shrewd rhetorical critiques of my writing never failed to make her English professor mom proud (despite her decision to pursue a career in neuroscience). My readers have her to thank for her ruthless excision of any word that smacked of the academy.

Finally, I could not have written this book without the loving support of my husband, Jerry Wetlaufer. His keen interest in the civil rights movement, which began when he visited black universities in the South with his high school church group and continued when he returned to Mississippi as a college student to help register black voters, meant that he was not only deeply committed to my project, but always willing to serve as a sounding board for my ideas. It also meant that our bookshelves were well-stocked with the classic studies of that era, and he took it upon himself to keep me well supplied with interesting new books on topics relevant to my project. A law professor, Jerry was a valuable resource when I wanted to learn more about the *Brown* decision and other legal matters regarding the desegregation of the public schools. I also relied on him, more times than I would like to admit or he would care to remember, for tech support when I encountered computer problems, and I learned to count on him to give me thoughtful and helpful feedback on my writing. I hope he recalls with as much pleasure as I do our many discussions—sometimes passionate and always productive—that fueled the writing of this book.

# sightline books
## The Iowa Series in Literary Nonfiction